The
Slave Book

Rayda Jacobs

Kwela Books

Jacket design by Jürgen Fomm
The illustrated motive used throughout the book,
is after a watercolour by H. C. de Meillon from
the book *300 Years of Cape Wine* by C. Louis Leipoldt,
Tafelberg, Cape Town, 1974
Set in 10.5 on 12.5 Monotype Plantin
and printed and bound by National Book Printers,
Drukkery Street, Goodwood, Western Cape
First edition, first printing 1998

ISBN 0-7957-0078-4

To Faramarz and Zaida

Heaven and Earth

ACKNOWLEDGEMENTS

A book of historical fiction is an arrogant attempt by a writer in a few hundred pages to recreate and inform. The best you can hope for is a glimpse, and trust that the glimpse will open a much larger window in your mind. I couldn't possibly speak on behalf of those early people, and don't pretend to know what it was like. This book is merely a scratch at the surface.

I want to thank Dr. Robert C.H. Shell, for finding the time to read the first draft of the manuscript, my brothers, Hymie and Ghalick, for their help and support and all those visits to Hangklip (Hanglip in those days) to find "Drostersgat", "Boeta" Achmat Davids for his invaluable input, manuscripts, generosity, and countless other wonderful people I've met along the way who have enriched my understanding of the slaves. Real praise, however, belongs to those writers who spend years researching the past and whose works we historical scavengers ruthlessly plunder for atmosphere and ideas. We cannot write these books without them, and I am particularly grateful for the following: *Children of Bondage, A Social History of the Slave Society at the Cape of Good Hope, 1652-1838*, Robert C.H. Shell, Witwatersrand University Press, Johannesburg, 1994; *Cape of Torments: Slavery & Resistance in S.A.*, Robert Ross, Routledge & Kegan Paul, London, 1983; *The Early Cape Muslims: The first and oldest mosques in Cape Town*, F.R. Bradlow & Margaret Cairns, A.A. Balkema, Cape Town, 1978; *Lady Herschel, Letters from the Cape 1834-1838*, Friends of the S.A. Library, Cape Town, 1991; *The Mosques of Bo-Kaap*, Achmat Davids, the S.A. Institute of Arabic & Islamic Research, Athlone, Cape Town, 1980; *Wagon Road to Wynberg*, C.Pama, Tafelberg Publishers, Cape Town, 1979; *300 Years of Cape Wine*, C.Louis Leipoldt, Tafelberg Publishers, Cape Town, 1952, and many other books and essays I've read and consulted, among them the work of John Edwin Mason, Susan Newton-King, Christopher Saunders, and Wayne Dooling.

Some points of interest: Papendorp was later called Woodstock. Keizersgragt became Darling Street. De Drie Koppen, where there was an inn at which travellers stopped on their way from Cape Town to Wynberg or Simon's Town, became Mowbray. Graave (later called Graave Street, then Grave Street) became Parliament Street. "Bosheuvel", where Jan van Riebeeck first established his own farm in the 1650s, is now Bishopscourt. It should also be noted that Dutch-speaking settlers at the time were called Boers, colonists, settlers, inhabitants, Christians, whites, Afrikanders. The Khoi of today were called Hottentot by the Dutch. The San were called bosjesman, boesman, and boshiesman. Koi-na and Sonqua are how the Khoi and San referred to themselves. The slaves came from many different countries and spoke a variety of languages; chief among them, Melayu, a creolized Dutch, and Portuguese.

Rayda Jacobs
October, 1998

ACCORDING TO THE TULBAGH SLAVE CODE OF 1754

SLAVES

* ★ are to be indoors after 10 p.m. or carry a lantern
* ★ are not to ride horses or wagons in streets
* ★ are not to sing, whistle or make any other sound at night
* ★ are not to meet in bars, buy alcohol, or form groups on public holidays
* ★ are not to gather near the entrance of a church during church services
* ★ are not to stop in the street to talk to other slaves
* ★ who insulted or falsely accused a freeman, would be flogged
* ★ who struck a slaveholder – put to death
* ★ are not permitted to own or to carry guns
* ★ Free blacks aren't equal to free white burghers
* ★ Freed slave women are not to wear coloured silk or hoop skirts, fine lace, or any decoration on their hats, or earrings made of gems or imitation gems

It rained that first day in 1838. Just a light drizzle, a weepy day with puffy skies. People said it was God crying. Ashamed of what we'd become. I remember it as if it was yesterday. The slaves had prayed and waited for it, and when January first arrived, most of them had nowhere to go. Some even begged to stay on with the masters who'd maimed them.

This drawing here, it's faded now. Hanibal did it. He could look at something, then put it to paper from memory. He had a good hand and was always looking for paper or cloth or stone. No one knew he had this talent. They didn't know anything. They didn't know Salie could sew. They didn't know I could read. But there was a tailor, an interpreter, a painter, a yellow-skinned Sonqua who could pick up the spoor of the devil, and of course, him. That child there in the picture, is his. He loved that child, and loved Somiela. She changed him. A white man with a bigheartedness too dangerous for his own good. But, let me go back to that first day, the day they put us all on the block and separated me and Noria . . .

I have found that, to make a contented slave, it is necessary to make a thoughtless one. It is necessary to darken his moral and mental vision . . . He must be able to detect no inconsistencies in slavery; he must be made to feel that slavery is right.

(Frederick Douglass, American fugitive slave, autobiographer, and abolitionist leader, 1845)

The auction was held under the tree. The tree which everyone knew near the well, behind the Slave Lodge. Where the Company slaves used to be. There were no longer Company slaves in 1832 – the arrival of the English had changed things, and the Lodge slaves had been freed in 1828 to serve as an example to the settlers who were facing the emancipation of their own slaves. But people still bought and sold human beings, and this sale was special. People had talked about it for days. Three slaves. Valuable. Crafted. Come on the day of the auction and thereby make profit, the poster said.

The morning was hot already for 9 o'clock. Andries de Villiers loosened his collar and stood slightly away from the crowd and cast his eye over a variety of articles, utensils, and horned cattle for sale. He wasn't interested in any of these, and walked to the end of the small platform from where he studied the slave up on the block. Tall and husky, in a vest and pantaloons, the man's long hair stood wild about his face. An intense face, defiant. But Andries was curious about the scars about the ankles. They appeared to have been made by leg irons. Had the owner been brave enough to defy the law? And why was such a strong and crafted slave being sold?

He turned to the man who'd first heard of the auction and told him about it. "Why're they selling him?"

Joost van Heerden shifted his weight to the back of his heels, and surveyed the slave up on the block. "He's Mohametan. Word is he preached to the other slaves, converting them, giving them ideas."

"What kind of ideas?"

"Does it matter? You don't want a slave having any ideas at all. Still, it's hard coming by fresh labour, and a carpenter – where can you find one today? If I didn't have one myself, I'd take the chance. You can always tame him."

Andries agreed. With the oceanic slave trade abolished, it was hard coming by new slaves. No one sold healthy and obedient slaves, and no slave wanted to be sold up country or over the mountain to a sadistic master. It was better to remain with the devil you knew than the one you didn't. The slave before Andries didn't have the demeanour of one who obeyed. The set of his jaw challenged any onlooker to buy him.

Andries wanted to know more, but the auctioneer was up on the block with the slave and had started the proceedings.

". . . nine hundred rix dollars . . ."

A throng of farmers had moved up to the front and a man close to the platform put up his hand.

"Nine hundred and fifty," someone else raised the bid.

"One thousand," the first man countered.

"One thousand and fifty."

"One thousand, one hundred."

Andries watched the proceedings. The price was high – not unusual for a skilled slave. But Andries wasn't sure he wanted a Javanese. He had slaves from Malabar and Ceylon, and to have them all from the same part of the world, speaking the same language, was asking for trouble. You mixed up the races to avoid mutiny. And the Malays were a sly lot, taking every opportunity to rebel. They were also not as suited for field work as the Mozambiquans and Madagascans. His prize negro, Kananga, captured by a Portuguese slaver off the coast of Mozambique, was an excellent mandoor. Prize negroes were introduced into the Cape after British involvement in the slave trade ceased in 1808. Although not technically slaves according to official documents, prize negroes belonged to the category of "slave" rather than "free", and had to serve a fourteen-year apprenticeship. Seized as slaves by the British naval squadron from the ships of other nations, they were to be liberated and bound to prudent masters and mistresses to learn trades or handicrafts so that they could gain their livelihood when their apprenticeships expired. Colonists were keen to have these slaves despite the fact that they came from up the east African coast and were regarded as the least valuable. Whereas masters had to buy slaves – and prices shot up after the ending of the slave trade – prize negroes were distributed by the state without cost. A master could find many uses for a prize negro, even hire him out, and keep most of his earnings. Andries wished he had more like Kananga, but one prize negro was all he'd been allowed.

He studied the slave up on the block. A proud bastard, he thought. He knew the maleier mentality. These people thought they had special avenues to God, and took pride in their suffering. There was another one on his farm, Salie, who also had an annoying way about him. Still, the Malays didn't drink, and being natural craftsmen and clever slaves, had skills the Africans didn't possess. There was a lot of wine on the premises, and the benefits of sobriety had to be weighed against the trouble they caused. Andries was two-minded. The slave looked as though he may be trouble, but for Andries this was an opportunity to increase his work force. He needed barrels, benches, a new barn, and was spending too much money hiring Van Heerden's carpenter when he could have his own. A part of him said yes, another, to walk away.

"Sangora van Java! Any advance?" The auctioneer was a dapper little man in a waistcoat and hat, the words rushing out of his mouth at great speed. He pointed to the shoulders and arms of the slave on the block. "He's strong. All his teeth. No sickness. Do I hear one thousand, two hundred for Sangora van Java . . ?"

No one responded.

"Once, twice . . . going to . . ."

"One thousand, two hundred!" Andries raised his hat.

The hammer fell, and Andries realized he'd bought the slave. A moan behind him made him turn. It was a female slave with an astonishingly beautiful girl waiting to go up on the block. The woman's colourful dress and shoes spoke of respectability, and although she was black as any Madagascan, the smoothness of her hair and sharp features told him she was also Malay. But it wasn't her countenance or finery that intrigued him, it was her grief. For the slave he'd just bought. Were they husband and wife? The arrival of the English had greatly upset things. They had come with their boats and artillery, killed the Boers, and given the heathens ideas. A slave could now marry and lodge a complaint. A Christian slave couldn't be sold. There were too many laws, and with talk of emancipation, a farmer had his hands full to control his slaves. Andries wished the English had stayed in their country and never set foot in the Cape. A tug on his jacket made him turn.

"Please, Seur," the woman beseeched him, speaking a creolized Dutch. "I am Noria, and this is Somiela, my daughter, sixteen years old. I can knit and cook and make clothes. My baby has died recently, there is milk still flowing from me. I can be a wet nurse if there are babies, and Somiela can carry water and bring wood and do many things in the kitchen. I am begging, Seur," she bowed her head, "to please buy us."

Startled by her boldness, Andries was nevertheless touched by the sincerity of her plea. "You know the slave I have bought?"

"He's Sangora Salamah. The father of the baby that has died."

She did not volunteer the name or origin of the father of the girl at her side. The girl wasn't of the same hue as her mother, and had a tawny complexion, with green eyes and brown hair; a half-breed. The half-breeds were the favoured slaves, and the price for both mother and daughter would be high.

"Why are you being sold?"

The auctioneer, spotting the farmer in conversation with her, approached Andries.

"It's against the rules to talk to the slaves."

"I wanted to know the reason she was being sold."

"That information is available for the asking. Not from the slave."

Noria and her daughter were led away, and a few minutes later, were up on the block.

The girl was offered first and Andries watched as several men moved to the front.

The auctioneer stood between the two slaves and pointed to the young one on his left. "Somiela van de Kaap, sixteen years old. A slave with kitchen skills, who can cook and sew. A good playmate for young children. Who will start the bidding for this excellent slave born in the Cape?"

The bid opened at five hundred rix dollars and was immediately taken up by several anxious bidders. Andries looked at the men casting their bids for the girl and wondered whether they were responding to her looks or her skills. It was an unusual looking slave. Too handsome. Dangerous to have on the premises. When the eight hundred mark was reached, the last bidder waited anxiously for the hammer to fall.

Andries tried not to look at Noria. He could sense her anxiety from where he stood. She was terrified. If he didn't buy her and her daughter, they would be separated from Sangora for good.

"Do I hear eight hundred and fifty?"

"Nine hundred."

"Nine hundred and fifty."

"One thousand!" Andries raised his hand.

There was silence. Everyone turned to look at him. One thousand rix dollars for a young girl, even a Cape-born half-breed, was high.

The hammer fell. "Yours, sir. Somiela van de Kaap for one thousand rix dollars."

Andries glanced briefly at Noria. Her eyes were closed, and something like a sigh escaped her lips.

Then it was her turn.

"Noria van Malabar," the auctioneer started. "The mother of Somiela van de Kaap. A wet nurse whose infant has died, about two months from her child bed, being also a clever seamstress, and irons well. Five hundred rix dollars!" He looked directly at Andries. "Perhaps the good gentleman will take the mother also?"

"Six hundred," a voice sounded from the back.

Andries looked around. He didn't recognize the man, but could tell from the cloth and cut of his jacket, the tall black hat on his head, and his distinguished voice, that he was English. He had increased the bid by a whole hundred rix dollars. The Englishman was serious about obtaining the slave.

Andries looked at Noria. He saw fear in her eyes. She didn't want to be separated from her daughter and Sangora, and was waiting for him to bid.

"Who's that man?" he asked Joost.

"He's a doctor of women's complaints, a friend of the new Governor. I believe he'll settle here for six years on the land below the Table Mountain, on Roeland Street."

"An Englishman."

"Yes."

Andries stole a glance at Noria. She was trembling as the bidding went back and forth. The amount reached the figure of eight hundred rix dollars.

"What do you think?" he asked Joost.

"You'll have to move fast if you want her. The Englishman looks serious."

Andries looked at Noria. He had no doubt that she would make a good worker. His wife would also benefit from the help, what with ten-year-old twins, a grown daughter preparing for marriage, and only an old female slave in attendance.

"Seur!"

She was actually calling to him, drawing attention to herself. He didn't look. The bidding reached its peak and he watched the auctioneer ready himself to seal the transaction.

"Bid, man," Van Heerden prodded him in the arm.

"Nine hundred once. Nine hundred twice . . ."

Andries de Villiers looked at the Englishman, waiting anxiously for the hammer to fall. He had seconds left to enter the bidding and stop the mother from going to the foreigner. But Andries did nothing. He kept his hands in his pockets and watched the hammer come down.

Andries took leave of his friend, told the slaves where to sit in the back of the wagon, then got on himself and made his way slowly down Keizersgragt. To his right, Table Mountain rose majestically above the farms on the slopes of Oranje Zigt. To his left lay the Company Gardens, the sea a glittering silver below them. Leaving town, he heard the loud boom of the cannon up on the hill in Waalendorp. It was twelve o'clock.

Andries was tired, and didn't relish the trip ahead. Still, it wasn't the long, arduous journey that it had been a decade ago. Travelling with his father as a boy along the old wagon road from the market to Papendorp used to take a whole morning. All the way to the Wynberg Hill, where Jan van Riebeeck had established his own farm, Bosheuvel, in the 1650s, would take a full day. That road, a curve around the base of the Devil's Peak, had been improved and later formed the route from the seaward side of the Castle in a more or less straight line to the first bastion of the French Lines, then back to the main road. But a new road had since been built. Ten years ago a journey from Cape Town to Simonstown took two days, with an overnight stop at Wynberg. Today, with the new road – providing there was no rain slowing down the horses in the mud, nothing blocking the road, and the load was light enough – the trip to his Wynberg estate from the market in town was less than two hours. It was said too, though Andries found it hard to believe, that letters could be delivered from Cape Town to Simonstown via Wynberg in only three hours.

In the back of the open wagon, Somiela looked forlornly about her. As the horses cantered along the hard road, kicking up dust, taking her further and further away from her mother and the Englishman who'd bought her, she felt a crushing emptiness. It was a feeling not of hunger or pain or anything she'd known before, but of dull despair. Her senses were numbed. She was too dead of spirit to cry. What would she do without her mother? Where was the house she was going to? What kind of place was it? Who would be there? Who would protect her? She had an indication of the kind of people to expect from the man who'd bought her. If he could separate mother and daughter, what kindness could she expect?

She looked at her stepfather sitting across from her. They wouldn't talk. Not in front of the farmer. But they communicated with their eyes, and had had a few minutes alone before being hurried up onto the wagon. What was going through Sangora's mind now, she wondered?

The wagon passed a turnpike, and came upon some fields. On each side were mules, horses, and oxen quietly grazing; here and there a windmill sailed gracefully in full working order. Somiela had been on this road before, as far as the turn-off for the Liesbeek, where she and her mother and Sangora had lived on the Muller farm just a few streets further along until that morning.

She knew the road from the few times she'd been allowed to visit the house in Dorp Street with her mother, when the grootbaas took them in his wagon on a Sunday morning. He would drop them off at the Company Gardens while he went visiting a farmer in the Oranje Zigt area. She recognized some of the places they passed now. They were not even near where the turn-off was to their previous place. Where was this place they were going to?

The wagon was loaded with all the goods that the farmer had bought, and Somiela and Sangora rocked back and forth between the barrels and sacks. She didn't have to look at Sangora to know his thoughts. In his head he would be saying a prayer. In his eyes, nothing would show.

On and on the wagon rolled, past the road where they had turned towards their previous place. The scenery changed yet again and the road became a shady avenue of majestic oaks. Every few hundred yards or so the entrance gate to some private dwelling showed itself, the building in many instances almost hidden by a grove of pine trees. And there were people along the road – women with pitchers of water gazing at them as they passed, a slave laden with fruit strung in bunches at each end of a long bamboo cane which he carried across his shoulder, several olive-complexioned, well featured, half-caste women like herself, quietly trudging towards town – and many children, laughing and playing, gathering acorns that fell from the branches of the aged oaks.

They were now well past any sights that she knew or recognized, and Somiela sensed from the pace and the snorting of the horses that they were reaching their destination. She looked at Sangora. They both looked about them. The wagon had turned off the main road along which they had come, struggled up a rise, gone down halfway the other side, taken another turn, and now was slowing down, heading for the entrance of what seemed to them to be a very large estate.

On no village in the peninsula had the building of the new road a greater impact than on Wynberg. Between the Castle and Westervoort the new road traversed villages and hamlets in much the same way as the old road had done, but after the bridge it went more directly towards Muizenberg and bypassed Wynberg by nearly a mile. The village was a cluster of houses on the slopes of Wynberg Hill and had grown up round a spot on the old wagon road where it crossed a stream known as Krakeel Water.

In 1795 the Dutch were already encamped on Wynberg Hill to meet the British advance from False Bay. After the Battle of Muizenberg, the intention was to make a stand there, but when the British advanced from Bergvliet the Dutch retreated to surrender two days later. The presence of a military camp and Wynberg's reputation as a health resort contributed to the development of the village – soldiers needed food, fresh vegetables, artisans, and officials to serve their needs – and attracted officers and civil servants from India who spent their leave here with their families for a year or more. At the end of the Napoleonic Wars the garrison at the Cape was much reduced, and many of the houses at Wynberg Camp were let to civilians as well as to half-pay officers. After 1815, small pieces of government land were granted to private individuals who built cottages on them. The owners of adjoining farms also began to build huurhuisies, rental cottages, to accommodate visitors.

Zoetewater was a way up from the new road, nestled on twelve morgen of fertile land in isolated splendour at the foot of the Wynberg mountains. It was a magnificent estate with a murmuring stream, forested land, and vineyards stretching up into the hills. The house had started out in the previous century as a simple rectangular room with partitions, known as a longhouse. The only external adornment was a cross on the roof over the door, signifying a Christian inhabitant. It became the home of Marieta and Jasper de Lange in 1812 and they enlarged the house after the birth of their daughter, Elspeth. When Jasper died a decade later, the widow married Andries de Villiers, a man six years younger than she was, with few prospects and many aspirations. With the assistance of a slave with architectural knowledge, and without plans, Andries pulled down the longhouse and erected the dwelling presently standing. The house was flat-roofed, the cross gone, and had a voorhuis for receiving guests, bedrooms with doors, a lofty kitchen, and a bathroom for the family where they could perform their ablutions in privacy. Outside, a light under the huge central gable above the front door was lit at dusk to prevent slaves from gathering in the dark to plot. A jongenshuis housing the male slaves was erected next to the stable, in front of which stood an impressive bell tower. The tower held a bell from a salvaged ship that was rung to summon the slaves to work or to enlist help in case of fire.

The morning at the auction had tired him, and Andries was grateful when he reached the entrance to the oak-lined estate and steered the wagon up the drive. Alone in front, he had listened for conversation from the slaves in the back, but they had not spoken. Once, when he had looked around, he saw Sangora staring impassively at the passing land, the girl with her head on her knees.

The ride from town had given Andries time to think. One thing he knew was that Sangora was no ordinary slave. There was intelligence in his brow. He had an inner demon. Was proud. But that too had its usefulness. There was a lot of work at Zoetewater, and Sangora would fit well into his plans. The agricultural year started in May with the coming of the first rains; Andries hired out some of his slaves to Joost van Heerden after the grape-picking and pressing season in April when the soil for barley and wheat had to be prepared with manure and ploughed. It was heavy work needing heavy labour. Van Heerden needed six to eight ploughs going at a time, each of them drawn by ten oxen. Three slaves attended each plough: one to lead the team, one to drive it on, and the third to guide the plough. The wheat farmer depended not only on his own workers and Andries's, but also on the nomadic Koi-na who came looking for seasonal work. The threshing and harvesting of the grain co-incided with the grape-picking season on Andries's own estate, and it was February already, the hottest month of the year, when the vines were top-heavy with fruit. Two of his slaves were at Joost van Heerden's now, harvesting the grain before the onset of the strong south-easter winds; the rest of the men were keeping birds and stray animals out of the Zoetewater vineyards as well as picking grapes. Andries's plan of strategy with Sangora would be to use the slave out in the field to break his spirit – maleiers didn't like outside work – then install him in the barn to do the carpentry work.

About the half-breed, Andries wasn't sure he'd done the right thing. Had his true motive for making the purchase been so the girl could help in the kitchen, or to increase the slave population on his farm? There were no females at Zoetewater except for Rachel, a full-bred Ceylonese of fifty years. Andries was all too aware of the unrest amongst the males and the fact that soon all slave trading would be stopped. He also had a suspicion that his wife, Marieta, wouldn't like this girl. She hadn't liked the look and manner of the last one, and he had swapped her with a farmer from the interior for sixty wagon-loads of wood.

The wagon arrived at the stable next to the jongenshuis, and Arend, the bastard interpreter, was first on the scene. It was his duty to outspan the horses when the master or visitors arrived. As the interpreter, Arend was furnished with a hat to signify that he understood Dutch, and also spoke English and Melayu, as well as Portuguese and the language of the Hottentots. Arend was the son of the aia, Rachel van Ceylon, and had been fathered by a Frenchman who had promised Rachel he would purchase the boy's freedom. But he had reneged on his word, and had given her money instead.

Andries got down from the wagon. "Any visitors while I was gone?"

"Yes, Seur. Mijnheer Martinus is here, for the kleinnooi."

Andries nodded. It was a stroke of luck that his stepdaughter, Elspeth, was being courted by a landdrost. The law was on the premises – a good thing for the slaves to keep in mind.

"Tell them to get down," Andries gestured towards the wagon. "And ask them their names."

Arend looked at the two slaves sitting upright in the back of the wagon. The male appeared to be in his late twenties, of slim build, sharp-featured, and dark, and the girl – Arend had been at Zoetewater for eighteen years, and had never seen a half-breed with green eyes – the girl was more beautiful than any he'd seen. His first concern was for the adornment of lace on her dress and the bangles on her arm. Slaves were forbidden such finery, and the lace and bangles would stir the anger of the farmer's wife. Arend helped her down from the wagon and said something to her in Melayu. She looked down at her arms, and answered him without looking up.

"Her name is Somiela van de Kaap, Seur."

"Tell her she can keep her name."

Arend related this to the girl. Somiela nodded that she understood. She looked nervously about. They were at the lower end of a rise, in front of a stable next to which there were barns and a long, low building, away from the main house which was higher up. They were on a wine farm. She had never been on a wine farm before: coming onto the property along the drive flanked on both side by tall trees, she had seen an apple orchard on her left, vineyards on her right. She did not have to be told that her new owners were rich. She could tell this from the vineyards, the neat rows of trees, the stable, the wagon house, barns. It would take many people to run such a place. But there were no slave women or children that she could see.

"And his?" Andries asked, although he already knew.

"Sangora Salamah," the Javanese answered himself in Cape Dutch. "Somiela's my stepdaughter."

Andries narrowed his eyes as he looked at the slave. He hadn't invited Sangora to speak. But the response was informative. It showed courage. Also that the slave was articulate.

"From today onwards," the farmer said harshly, "your name will be February. You understand? You'll work under the mandoor, Kananga, and do as he says. I see you have scars on your legs. What are they from?"

Sangora looked down at his ankles, then up at the farmer. "Chains."

"What for?"

"For speaking the truth."

Andries didn't expect this answer. "What's the truth?"

"That we all need God."

"That we all need God, Seur. Don't you know how to speak?"

"That we all need God, Seur."

Andries looked at him. "We don't need the truth here. There's only my truth. And no slave here's been in chains. I don't like chains. But I won't hesitate to use them on you if you're trouble. Understand?" He turned to Arend. "Take him to the jongenshuis. And tell Kananga I want to see him."

Sangora turned to Somiela. "It won't be forever," he said to her in Melayu. "One day we'll be free."

"What did he say?" Andries asked Arend.

"He told her to behave."

"Come," Andries said to Somiela.

Somiela stared after the departing figures, then followed the farmer to the back of the house. They entered the kitchen and came upon Marieta, a stern-faced woman in a common calico bonnet. She had a shawl draped over her shoulders despite the February heat, and she was drinking coffee at the table with her daughter, Elspeth, and the landdrost, Martinus Kloot. At the hearth, the aia, Rachel, was wiping the hands and mouths of Leentje and Annie, the ten-year-old twins.

"Pa!" Annie exclaimed. "Did you bring us anything?"

"A playmate, who will also walk you to school, and look after you. Her name's Somiela."

There was silence as everyone stared at the girl who was standing silently behind Andries. Slaves came in various shades of swarthiness. This one was light-complexioned with green eyes and a heart-shaped face, with brown hair falling naturally past her shoulders to her waist. Her dress was trimmed with lace, tight across the bodice, with a full skirt, and even though it showed no skin, couldn't conceal her burgeoning maturity.

"A fine-looking thing," the words popped out of Martinus's mouth before he could stop himself.

Marieta's thin lips pulled together in a sneer. She didn't like the remark. It flattered the girl, and she didn't like hearing her prospective son-in-law talk this way about a slave.

"We didn't need more help in the house. What good will she be except to cause havoc amongst the males? Can she speak the language?"

"She's Cape-born, there's no problem. A half-breed."

"We can see all right what she is. A naai-mandje."

Andries was surprised to hear his wife utter such a slur. To naai was to sew or to have sexual intercourse; mandje was a basket. It was bad form in front of the guest. It also didn't bode well for the girl.

"Well, I've bought her, and she's here. She can help Rachel in the kitchen, and look after the twins."

Marieta got up. She had been pleasant-looking when she was

young, but time had been cruel and she looked older than her thirty-eight years. She came to stand in front of Somiela. "Where did you get these things on your arms?"

Somiela was standing just inside the back door, and was being prodded and inspected by the twins who had walked over to her and gazed in fascination at her straight hair so different from their tight curls.

"From my mother."

"A common slave has such things? Take them off and give them here."

Somiela hesitated.

"Take them off, and give them to the nooi," Andries said.

Somiela looked at the bangles above her wrists. The four delicate bangles carved out of yellowwood had been given to her by Sangora when she was ten years old. Sangora had been with her mother a few years by then. She liked the dull sound the bangles made when they swung on her arms and she had never taken them off. No one had asked her to take them off before, not even the nooi or the seur at the previous place. She didn't even know if the bangles would come off her wrists. Her arms would feel naked without them. But she knew from the faces around the table, except for the man who had spoken, that she should obey. She worked them off over her hands and handed them to the farmer's wife without looking her in the face.

"Mother and daughter were on the block together," Andries said. "I couldn't take the chance buying a whole family."

"But you bought *her*. Why? Take her to the back, Rachel, and get rid of the lace on that dress. Why didn't you buy the mother instead?"

Rachel left with Somiela through the back door.

"I bought the stepfather," Andries responded.

"You mean you bought two?"

"It was a good morning for bargains. And I can use a carpenter. You don't come across them every day."

"No one sells carpenters. There must be something wrong with him."

"There's nothing wrong with him. He just preached his religion and converted some slaves."

26

"*Just?* You've brought a troublemaker here? We could all be killed."

"His crime isn't one of violence."

Martinus coughed politely. "A slave with power over other slaves is perhaps more dangerous, if you don't mind me saying so, Oom Andries. It seems like this one has powers, if he can convert people to his beliefs."

"He won't give trouble. The maleiers are good craftsmen. They're also sober slaves, they don't drink. And I have plans for him. I'll work him in the field under Kananga. Kananga will know how to cut his wind."

Marieta looked at her daughter and the landdrost. They had just finished talking about Kananga. "You'll have to do something about Kananga, and quickly," she said. "I wouldn't sing his praises if I were you. He's beaten Siek Klaas senseless and broken his ribs for losing one of the cows."

"What?"

"He's gone too far this time. There'll be consequences if the slave dies. We've had the Protector of Slaves here already, we can't afford to have him here again."

Andries knew well what would happen. "Did they find the cow?"

"No."

He pulled up a chair. "I've sent Arend to call Kananga. I'll talk to him. He's not stupid. He knows what happens the second time." He wondered how Kananga and the new slave would get along. Kananga took his pleasure with the males, and Sangora, with his straight hair and fine features, would be hard for him to resist.

A shadow darkened the doorway and the massive bulk of the Mozambiquan rose up before them. Kananga had thick features, big hands, and clumps of wiry hair flattened with grease. He had on pantaloons like the others, but wore a waistcoat over his shirt to indicate his mandoor status. In his hand he carried a sjambok, a heavy whip made of rhinoceros hide the width of a man's finger, with which he prodded and whipped the slaves. A prize negro, he had served five years of his fourteen-year apprenticeship as a hangman's assistant, then had worked three years on the farm, with six more to go. But even though Kananga had come free of charge, he had cost Andries money when two slaves absconded as a result of the mandoor's cruelty. For Andries, however, he was invaluable. Kananga got extra performance out of the slaves, freeing them up faster for hire to other farmers – all resulting in profits for Zoetewater.

Andries got up and went to the back door. From there he could see all the way down to the chicken run, stable, wagon house, and jongenshuis on his right. There was an apricot tree to the side of the jongenshuis, under which the men ate, and a mulberry tree at the back of it, with several tree stumps and a water barrel where they washed. To the right of this was a small kraal. The woodworking barn was to the left of the property, next to the buitekamer. To cross from the barn to the jongenshuis was a good two hundred yards, and you had to pass the barn to go out down the drive. The vineyards spread out from below the jongenshuis, up into the hills.

"There're two new slaves," he addressed Kananga. "A carpenter and a house servant. The male's name from today on-wards is February. Work him. He's not a field slave, but I want him outside for a while." He paused to lend gravity to what he was about to say next. "I don't want you touching this slave."

Kananga looked up.

"You know what I mean," said Andries. "You leave him alone. I don't want trouble. The female's his stepdaughter. Discourage the men. I don't want Arend or Salie thinking there's something for them here to play with. Understand?"

Kananga grunted. He hardly answered, and never added "seur" when he did. Andries let it go, aware that all he could do was sell Kananga if he was unhappy with him. There was no punishment he could inflict. Kananga was mean and cruel, and while this had its benefits in the field, it was hazardous for an owner. Andries's only control over the Mozambiquan was the threat of sale.

"Now, what happened to Siek Klaas? I hear you've broken his ribs."

"He lost a cow."

"So you beat him unconscious? Didn't you learn anything the last time? You want the Protector of Slaves on my neck again? They'll sling your heathen's arse on Robben Island if he dies and there's nothing anyone will be able to do about it. You want that?"

The mandoor's nostrils flared slightly.

"Where's the cow now?" Andries asked when he saw that no answer was forthcoming.

"I don't know."

"How can a cow just disappear? How do you know he didn't sell it for dagga or money?"

"He didn't. I questioned some drosters who came begging for food. They don't know anything. No one's got a cow. Siek Klaas grazed the cattle on the other side of the mountain, and was gone for three days. When he returned, one was missing. He forgot to count them. That's why I beat him. I didn't want to kill him."

"That may be so, but you're responsible for what goes on with the men out there. Cows are expensive, and this one you're paying for. There'll be no money coming to you for months."

Kananga's left eye twitched. But he said nothing.

In the yard, Rachel led Somiela to a barrel of water at the back of the jongenshuis where the males washed their hands and feet at the end of the day. She didn't know what it was about the girl – her unhappiness, bewilderment, the separation from her mother – but Rachel was reminded of her own arrival at Zoetewater two decades ago. She too had been separated from a loved one – her female child was living elsewhere. She had not seen that child in twenty years, did not know where she was, what she looked like now; if she was married, free, or even alive. Rachel understood pain, and the pain of loss was the hardest. It would swell and subside, but forever lay buried like a pebble inside the heart. Somiela was only at the beginning of her grief.

"Take off your dress and get into the water. I've got a pinafore here for you to put on. It's the kleinnooi's and should fit you. Later, I want you to take off the lace on your dress."

"I want to keep my dress."

"You will. Take it off now, and get in."

Somiela looked about her. They were out in the open behind the jongenshuis where the vineyards started up the hill. In amongst the rows were men with baskets of grapes staring at them.

Rachel saw her concern. "They're far away, they can't see. I'll stand in front of you."

Somiela stepped into the barrel and slid off her dress.

"What's your name?" Rachel asked.

"Somiela."

"And the one who came with you?"

"He's my mother's husband, Sangora. My mother had a baby a few weeks ago. He died in his sleep. An Englishman doctor bought my mother. Someone told Sangora he lives at the foot of the Table Mountain, on Roeland Street. Sangora says he'll find him, and my mother. One day we'll all be together again."

"Listen to me," Rachel said, taking a bar of soap from her apron pocket and giving it to Somiela to wash herself with. "I know it's hard being away from your mother, not knowing where she is or when you'll see her, but you'll make yourself sick working up all these ideas in your head. You must think of yourself now, how to survive in the house. Listen to Rachel and you won't go wrong. Are you listening?"

"Yes."

"The benefit of being in the house is that you'll have food to eat and clothes to wear, and you'll sleep warm next to the fireplace. But you'll also be constantly under the feet of the family. The master's kind if you do as he says. The women come upon you like the wind, fast and unexpected, even the twins. Children learn early how the game's played. Don't argue back, and don't make yourself grander than them. That man's right, you're a fine-looking thing, but on Zoetewater, it's not a blessing, it's a curse. Your looks are not to your benefit here."

Somiela lowered her gaze to the inkiness of the water.

Rachel softened. "It's not so bad, you'll see. And there's hope. In the kitchen you hear many things. The landdrost always brings news. One day we'll be free. God won't keep us like this."

Somiela's interest was piqued by the reference to God. "You're Mohametan also?"

"No. They'll punish us if they think we listen to the religious nonsense of the Mohametans. They don't mind the Mohametans working for them – we have one here called Salie van Celebes – but they don't want us listening to them. There's a house in Dorp

Street where the Mohametans teach people. Arend and Salie go there on their day off. They leave early on Sundays and are back by the time the bell rings."

"I know that house. I've been there with my mother when we cut the orange leaves on the Prophet's birthday. It's high up on the hill. After we cut the leaves, they serve tea and cake."

"Your owners were good to let you go."

"We were allowed to do things in private, but not to talk to the other slaves about it. The trouble started when Sangora took them to the house. The master warned him. He didn't listen. When three of the slaves converted and refused to do certain things because they interfered with their new beliefs, Sangora was put in chains."

"They can't put you in chains any more."

"Our master did, for a whole week, and gave all of them twenty-five strokes. He'd taught all the slaves how to read."

"Sangora can read?"

"Yes. And me, and my mother."

"My son, Arend, the interpreter – the people in Dorp Street have converted him. He has a Mohametan name also, Ali, but they don't know in the house. They don't know he's converted. We're not allowed to turn Christian, so what god do we have? How can we marry? The Mohametans will marry you. God recognizes this marriage even if the law doesn't. When I was young, there was a man who wanted to marry me, but the seur wouldn't let me be baptised and wouldn't give me my freedom." Rachel stopped at the sound of voices. "Someone's coming. Dry yourself with this. And remember what I said."

A few minutes later Elspeth and Martinus appeared round the side of the building just as Somiela had pulled on the pinafore Rachel had handed to her.

"Here you are, Rachel, I was looking for you. I need you to iron my dress. The half-breed can rub up my shoes. Show her how to do it."

"Yes, Kleinnooi."

"And do something about that long hair. It's not necessary to hang so in her face. Cut it, it's too long."

Rachel looked at Somiela who reached instinctively to protect her long tresses.

"Kleinnooi wants me to cut her hair?"

"That's what I said."

"No!" Somiela blurted suddenly.

They all stared at Somiela.

Elspeth came forward. "What did you say?"

Somiela realized with a start what she'd done. But even as she flinched from the reproach which she knew would follow her outspokenness, she couldn't stop herself. "I said no. You can't cut my hair."

Elspeth had never been openly defied by a slave. And in front of a guest and another slave. "You dare to speak back to me?" She raised her hand to strike her.

"No, Elspeth," Martinus said. "Give her a chance."

"Didn't you hear what she said?"

"She's new, she doesn't know."

"She's not a slave from yesterday. She knows."

"She just got here. If you're concerned that her hair will fall into the food when she works in the kitchen, she can cover it, like Rachel here, with a doek. Let the girl keep what she has."

Rachel felt a horrible foreboding. It was the second time the landdrost had spoken impulsively. And to defend a slave. Elspeth hadn't snared the landdrost yet, and had to keep up some sort of pretence. Still, it wasn't in her nature to be kind, and the landdrost, by accident or design, had made things worse for Somiela.

"Get the scissors, Rachel."

"The scissors, Kleinnooi?"

"Are you deaf? Get the scissors, and hurry up."

Rachel mumbled something under her breath, and walked off. She had to obey. To do anything else would make matters worse. She knew Elspeth. Had nursed her, washed her, knew her inside out. Elspeth felt threatened. The slave had a beauty you had to be born with. Elspeth wanted to shame her, make her look ugly, take the little she had away. What chance did Somiela have in the house?

Rachel found the scissors in the sewing box in the voorkamer. She returned to the scene behind the jongenshuis and handed them over.

"Hold her," Elspeth ordered.

"No one has to hold me," Somiela hissed.

Elspeth smacked her across the face. "Shut your mouth!"

Somiela's eyes flashed. She stood silent, daring Elspeth to go ahead.

"Really, Elspeth," Martinus said. "It's not necessary." He could bear it no longer, and turned to go back to the house.

Elspeth didn't care how she appeared to him now. She jerked Somiela's head back, gathered the hair in a bunch, then cut straight across it, chopping it off high in the neck. She flung the queue, a foot long, into the wind. Farther away, watching all this from where he stood under a tree, a young slave dressed only in pantaloons picked up a clump of wet hair.

Elspeth handed the scissors back to Rachel and ran after Martinus.

Somiela felt with her hands about her ears. "My hair's gone, Rachel," she burst into tears. "It's gone! How could she? My mother never cut my hair. It's *my* hair. How could she do it? She cut it, Rachel. She cut my hair . . ."

Rachel didn't know what to say. In a moment of mean-heartedness, Elspeth had killed the girl's spirit. She wanted to put her arms about Somiela and reassure her, but would not make up words and deliver false promises. There was no room for self-pity if Somiela was to survive.

"I told you not to blurt out feelings and argue back. She had no right cutting your hair, but that man defended you, and you pay a price for kindnesses like that. Don't you see? You're a threat to her. You're a slave and you dare to look white, dare to have straight hair, green eyes, and then have the cheek to open your mouth. Slaves don't have opinions. They stand with their mouths shut and take it."

"I won't take it, I won't!"

"Then pay the price. It's your choice."

"What did my hair do to her? I did nothing, Rachel, nothing! My dress, my bangles, and now my hair." She sank down to her knees and sobbed into her hands.

Rachel stood by helplessly. "Listen to me. You want them to see what they've done to you? You want them to see that they've broken you? You're a slave, child. The faster you see that, the better it'll be for you. You can't do anything about your hair, your hair's gone. If you want to keep it in future, I suggest you wear a doek from now on."

"I don't want a doek."

A noise behind them made them turn. The mandoor and Sangora were heading for the water barrel.

"Somiela!" Sangora rushed forward, seeing her huddled on the ground. "Why are you crying? *Allah!*" he invoked God's name. "Who did this to you?"

"The kleinnooi. She just took my hair and cut it. I didn't do anything."

"But why?"

"I don't know. You can ask Rachel. She just did it, out of spite."

Sangora looked up at the house and started towards it.

"Where do you think you're going!" Kananga shouted. "Stop!"

Sangora pressed on.

"I said, stop!" Kananga lashed out with the sjambok, and the tip caught Sangora on the shoulder. For a moment it looked as if there might be a fight, but a look passed between them and Kananga's hand dropped to his side. "You have no reason to go up there."

"Who'll stop me?" Sangora snarled, and before Kananga could do anything, he was gone.

Andries, looking through the kitchen window, saw the slave he'd just purchased walk up hurriedly from the jongenshuis. He could tell from the stride – and from Kananga running up behind – that something was dreadfully wrong. He met them at the back door.

"What's going on?"

Sangora waited until he was directly in front of the farmer, and composed himself. "I've come to make a complaint. It's about my stepchild. Her hair was cut by someone in the house. I'd like to know what she's done to deserve it."

Andries was shocked to hear this, but even more alarmed by the audacity. "You will dare to come here and question me?"

"I am asking respectfully, Seur, what she has done to deserve such a thing. She is back there, crying."

"What is a slave's tears?"

"But – "

34

"Shut your trap! You're an insolent maleier. I won't have it. Now get back to work before I have you flogged."

"We have rights. I can go to the Protector of Slaves."

Andries turned red. "You will threaten me? How dare you!" He spotted Arend near the stable, and called out to him. "Arend, get the chains from the barn!"

"Chains are against the law," Sangora continued, unafraid.

Andries had had enough. "Kananga, teach him a lesson!"

Kananga looked from the farmer to the slave, and raised the sjambok. He hesitated for a moment, then did as he was told. The whip came down again and again. Sangora flinched, but made no move to ward off the blows. He kept the farmer in his sight, as well as the man and two women who had come out on the stoep. He could tell from the smirk on the young woman's face that it was she who had cut Somiela's hair. His eyes ate into hers. Her smile faded. The man at her side looked away.

Arend came with the leg irons and handed it to the farmer.

"Where're the keys?"

"There're no keys, Seur. They're not locked."

"I can see they're not locked. But they will be when they're on. Go back and look for them."

"Yes, Seur."

"Put them on," he ordered the mandoor. Then he turned to Sangora. "If no one's taught you how to behave, I will. There's no law here except mine, I told you. You follow it or suffer the consequences." He looked at Martinus behind him. Martinus was a landdrost. He *was* the law. But Martinus was soon to be family. Things happened when you had slaves, and what happened in a man's house, stayed in his house. Andries had no fear of Martinus. But he noted the look on his face, and knew then that Elspeth had cut the girl's hair.

Sangora felt the irons clamped onto his legs; cold, heavy, the chain between them short. He looked up from his ankles to the farmer. He didn't hate people, but hated this man. And hated the women beside him.

"You won't break me," he hissed.

Andries narrowed his eyes. In his gut he knew he had made a serious mistake buying the slave.

"Ten strokes, Kananga – give it to him!"

"Oom . . ." Martinus pleaded.

"Flog him!" Marieta added. "I've heard enough!"

Rachel and Somiela watched everything from where they stood hidden by the mulberry tree. They heard the voices, saw the leg irons clamped on, Sangora falling down to his knees under the blows from the sjambok.

"It's all my fault," Somiela lamented.

"It's not. It was his choice to go up there. He'll learn. And so will you. I just don't want you to learn the hard way. Come on, I want to check on Siek Klaas before we go back."

Somiela stole a last look. The flogging had stopped. Sangora struggled to his feet, fell. Kananga straightened him up and led him away.

"This is the jongenshuis, where the men sleep," Rachel said, leading Somiela around the side of the building. "Don't come here on your own unless the seur sends you. These men are bereft of the rights of nature and starved for a woman's flesh. Stay out of their way." They reached the doorway and saw several slaves standing about.

"What're you all doing here? You have no work to do?" she asked.

"We saw what happened," an old slave in pantaloons and a torn jacket said. "They can't do that. It's against the law."

"And who will enforce this law?" Rachel asked sarcastically. "Get back to work, all of you, before he comes down here and find you loafing around. Where's Arend?"

"Inside, with Siek Klaas," Geduld said.

Rachel liked the soft-spoken little mountain man from the north. Geduld was a sallow-skinned Sonqua who came during the grape-picking season to Zoetewater where he took off his loin cloth and worked alongside the slaves. When the season ended, he wiped down his arrows, tied on his flap, and disappeared into the interior until it was time to come down to the Cape again. A fast runner and an excellent tracker, it was he who had led Andries along the Muizenberg mountains a year ago to a cave where two runaway slaves had hidden. He had been given the nickname

Geduld because of his ability to persevere: it was said that he once sat nine days at a stream in the Drakenstein mountains waiting for a group of Sonqua to arrive.

"How's Siek Klaas?"

Geduld's eyes became sad. "His ancestors are waiting."

"He's dead?" Rachel asked irritably, not sure of his meaning. Geduld never spoke in a straight line, and was always on about the moon and the stars and the gods. She didn't have time for it now.

"Not yet."

"Well, speak so I can understand you then." She stepped through the doorway.

Somiela stood a few feet from the entrance, surrounded by strange men. She didn't know where to look, what to do. She was in an ugly old pinafore with chopped-off hair, and felt everyone staring at her. The dress she had taken off was rolled in a small bundle in her hands and she picked at it nervously.

"You're new here," a slave said in Melayu. He was sharp-featured, with smooth brown skin, very white teeth, and a mane of black hair. His chest muscles glistened with sweat.

She looked at him. It was the same slave she had seen under the tree picking up her hair. The hair was plaited in a coil, stuck in the waist of his pants. It gave her a strange feeling to see it there.

"I'm Salie," he came forward. "You're the carpenter's step-daughter?"

"You've got my hair."

He looked down at his waist. "Yes."

"Why?"

"Do you want it back?"

"I just wanted to know why you took it. It would've been better if it had blown away in the wind."

He caught her meaning and tried not to look at her head. "I saw what happened. But it will grow back. Hair grows back. They can't grow a conscience, but you'll get back your hair. Here," he said, handing her back the coil, "you can have it."

Somiela looked at him. He was very handsome.

"No. Keep it."

He looked at her, smiled. "You are sure?"

"Yes," she replied, knowing instinctively that by allowing him to keep the hair, she was acknowledging a connection between them.

Rachel saw what was happening. "Hai!" she called roughly. "Leave her alone. Somiela, come here."

"We'll talk again," Salie said. "I'm Mohametan also."

Somiela entered the jongenshuis: a long room, windowless, foul-smelling, the floor strewn with coir pads. Her eyes adjusted to the dark and she saw an old slave comatose on the mattress closest to the door. The front of his shirt was soiled with blood, and Arend was down on his knees, his ear to the slave's chest.

"How bad is it?" Rachel asked.

"His heart's still beating, but it's not only his ribs. He has other sickness, the doctor said. Kananga's beating made it worse."

"There'll be trouble now," Rachel said. "Kananga knows the Protector will come if Siek Klaas dies. Go back to your work, you can't do anything for him."

Arend left the room and Rachel took a clean cloth from her apron with which she wiped Siek Klaas's face and hands.

Somiela looked down at the battered old face and for a moment imagined that it was Sangora lying there, all broken up, with his eyes closed. She shuddered. The Zoetewater people were cruel. She hoped nothing like this ever happened to her stepfather.

"Come," Rachel said. "We can't stay here forever, we have to go back and serve supper. When we're done in the kitchen, I want you to take the lace off that dress and wash it. And don't forget the kleinnooi's shoes. They don't like to see you do nothing even when there's nothing to do. You must always keep busy. Do you understand?"

"Yes."

"Yes, Rachel," Rachel said gently, teaching her the correct way to speak.

"Yes, Rachel."

"And don't blame yourself for the chains. He did what he had to do. Any parent would've done it."

"Yes, Rachel."

Rachel hastened her stride to the house. In her breast was a lightness. Zoetewater would have fresh troubles now, but the arrival of the girl had renewed her. She was not alone. She had someone to fuss over, someone she could talk to and pretend was her own. There was also a chance her son might find his bride on the farm.

Restore the country of which our forefathers were despoiled by the Dutch and we have nothing more to ask . . . We have lived very contentedly . . . before these Dutch plunderers molested us, and why should we not do so again if left to ourselves? Has not the Groot Baas given plenty of grass-roots, and berries and grasshoppers for our use; and, till the Dutch destroyed them, abundance of wild animals to hunt? And will they not return and multiply when these destroyers are gone?

(The rebel leader Klaas Stuurman Barrow, *Travels*, Volume II, p.111)

Far, far north in the Karoo, the day broke silent and hot over the scarred, cracked land of the Hantamberge. The morning was like a hundred mornings before and arrived cloudless and dry, with no sign of rain, no hint of life on the still, desolate terrain.

A group of Sonqua heading north saw a brood of vultures swooping up ahead, and moved faster. What had brought the scavengers, what had they seen? The drought had squeezed out every last drop of moisture from the land, and deadened the spirit of all creatures. The animals had left this shrivelled wasteland long ago for other pastures.

"There's something there," one of the little hunters said.

"Maybe only a snake."

"Even a snake. We are hungry."

They neared a cluster of rocks and came suddenly upon the carcass of an eland in an open clearing. Their surprise at finding this gift waiting for them in this forsaken land was so great that the women dropped their loads and rushed forward, leaving their husbands and children staring after them.

"Wait!"

They stopped and looked at the one who had spoken. It wasn't their leader, Tuka, the son of Toma who had been gored to death by a buffalo, but the white man trotting alongside on his horse who'd picked up their trail two days south and accompanied them to the Oorlogsrivier. His eyes were grey, his silver hair long, his eyefolds slanted like those of the Sonqua; he was the half-breed son of Eyes of the Sky, Toma's old rival from years ago. They knew this man's history. Harman Kloot was a friend, spoke their language, wore their skins, and frequently showed up at their camps to come and shoot springbok or eland for their fires.

"What is it?" Tuka came up.

Harman kneeled beside the carcass. "Something doesn't look right. Where did this eland come from, and what killed it? There're no antelope in these parts." Then he saw the bullet hole in the soft belly, oozing blood. The body had been moved there. It was a trap. Before he could say anything, there was a thunder of hooves and three riders with rifles materialized over the rant and came galloping towards them.

"Run!"

Women and children scattered in all directions. Tuka and Koerikei reached for their bows. Koerikei was the oldest member of the group, bent with age, but had lost none of the agility that he possessed as its leader when he was younger. He stood steadfast next to Tuka, dropping to one knee at the last moment to aim his arrow.

Harman's heart raced in his chest. He should've recognized the situation, and investigated when Tuka said he'd smelled blood. It was an old ploy, killing game and leaving it for the hunters to find, only to attack them while they were eating. He had no choice. He cocked his rifle and fired. The bullet flung one of the men from his horse, and the riders, shocked to find themselves being fired at, came to an abrupt halt.

"It's him!" one of them shouted, aiming his rifle. "Roeloff Kloot's son!"

Harman sprang to the attack. He had already reloaded, and fired a second shot over their heads. At the same time there was a murderous scream as one of the Sonqua's arrows struck a horse.

"Go back, I'm warning you!" he shouted.

The attackers knew they were beaten. They had an injured man and a wounded horse. They waved their rifles, promising revenge, then turned around and rode off.

Harman stood for a few moments watching them. They rode a short distance, then stopped. There was poison on the tip of the arrow. They had to cut open the wound and clean it or they would have a dead horse.

"They tried to kill us," Tuka said, visibly shaken.

"And to steal your children and your women to work on their farms. They killed this eland to lure you here. You must leave right away, they're coming back with reinforcements. I've injured one of their men. They'll have no mercy when they return."

"What about all this food? Our bellies are empty. We can't just leave this eland for the vultures."

"I'll bring it to you. They'll be looking for all of us. Split up in two groups. I'll find you by nightfall."

Tuka looked at the slain animal, then at Koerikei.

Harman waited. He knew that even though Tuka was the leader, he would wait for Koerikei to speak. Tuka was the same age as him, young for a leader, but in Sonqua culture, age mattered less than courage and strength. Still, even leaders had to listen to the wise counsel of elders.

Koerikei looked wearily at the shrivelled land around him. The faces of his people were painful to behold, but they had suffered the spite of the gods many times before. Food was essential and sorely needed, but the group's safety came first.

"We haven't eaten in days, and we're hungry, but the son of Eyes of the Sky is right. We can't waste any time here. We must pick up our arrows and leave right away. They'll expect us to continue north. We'll go east until the sun is directly overhead, then turn north again."

"Can't we take out the liver quickly?" someone asked.

"We must go."

The women looked with sad eyes at the carcass, then dutifully took their babies to their hips and followed Tuka and Koerikei.

Harman set quickly to work on the carcass. He wanted to disembowel it to lighten the load on his horse and knew he didn't have much time before the riders returned with their flintlock muskets, this time to steal *and* to kill. He knew one of them, Gerrit Malan. Malan bought sheep from his father. And if he had recognized the bushy-haired Malan, Malan had also recognized him. The news would be out by day's end. Harman Kloot had been with the Sonqua and shot a farmer. There would be a price on his head.

He slit open the belly and fought down his nausea at the stench of the gases released. He reached into the warm flesh and pulled out the entrails. The vultures formed a dark cloud overhead, their sharp eyes boring into his back. Then a swoop of wings as they settled on the ground a few yards away. He tossed them a handful of guts. They seized upon it and danced off a short distance, the bloody intestines trailing from their beaks. Yet his work wasn't done. There was still the covering of the tracks. It would delay him, but give the Sonqua extra time.

He walked to a nearby bush and pulled off a branch. Following the hunters' tracks for almost a mile to a dry riverbed, he walked back carefully on the same trail, sweeping the branch lightly over the tracks, careful to leave the surface dotted with stones and twigs and odd chips of bleached bone to give the appearance of undisturbed ground. The sun was reaching its midway point when he slung the eland over the mare, and set a false trail leading west.

But he rode uneasily. What he'd done would come back to haunt him. He'd aided the Sonqua and injured a farmer. A white man. Who would understand? Who would care? The Sonqua were of no consequence to farmers. They were savages, thieves. He was also concerned that his father, who didn't know where he was, might get the news before he'd had a chance to explain. Well-known for his merino, his father was a complex man, easy to misunderstand if you didn't know his philosophy. But Harman understood the way his father's mind worked, better than his younger brother, Karel, who worked on Oupa Wynand's farm in the Cederberg, hoping to some day inherit it, and his older brother, Martinus, who was a landdrost in the Cape. Harman hoped his actions would have no repercussions for the family.

For the farmer, the land was an economic resource. For the Sonqua, the natural world and the world of spirit were one. Thus the eland, favourite of the trickster god /Kaggen, was also a valued source of food. Humans and animals were closely linked. The people of today were the animals of the past and the animals of today were the dawn-time people. The people of today still carried within themselves aspects of their dawn-time animal identity, and the animals retained certain human characteristics.

Loss of territory, or the invasion of hunting grounds, involved more than economic loss; it was also a spiritual crisis. The coming of the settlers with their attitude to man and nature was something to which the Sonqua couldn't adapt. Every krans, fountain, pool of water carried reminders of an order whose foundations had been laid long before the coming of the farmers. These people had blundered into this world, ignorant of its principles, unaware of its secrets. They had desecrated its landscape and destroyed its most precious treasures, killing eland, piling the carcasses high on their wagons, without regard to the meaning of their actions.

The Sonqua had been shot at and killed and rounded up to work as servants on farms. After this incident, Harman had no doubt that the kommando would come after them in full force.

Would his father be angry when the news reached him? Harman's visits with the Sonqua were not secret, and his father should be first to understand. It was he, after all, who'd started it. *You are not from the same mother as your brothers and sister, Harman. Your mother is Sonqua. We played together as children. I won't make apologies for my youth.* Harman was sixteen when his father told him, just the two of them sitting around a fire, on one of their excursions into the bush. Sanna, the old Koi-na servant, had filled in the gaps.

. . . Zokho was captured and brought to the farm as a girl. Smoke in the Eyes, they called her. Your father had great feeling for Zokho. But there's no place for people like them in the Karoo. It was perhaps better that she did what she did. Neeltje took you, just a few hours old. She's your real mother, Harman. Not the one who gave you birth, but the one who saved you and loved you ever since . . .

A sudden change in the spoor made him dismount. The tracks were fresh. Six horsemen! While he'd wasted time setting a false trail, they'd already gone and come back; seen through the ruse and come from a different direction. How could they have travelled so quickly? A new panic seized him. He got back on his mare and pressed it to go faster. A short while later, he came to a cluster of rocks and saw Tuka running towards him.

"It's the son!" he shouted.

Harman looked at the bodies strewn on the sand. "What happened here?"

Tuka clamped his left hand over a dripping wound above his right elbow. "They've killed Koerikei and Tau, and thought they'd killed me. Only Karees, hidden behind that rock, escaped their fire. They took Karees's two children, and also my brother's child! Three children are gone!"

Harman was stunned. Koerikei was face down in the sand, his head leaking blood, his wife, Tau, spreadeagled on her back, a gaping hole in her chest.

"And the others?"

"They went to the cave."

"We must fix your arm and go after them to make sure they got there safely. Do we have water?" he asked Karees.

"No," she said. Harman could see that she was badly shocked, too devastated to comprehend everything that had happened.

"What about the children?" Tuka asked. "We can't leave them where they are."

Harman unbundled his clothes roll and tore up an old shirt. He started to clean Tuka's wound. "We'll take back the children."

Tuka squinted at him through the pain. "How? You have one horse and one rifle."

"And by now they've probably divided the children among them. But I know where one of them lives. We must plan."

"You know one of these men?"

"Yes. If we rush off blindly, we'll lose the advantage of surprise. I think I know of a way to distract them. It'll give us time to get away. But there'll be danger."

"They'll come after you."

"You want the children, Tuka?"

Tuka said nothing. Harman bandaged his arm and turned his attention to the corpses. "Look," he pointed to the sky. "All this blood's drawing scavengers. We must bury these bodies and get this eland to the others." He looked around for a burial site and selected a spot near a cluster of skaapbos. He, Tuka and Karees got down on their knees. They started chopping into the hard soil with sharpened stones and scooping sand with a tin plate and a large tortoise shell Karees used as a food platter. It was hard work and they had to do it quickly, making a deep hole – square rather than long – using Tuka's leather pouch to lift out the soil. When it was deep enough, Tuka stepped into the hole, and Harman and Karees lowered Koerikei's corpse down to him. It had not yet stiffened, and he arranged it in a sitting position with the head tucked forward over the knees. Then Tau's corpse was lowered, and this was arranged facing Koerikei's, the two bodies closely huddled together, heads bowed, hands intertwined. There were no words for the departed except a mournful sigh and the lonely whistle of the wind as it swept across the wilderness. They filled up the hole with sand, laying stones on the grave to prevent it from being dug up by predators.

Fifteen miles north, Roeloff Kloot was woken out of a deep sleep by loud knocking. It took him several seconds to realize that someone was banging on his door.

"Oom Roff! Open up!"

Roeloff recognized the voice. It was Jan Joubert's son-in-law, Lourens. What was he doing knocking on his door in the middle of the night? Had Jan Joubert died? Only tidings of death warranted a call this time of the night. He got out of bed and pulled on his pants.

Neeltje, asleep next to him, woke up with the disturbance.

"What is it, Roff?"

"It's Lourens at the door. Coming!" he shouted, moving to the door while fastening his pants.

"Lourens. What brings you here at this time – is something wrong?"

"Oom Jan sent me!" Lourens said breathlessly. "I came as fast as I could. We've just had a visit from the kommando. They're out looking for Harman! They say he went with the bosjesmans to Brinkman and Van Niekerk's and took three children and set fire to the barns!"

"*My* Harman?"

"Yes."

"It can't be," Neeltje said, coming up behind them. "Harman would never do such a thing."

"Gerrit Malan said he shot one of their men. The man's alive, but barely breathing. The bosjesmans also wounded a horse."

Roeloff was badly shocked, but there was no time to stand

around trying to work out whether or not his son was responsible. He had to get to Harman before the kommando did. Still, he was surprised from which direction the warning had come. Joubert was an old enemy. They hadn't spoken since his father Willem Kloot's funeral twenty years ago, and when they did meet at a nagmaal or a wedding at a neighbouring farmer's, they gave each other nothing more than a cursory nod.

"I must go," Roeloff said, pulling on his boots. "Throw some of his clothes together for me, Neeltje, quickly! And some money. Lourens, you'd better make yourself scarce before they get here. Thank you for the warning."

Beatrix had woken up with the commotion and stood in the doorway. "Where are you going, Pa?"

"Look after your mother. I'll be back soon."

He left for the stable, and minutes later came out on the stallion.

Neeltje handed him two bundles. "Why do you need his clothes?"

"He can't come back here."

"What do you mean?"

"Come now, Neeltje, this isn't the time."

"For how long can't he come back?"

"Not for a long time. I'll tell him to go to your father in the Cederberg, then down to Martinus in the Cape. Harman has his half-sister there also. He and Bessie always got along. Come, both of you, back to bed. It mustn't look like anyone's been here. If they ask where I am, I'm away delivering sheep."

Roeloff turned the stallion south and galloped off into the night. No one understood better than him Neeltje's feeling for Harman. Harman was not the son of her loins, but the one of her heart. More hers than his. The one she'd raised first. The one she'd loved while he still dealt with his grief.

He rode steadily throughout the night, and arrived with the first thread of dawn at the Sonqua hideout which Harman had told him about. Roeloff had pretended to be hearing about it for the first time so as not to spoil the telling of it for his son, but knew of its existence in Twa's time. *The place of some of my ancestors, Kudu. Bring me here when the big sleep comes.* He had brought Twa to the cave, and buried him with his quiver and tobacco pouch in a deep hole at the bottom of the cliff. It was a place only the little hunters knew about, the mouth of the cave on a high precipice, overlooking the broken land below.

He got off his horse and for a moment thought he was at the wrong place. The path leading up to the cave was hidden by dense bush and he stood for a few moments inspecting the scene. Everything was still, undisturbed. There were no footprints, no evidence that people or animals had recently been there, the entrance completely overgrown. He examined the bushes, and sniffed at something he found on the ground. Then his heart lurched as a body loomed up before him.

"Harman!"

"You found us," Harman whispered, putting a finger to his lips. He had been there all the time watching his father approach. Harman's long hair was tied back with a thong – much as Roeloff had worn his when he was younger – his only clothing, a leather flap held up by a cord around the waist.

Roeloff was shocked to see his son dressed like a bosjesman. With his hair back and out of his face, in the grey light of dawn, it was like looking at Zokho.

"The kommando's out looking for you. Word is you went to Brinkman and Van Niekerk's with the Sonqua and took three children and set fire to the barns."

"Malan and his pack killed two Sonqua, Pa, and stole their children. I was with Tuka's clan yesterday when the three men lured them with a slain eland and attacked them. I couldn't just stand there and do nothing. I fired. One of the men fell from his horse. When they left, we split up. They came back and slaughtered Koerikei and his wife-"

"Koerikei?"

"*And* Tau. They took three of the children. I went after them to take back the children."

"And the barns? You didn't set fire to them?"

"I set fire to the trees at the back to create a diversion to give us time to get away. Tuka took it further. I couldn't stop him."

"It's not safe for you here, they're looking for you. I've brought clothes and money. Go to Oupa Wynand for a few days, then

48

leave for the Cape. I'll take care of things from this end. Go to Martinus, but it will probably be safer for you at Bessie's. Martinus is a Kloot. She's not. She's under Braam's name and will be harder to locate."

Harman stared at him. "You want me to leave the Karoo?"

"There's no other way. I'll send word when it's safe to return."

"And Ma?"

"She's not taking it well. She's already got one son in the Cape, and one in the Cederberg. Still, she'll take comfort that you'll be with your brother. Bessie and Braam live near the docks. Martinus can tell you where they are." He patted Harman on the shoulder. "Day's breaking, I must go."

"But, Pa – "

Roeloff hardened himself. "Come back, you hear?" He got on his horse. "Don't have your head turned by the Cape. Your mother couldn't take it if you stayed."

Harman watched his father ride off into the stillness. He went up to to the cave where Tuka was sleeping curled up in the sand. "Wake up, Tuka." He was already pulling on his clothes.

"What's going on?" Tuka squinted up at him.

"My father's been here. The kommando's out looking for me. I must leave. You're safe here with the children. No one knows about this place."

Tuka got up and stumbled after Harman to his mare. "Where will you go?"

"To the Cape."

"Will it be safe?"

"I have a brother there. He knows the law."

"This law will protect you?"

"I don't know."

Tuka shook his head sadly. "When will we see you now, son of Eyes of the Sky?"

Harman tied his few belongings to the front of the saddle, and got on his horse. "Soon, Tuka. Very soon. You will look up, and there I will be coming towards you from the south."

Wine and brandy may be considered, with wheat and barley, as the staple commodities of the Cape of Good Hope. Grapes grow with the greatest luxuriance in every part of this extensive colony; but the cultivation of the wine is little understood, or to speak more properly, is not attended to with that diligence which in other countries is bestowed upon it. Hence the wines are susceptible of great improvement and the quantity of being increased indefinitely.

Ten or twelve distinct kinds of wines are manufactured at the Cape and each of those has a different flavour and quality at the different farms on which they are produced. From difference of soil, from situation and management, scarcely any two vineyards of the same kind of grape give the same wine. By throwing under the press the ripe and unripe grapes, together with the stalk, most of the wines have either a thinness or a slight acidity, or, for want of a proper degree of fermentation and from being pressed when over-ripe, acquire a sickly saccharine taste ...

(John Barrow)

In 1814 the government widely distributed a general advertisement giving wine farmers the benefit of expert opinion on what could be done to improve matters in their vineyards. The advice given was that vines, far too closely planted, should be more widely spaced, and trained on espaliers of bamboo or reed, not more than four feet high to prevent damage by the south-easter wind; that all vineyards be scrupulously weeded; that existing vine plots be drastically thinned; and that great attention be paid to removing shoots and leaves so as to give the grapes sufficient air and sunlight. Further, that the greatest care should be taken in gathering the harvest, and in pressing the grapes and eliminating all rotten and immature berries. The grapes should be pressed out by men's feet. All casks should be washed out with brandy and the greatest cleanliness observed. Farmers were to be allowed to send their wine into town after the first fermentation and the wine merchants were to take it over at that stage. The wine merchant had to further improve the wine by keeping it in his possession for at least sixteen months, separating it at the end of that time into four different qualities and blending his final wines accordingly.

Andries de Villiers was not yet with Marieta at that time, having married her only in 1822, but had learned the business of wine farming first hand as an overseer on a well-established farm producing three very popular wines, just a short distance away in Constantia. The government at that time were granting gold medals with values ranging from one hundred to three hundred rix dollars for farmers who planted the greatest number of new vines, produced the best Cape Madeira, and submitted the best sample of wine considered to come nearest in flavour to real Madeira. Andries remembered well the medals collected by the owner of the farm where he had worked.

When he married Marieta and took over Zoetewater, he saw immediately what had to be done and gave himself two years to turn things around. The vines at the time were growing like currant bushes close to the ground, giving the wine an earthy taste. There was too little sun, no air, and leaf blight. Andries had hardly corrected the problem when he was faced with a more serious one, a rust disease affecting the Hanepoot grapes, and there was the added nuisance of having to sulphur the vines. To make matters worse, Cape wine was now considered to be so inferior that the London agent had written to say it was hardly worth financial consideration, and together with the imposition of further excise duties, Andries was so frustrated with the whole business, he considered giving it all up to go into horse breeding. But there was a doggedness to succeed; his saving grace, Joost always said, and in the end it was Andries's persistence, his knowledge, hard work, and the right hands, that paid off. It took a long time, but he pruned back the vines that were there, trained them on low palings to raise them from the ground, then cleared the land at the back behind the jongenshuis, and planted new vines. Vines liked a warm, temperate climate, shelter from cold and dry winds, a moderate altitude. Andries planted them in rows running from east to west on the slopes facing north to avoid extremes of cold. Over five years, he transformed Zoetewater from a struggling enterprise into one of note, producing a very fine, high-coloured Madeira and Muscadel.

But it took a further three years before he could show any real profit. There was the cost of upkeep of the slaves; clothing, corn for bread, tea, coffee, sugar, clothing for the family, implements for pressing and distilling, contingencies. Oxen died, wagons had to be fixed, there was wear and tear, duty at barriers. A farmer had to have capital to keep his estate in good running order. Expenses were high, the returns hardly worth the sweat that poured off a man's back. Every hand was accounted for. There was no room for sick or idle slaves especially during the grape-picking and pressing season. It was under such tight conditions and meticulous accounting that Andries de Villiers brought the estate to its present strength, attributing part of his success to his ability to assess a slave's worth and temperament, putting him to the right job – and also selling him again if it turned out the slave detracted from the general growth and well-being of the farm. He had sensed something problematic in Sangora from the start, yet he'd ignored it and bought him. And now there was Kananga, his second set of eyes and the best overseer he'd had if one looked at the results, whom Andries now had to get rid of and replace. Selling the mandoor wasn't the problem – it was finding the right overseer which worried Andries. And what about Sangora? Was he going to live to regret his purchase? Should he take a different tack with the maleier, take him out of the vineyards and put him to use as a carpenter to mute his anger? Andries had had to keep him out of sight when the fiscal appeared at the farm to investigate Siek Klaas's death, but at some point, he knew, he would have to remove the chains. If that was to be discovered, he would get much more than a fine. Andries grimaced. He hated the English. They had come here and caused nothing but trouble, invading their land, overcrowding his village, making things easy for the slaves, giving them the right to complain against their own masters. He wouldn't have had this problem ten years ago.

Concealed by the lush cover of the vines where he was picking grapes and placing the bunches in a basket at his feet, Sangora watched from the top of the hill as Kananga forced the fourteen-year-old Madagascan slave, Hanibal, into a sexual embrace. Hanibal spoke a creolized Portuguese, and while he understood the others when they spoke in Melayu, could not speak it himself, and communication often was difficult. They had all been privy to the assault the previous night when Kananga forced the young slave from his bed and dragged him to the room next door. Hanibal had fought against it and cried out for help, but everyone shut their eyes and ears to his pleas. To interfere was to find themselves face down in the mandoor's mattress.

Sangora had been on Zoetewater only a few weeks, but saw quickly how things worked. He knew who were the inciters, the complainers, the helpless, the good, the ones with too much female blood. Kananga liked boys, and the seur turned a blind eye to it. Not only had Hanibal complained to the farmer through the interpretive skills of Arend that he was being assaulted by the mandoor, but Sangora had heard that the farmer had actually caught Kananga in the wagon house with his hand down the front of Petroos's pants, and done nothing about it. Petroos was the brown-skinned, Cape-born slave, not yet twenty. He'd never had any of these inclinations when he first arrived at the farm five years ago, Arend said, but now he acted just like a woman, as Sangora could see from that silly laugh he had, and the way he waved his arms about when he talked. The aia, Rachel, seemed to be the only one who cared anything for the men. She had a rough tongue and a quick hand, and he'd seen her thump Salie, big as he was, against the head for arguing with her, but she had a huge heart, and a generous nature to go with it.

Sangora cut off a heavy bunch of the sweet-smelling, golden green grapes, and put it on the basket at his feet. Separated from his wife, chains on his feet, and forced to help in the production of wine. This work was against his beliefs. What was the point of not drinking alcohol if a man was forced to produce it for others?

He watched grimly as Hanibal struggled with Kananga two rows away. There was nothing he could do. In the end, the Mozambiquan simply forced Hanibal's head down to his crotch. It sickened Sangora. He couldn't look any more and turned away. He was glad that Somiela was lodged in the house. He had spoken to her only a few times, but knew from Arend that she was safe under Rachel's care. It was God's mercy that there was a woman like Rachel in the house.

He had developed a sore above his left ankle, and bent down to massage his foot. Arend, working a few rows away, saw him and came over. "That sore looks bad, Sangora."

Sangora looked up at him. He liked Arend although he was all too aware that both Arend and Salie had designs on his stepdaughter. Arend was newly converted. Salie was Mohametan. Which one he preferred, if either, he couldn't say. Sometimes a convert turned out better than one born to the faith. Still, Arend was likeable, with a clean heart.

"It won't get better with these things on. I didn't think I would have them on this long."

"The landdrost said something to the seur about it, my mother says."

"What did he say?"

"He said if someone were to see it and report it, the seur would be in trouble. The seur knows it's wrong. But we know how the seur thinks, and the fastest way to get them off is for no one to say anything to him about it. He must come up with it on his own. He won't do it if someone tells him." Arend looked behind him to see where Kananga was. He pulled out a wad of cloths from a shirt pocket. "My mother gave me this for you. It's clean. Stuff it between the chains. She'll give you salve later on."

Sangora took the cloths and inserted them gingerly between the leg irons. "Thank your mother for me."

Arend leaned forward conspiratorially. "I have keys."

Sangora looked up. He wasn't sure he caught the interpreter's meaning.

"I found them that day when he sent me for the chains," Arend continued. "I didn't give them to him. I hid them."

"You mean keys that might unlock these chains?"

"They might. I don't know. Tonight, when the candle's out and Kananga's gone, we can see if they fit."

"Why would you take such a risk? If the keys fit and I ran away, you'd be in trouble."

"You won't run away. You know what will happen if they catch you. And you won't leave Somiela here on her own."

"But if I did, they would know you helped me. You'd get twenty-five strokes. They'd get Kananga to do it."

"Kananga doesn't have long. They're talking of selling him.

They're looking for someone to take his place. A white man. That was one of the conditions. The fiscal said they didn't want any more slaves killing slaves on Zoetewater. Kananga's lucky they didn't take him away."

A low whistle from Salie a few rows away warned them of Kananga's approach.

Sangora and Arend busied themselves moving the grapes around in the basket, but it was too late. Kananga had seen them wasting time. He flicked his sjambok, and it caught Arend across the back.

"Didn't I say to leave the maleier alone! And why are you working in the same row with him?"

"The basket's full. I was helping Sangora make room in it before getting another one."

"His name's February!" Kananga struck him again. "How many times do I have to tell you?" The mandoor hardly ever washed himself or his clothes, and gave off a powerful odour of rotting onions.

Arend hopped around on one foot, yelping like a dog who'd got his tail caught in a trap. "I forgot . . ."

"You forgot? See if you'll forget this." Kananga loomed over him and raised the sjambok to strike him again.

"Stop it!"

Kananga turned to Sangora, surprised. "What did you say?"

Sangora stood up and looked Kananga straight in the eye. "You're not stupid, Kananga. Why do you do this?"

Kananga made a move as if to strike him. No one questioned his actions. The sjambok had the last word. But something held him back. The voice. Quiet, unaccusing, no fear. He didn't know why the maleier unnerved him. He looked at Sangora threateningly, then pushed Arend out of the way, and strode off.

Arend shook his head in disbelief. "I don't believe what I just saw. You don't talk back to that heathen and get away with it. Sometimes he's worse than the seur."

"I'm a maleier, that's why. He's afraid. In his eyes, we do doekoem work. I could toor him – take a hard-boiled egg, dip it in borrie, put it under his mattress, and he would die in his sleep. That's what they all think about us."

"You feel sorry for him."

"He's cruel. Not soulless."

"He's killed people for looking at him the wrong way. You care about his soul?"

"I care about everyone's soul. Kananga stands between the white man and the slave. Who does he have? Slaves have each other. There's comfort in that. He flogged me, he put me in chains, but he's following orders. Don't you see? He's forced to act against us. That's another way to keep slaves apart."

"I don't understand you, Sangora. He's responsible for the sores on your legs, and you feel sorry for him."

"He's not responsible. And you won't understand now."

Arend muttered under his breath, picked up the basket, and carried it down the hill.

That night, several things happened after the candle "went out" in the jongenshuis. The candle went out at approximately the same time every night to satisfy the owners up at the house – the slaves only received one candle a week, but had their own supply for late night discussions when they would block out the light and create the impression that they were asleep.

"Close up, Petroos," Salie said.

Petroos got up and stuffed his blanket into the small window high above their heads. Satisfied that no one could see the light from outside, he sat down next to Arend and Sangora and the others.

When they could see one another again, Arend presented Sangora with a long iron key and a set of smaller ones. He also brought out the poultice his mother had secretly prepared for the festering sores on the carpenter's ankles.

"Put this on later, it will draw out the poison. Remove it in the morning before Kananga comes. If he sees it, she'll be in trouble."

Sangora looked at Arend and smiled gratefully. "It's a good thing your mother's in the kitchen to give us all these things."

"He's the only one allowed in there," Petroos said.

"That's because I interpret for them."

"It's because of your mother. She's an inside slave," Salie added. "You get special treatment."

56

"I don't," Arend countered, getting cross.

"Never mind," Sangora interrupted. "Don't you two start."

"Try the keys, Sangora," Salie said. "We're waiting." They all knew about the keys, and knelt around the carpenter to see what would happen.

Sangora selected one of the smaller keys. He didn't want to know right away that the long iron one, the one most likely to slip into the lock, wouldn't work. He inserted the small key and fiddled with the lock. Nothing happened. He tried the second one in the set. That, too, didn't fit. He could feel the tension around him. Arend had found the keys in a rusted tin near the place where the chains were kept, but there was no guarantee that they belonged with the leg irons.

"Try the other one," Tromp suggested. Tromp was almost fifty, the oldest slave in the group, the most hardened and most outspoken in his hatred of white people.

Sangora picked it up. "Bismillah," he said, invoking the name of God as he inserted the key. It went in. He waited a few seconds before turning it. Everyone held their breaths. He snapped his wrist. The lock clicked.

"It's open!" Salie exclaimed, then quickly put his hand to his mouth, remembering Kananga on the other side of the wall.

Sangora removed the chains and massaged his ankles where the iron cuffs had broken the skin. He couldn't believe it. His legs were free. He moved them, spreading them wide apart. There was no weight, nothing restricting him. He stood up and lifted his knee. First the left one, then the right.

"That was clever, Arend," Tromp said, "that you hid the keys. A good thing."

Arend's feelings swelled. He was glad he could help. He liked the Mohametan carpenter. Sangora's arrival at Zoetewater had given them all hope. He was unafraid of authority, a leader without realizing it. His courage that first day had impressed all of them. Arend handed Sangora the poultice. "Put this on now. The sores will heal more quickly without the chains."

Sangora took the poultice and applied it to his left ankle, securing it with a torn shirt which he wrapped around like a bandage.

"If Kananga finds out about this, you're in big trouble," Salie said. "You have to make sure you have the chains on before he opens the door in the morning, or we'll all taste his anger."

"Not me," Geduld said. "He knows if he hits me, I'm gone. I can leave anytime I want."

The men were silent, acknowledging the truth of this.

Sangora considered the little hunter, a pleasant little fellow, with great knowledge of the mountains and slopes. Geduld was right. Slave owners had little control over the Sonqua and Koi-na. Many of them were indentured to owners until the age of twenty-five, some *for* twenty-five years, but they paid little attention to these rules. They were the indigenous people of the land, and came and went as they pleased. If a slave ran away, the kommando could go after him – most slaves were new to the land, and wouldn't know where to hide. But the Sonqua and Koi-na had their relatives and hide-outs in the north, the west, and the east, and could run off and disappear, and no one would find them.

"Where do you go when you leave here, Geduld?" Sangora asked him.

"I meet up with my people in the interior below the Orange River. It's very hot where I come from. Sometimes I go to Hanglip."

"Hanglip?" Sangora's interest was piqued. Hanglip was where the drosters went when they ran away. He'd heard stories about the caves there and at Rooi Els. "I've heard much about this place. Is it true what they say about it? That no one except the slaves know the entrances to the caves?"

"It's true. You can stand on top of Drostersgat – a deep cut in the rock leading down to the sea – and not even know it. That's where they lower themselves with a rope at low tide – runaways, escaped criminals, sailors whose ships have ended up on the rocks lining the coast. At high tide the sea thunders in, and they're safely out of reach of their pursuers in the caves underneath."

"What do the drosters eat?"

"Whatever they find in the ground and the sea. Mussels, kreef, fish. Berries, roots from the ground. When they want meat, or powder for their rifles, or clothes, they steal from farmers in neighbouring valleys. Some of them go to Elandskloof where they ambush passing wagons and take the cattle." The men sat silent, thinking about the way the drosters lived. Then Geduld spoke again. "Did I tell you about those two white children who were kidnapped by a band of drosters and taken to a cave at Rooi Els?"

"No."

"The drosters killed their parents and took the cattle and the children. One of the children managed to leave a piece of clothing for the people who came looking for them."

"What happened?"

"You want me to tell you?"

"Of course we want you to tell us," Petroos said.

Geduld settled back on his heels and told them how the drosters were tracked to the cave where they were barricaded behind stones and branches for several days. His bright eyes flashed at his remembrance of things.

"You're making this up," Salie said.

"He's not," Tromp wagged his finger. "I've heard the story, it's true. Go on, Geduld."

Geduld chattered on, laughing, sighing, pulling his face to imitate the various characters as if he'd been there himself.

Sangora looked at the faces about him. The night had taken on a strange reality. The candle had burnt down, the light was low, but the spirit of the men was ignited, and eased the grimness residing in their souls. For the moment they forgot where they were. They were free, united, the masters powerless against their strength. The carefree little nomad who trusted in the moon and the sun and the accuracy of his arrow had perhaps had too much wine, but was creating for them a momentary respite from the hopelessness of their lives. Sangora had come to know the men with whom he lived so closely. Tromp, the old herdsman, had no God, and wasn't looking for one. Hanibal, the quiet one – always carving or scratching or painting the face of a slave or a tree or a mountain on stone or cloth or paper which Arend bought for him on his visits with the seur into town – had arrived at the Cape a believer, but now joined Tromp in his bitter litany against God. Salie, the handsome, olive-skinned Mohametan from Celebes, who wet his hands and feet in the stream and faced east in prayer, but sat with the others when they drank wine. Petroos, the giggler, whose words and laughter most times belied the inse-

59

curities he felt, and Arend, the good-natured interpreter, who believed in his new faith, and thought everyone was honest like him. Where were they all headed? Where would it end?

Sangora listened to Geduld tell how the drosters were finally smoked out of the cave and shot. The men reacted with varying degrees of anger and outrage. Petroos laughed, but more out of nervousness than delight.

"If they were all smoked out and shot, who lived to tell the story?" Salie asked. "You are telling us a story passed down by the white man?"

Geduld looked at Salie. "Of course not. There was one who got away. An old sailor who wasn't in the cave at the time, but hidden nearby for several days. He passed it on."

Geduld came to the end of his story and the men sighed contentedly. They liked stories, especially ones with trickster gods and angry ancestors, and Geduld knew how to tell a good tale – even if they suspected that most of what he said came from an over-active imagination. Petroos blew out the candle and removed his blanket from the hole in the wall.

The men returned to their beds. It seemed that they had hardly closed their eyes when the slave bell sounded to summon them to a new day. Sangora got up and massaged his legs. He jumped up and down a few times, stretched his legs wide, then put on his leg irons and shuffled out after the men in the dark to meet with Kananga under the bell tower.

... and is effected in the following manner. Several farmers that are in want of servants, join together, and take a journey to that part of the country where the Boshies-men live. They themselves, as well as their Hottentots, or else such Boshies-men as have been caught some time before, and have been trained up to fidelity in their service, endeavour to spy out where the wild Boshies-men have their haunts. This is best discovered by the smoke of their fires. They are found in societies from ten to fifty and a hundred, reckoning great and small together. Notwithstanding this, the farmers will venture on a dark night to set upon them with six or eight people, which they contrive to do, by previously stationing themselves at some distance round about the kraal. Then they give the alarm by firing a gun or two. By this means there is such a consternation spread over the whole body of these savages, that it is only the most bold and intelligent among them, that have the courage to break through the circle and steal off. These the captors are glad enough to get rid of at so easy a rate, being better pleased with those that are stupid, timorous, and struck with amazement, and who consequently allow themselves to be taken and carried into bondage. They are, however, at first, treated by gentle methods; that is, the victors intermix the fairest promises with their threats, and endeavour, if possible, to shoot some of the larger kinds of game for their prisoners, such as buffaloes, sea cows and the like. Such agreeable baits, together with a little tobacco, soon induce them, continually cockered and feasted as they are, to go with a tolerable degree of cheerfulness to the colonist's place of abode. There this luxurious junketing upon meat and fat is exchanged for more moderate portions, consisting for the most part of buttermilk, gruel and porridges.

(Anders Sparrman, *Voyage to the Cape of Good Hope*, Volume I)

Somiela was in the kitchen preparing breakfast when Arend appeared at the back door "Come in, Arend. You're early."

Arend took off his hat. "I came to tell the seur the wagon's ready. Also, to ask my mother if she needs anything from town."

"The bread's ready. You want some?"

"Please." It wasn't every day he was fortunate enough to be at hand when things came hot out of the oven.

Somiela cut off a thick slice of bread and spooned some apricot jam onto it. She liked Arend. His clothes were clean, his hair smooth and shiny. He didn't wear anything on his feet – he wasn't free – but was always neat and looked every bit the interpreter in his hat. It was Arend who kept them informed of the goings-on at the back. She suspected that, like Salie, he had feelings for her, and had heard from Rachel that the two of them had had words over this. This pleased and distressed Somiela. She liked Arend, but not like that, and felt a little responsible for the way he felt. She had perhaps been too friendly, perhaps let him think the wrong thing. Salie was different. He was of the same faith, handsome, exciting to look at, and made her laugh. He'd spoken to her several times since that first day, and asked her more than once to meet him behind the jongenshuis. She'd declined. Her mother had warned her about the wild nature of men and cautioned against urgent promises and syrupy words. She sensed some of that in Salie, and while she was attracted to him, she was also afraid of where her curiosity might take her.

Rachel came into the kitchen and saw her son. As was her habit, she was always kinder to him behind his back, never praising him to his face. "Have you cleaned your ears properly? You'll sit next to the seur in the wagon, he'll see into those wax pits if you didn't wash."

"My ears are clean, and my nails. I won't be a sight for anyone."

Rachel grunted. "Finish that bread before someone sees you."

Arend stuffed the last piece into his mouth. "Sangora's leg's better. He says thank you."

"Good."

"Does he ask about me?" Somiela asked. "I hardly see him."

"He asks if things are all right in the house."

"What do you tell him?"

"I say, yes."

"I miss my mother. Tell him."

Rachel rattled the pan noisily on the stove, shaking loose its contents. "Come, come, don't be idling here in the kitchen upsetting things." She slipped her hand into her apron pocket and took out a small cloth purse. "I need some kapok, enough to fill a small basket, and some soft, white material. You'll find that in a place where they sell women's things."

"Women's things?" Arend turned red. He didn't know anything about women's things. "I don't know if I've seen such a place. How soft should this material be?"

Rachel became impatient. "Is the weather stuffing up your head, you can't think? Soft enough."

Arend was embarrassed. It was obvious that the material was for Somiela. His mother never cared for such things. And the kapok? Was that for her, too?

"This should be enough," Rachel said, handing him a few coins.

He took it. Slaves received money, especially at harvest time, but it was very little and they used it sparingly, saving for the day when they would be free. His mother had a small reserve, given to her by his father years ago to buy their freedom. The owner had reneged on his word, and his mother had saved it. She had once told him that the money was his and that she would give it to him when he married or was set free. She used none of it for herself. Spending some of it now on Somiela showed how much she cared for the girl.

"Anything else? A jar of honey? There's enough here." Honey was his mother's weakness.

Rachel relented. "A small jar."

Arend left and almost immediately Andries de Villiers appeared in the kitchen, fully dressed for his visit into town. The women greeted him and he sat down.

Rachel poured his coffee and set a plate of fried sheep kidneys and eggs in front of him. "The wagon's ready, Arend says."

Andries took a piece of bread and dipped it into his plate, scooping up a crisp kidney. "Did he eat yet?"

"No, Seur."

"Give him his breakfast. We'll be gone all day."

Rachel took this to mean that she could give her son something from the pan. She hastily placed a fried egg and kidney between two thick slices of bread and sent Somiela outside with it.

"The landdrost and his brother will eat here tonight. Make some of that food you made last week with the mutton and potatoes and cabbage."

"The cabbage bredie, Seur."

"Yes."

"Somiela made it, Seur. Here she comes."

Andries noted the doek on the girl's head, and the dress she had first arrived in. "Rachel tells me it was you who made that cabbage food last week," he said.

"Yes, Seur."

"It was tasty."

"Yes, Seur."

"You must make it for the guests tonight."

"Yes, Seur." Somiela had taken Rachel's advice and never spoke to the farmer unnecessarily. It had kept her out of trouble. Still, she took no chances. She had seen how quickly moods changed at Zoetewater with the other members of the family, who at one moment treated her civilly, and the next reminded her that she was just their slave. Her cheeks still burned when she remembered the incident that had taken place a few weeks ago when she had walked the twins to a neighbour's house near the main road where the girls played with the cooper's daughter on Saturday afternoons. They had arrived at the house, and Somiela had been on the verge of taking her leave, reminding them that she would be back an hour before sunset to fetch them, when Annie, pointing down to her right boot, told Somiela to tie her laces. Somiela had never helped the twins with their boots, Rachel having told them firmly long ago that they would dress themselves. Somiela gave a thin smile to show all present that she knew Annie was only playing with her, and said she had to hurry back. Annie had looked first at her sister, then her friend, then swelling her top lip and stretching her neck much like her mother, demanded that Somiela tie her laces and do it right away.

"No," Somiela insisted, still speaking nicely. "*You* do it."

Feeling her position threatened in front of her friend, Annie said, "If you don't do it, I'll tell my mother. My mother said you're our slave, you're to do anything we want."

Somiela was taken completely by surprise. It was the first time anything like this had happened. The twins had never displayed any kind of animosity towards her at home. She was so angry at Annie that she wanted to smack her. And she didn't tie the laces. Giving Annie a look that would send the girl diving into her blankets – Annie was a quick crier – Somiela left the property.

Fetching the girls later that afternoon, Annie sulked all the way home. Just before reaching the entrance to Zoetewater, she suddenly broke down in a fit of guilt. Both she and her sister enjoyed Somiela reading to them, and Annie knew somehow that threatening Somiela would result in the loss of this privilege, or even some of the other games that they played. Annie didn't say she was sorry, but said she never meant what she said. Somiela let it go, but never forgot it.

She watched them now as they entered the kitchen with Marieta, all of them dressed in long-sleeved dresses and bonnets.

Andries pushed back his chair and got up. "I'm leaving now. I'll be back in time for the guests."

Marieta resettled the shawl over her shoulders. "Couldn't you wait for Leentje and Annie? It looks like it's going to rain."

The school was on a nearby farm. The Germans were the most qualified teachers at the time, and the kneg on the Jansen farm had been giving lessons in reading and writing and arithmetic in the mornings for several years, together with his other duties. There was another place of learning closer by, but Andries did not want his children to go there. It was a thatched-roof building first used as an ambulante hospitaal, then taken over by the government; part of it was later converted to a schoolroom and schoolmaster's quarters, the other part used as an Anglican place of worship. The ride to the Jansen farm would take Andries a few minutes out of his way

"They haven't eaten yet, and I'm late. Somiela can walk them. I told her to make some of that food for tonight that she made the other day."

"Somiela can't cook."

"She can. She's the one who made the – what's it called again?" he asked Somiela directly.

"Cabbage bredie, Seur," Rachel spoke up for Somiela, sensing Marieta's hostility.

"Well, whatever it is, we won't have it," Marieta said with finality. "Not for guests. Rachel will cook what I tell her to cook, and we'll serve what we usually serve – roast meat and potatoes and carrots." She paused to blow her nose with a handkerchief she pulled from her sleeve. "You don't have time to wait for the twins, but can waste time talking to servants about food."

Andries studied her for a moment. He seemed ready to say something, but changed his mind. He took his rifle from the wall and walked towards the door.

"Make what the nooi tells you, Rachel. Somiela, you make that cabbage food for me."

"Yes, Seur," Somiela said uncertainly.

Marieta's eyes narrowed. She waited for Andries to leave, then got up and approached Somiela at the working table. "You little slut."

Somiela kept her eyes lowered to the bread she was slicing.

Marieta advanced on her, breathing heavily. "You want to cause trouble in this house?"

"No, Nooi."

"And why are you wearing that dress? Didn't I tell you I didn't want to see it on you again?"

"Yes, Nooi."

"Yes, nooi, no, nooi," Marieta mocked, then suddenly struck her. "Don't you listen the first time?"

Somiela touched her hand to her face. Marieta's knuckle had caught the tip of her nose, and her eyes teared.

"I'm talking to you! Why are you wearing that dress?"

Somiela kept her gaze down.

"Speak up!" Marieta pushed her into the table.

Somiela looked up, and from somewhere inside her, the devil reared its head. It had happened before at the previous farm when the owner's daughter had smacked her, and she had smacked her back, resulting in severe punishment. "Because I won't wear your fat daughters' ugly dresses!"

Marieta's jaw dropped open in shock. And from where she stood at the stove, Rachel wanted to slam the pan, eggs and all, on Somiela's head. She couldn't believe the girl's stupidity.

Marieta grabbed the whip from the wall and struck her. "Get Kananga!"

"Nooi," Rachel beseeched her. "She didn't mean it."

"Get him!" Marieta screeched, and lashed the whip full force across Somiela's back.

The twins ran to their mother and pulled on her dress. "Ma, don't!"

66

"Go!" Marieta shoved Rachel towards the door.

Rachel left the kitchen in a panic. Something terrible was going to happen. Outside, she could see the wagon in the distance. The farmer hadn't cleared the gate yet. Should she run after it and see if she could stop him? No, she thought, she couldn't run, but if she could get Hanibal or Geduld to chase down the wagon, there was a chance Andries de Villiers would turn back. She walked quickly to the jongenshuis, not daring to consider the consequences if the farmer took her warning the wrong way and punished her instead. She reached the door and found the slaves milling about outside, waiting for the breakfast call.

"Geduld, run after the wagon. The seur just left. Tell him there's trouble. Nooi wants Kananga to whip Somiela – he must hurry! Quickly now. Run!"

"What happened?" Sangora asked.

Rachel scowled at him. "She talked back to the wife. She was provoked, but she should've kept her mouth shut. I don't know how many times I've told her. Nooi wants Kananga to give her a flogging."

"A flogging?" Sangora's eyes smouldered. "A flogging for talking back? If anything happens to Somiela . . ."

"She called the daughters fat, said she wouldn't wear their ugly dresses. And what can you do? You're a slave like the rest of us. Don't you start talking nonsense. I thought you had a brain, Sangora. Use it. I've been here twenty-two years. I know how things work. You can't change things. Her job's to survive, not to show how clever she is."

"I promised her mother I wouldn't let anything happen to her."

"Slaves don't have the luxury of promises. You don't make promises you can't keep."

Sangora realized that he had under-estimated Rachel, who spoke from a place of knowledge, trust, and was a valuable ally. "I'm sorry."

"Sorry's no good after the horse has bolted from the barn. How's your ankle?"

Sangora looked down at his feet. "Much better. What do you think will happen now?"

"Depends on his mood. His wife upset him this morning. It might work in Somiela's favour. Then again not. You have to talk to her. She's headstrong. It seems everyone here's too headstrong for his own good."

Kananga came through the door and saw them talking. "What's going on?"

"Nooi wants you."

"What for?"

"I don't know, but whatever she asks you to do to Somiela, don't do it. I've sent Geduld after the wagon to get the seur. Seur won't want her punished."

Kananga gave a short ugly bark that passed for a laugh. "Makes no difference to him. Shit's shit. And makes no difference to me." He moved off.

"Kananga!" Sangora called after him.

The mandoor stopped without turning.

"You're one of us, Kananga. Don't do it."

Kananga tapped the sjambok against his leg, and continued on.

In the kitchen, Somiela was backed into a corner between the work table and the stove. The tip of the whip caught at the crockery in the dresser, and cups and saucers crashed all about the women on the wooden floor. Marieta shrieked, the twins cried, Elspeth implored her mother to stop. But Marieta couldn't. Her bonnet was sitting askew on her head, the shawl hanging off one shoulder. She was consumed with rage. The meid had no respect. Her tongue was too big for her head. She had too much wind for a half-naartje.

"You little bastard!" she shrieked, hitting Somiela again.

Somiela held her arms up to her head to ward off the blows. She felt the whip cut into the soft flesh of her skin where it caught her under the armpit, across the breast. She stood silent. She wouldn't cry out. She wouldn't touch the spot where it burned. The whip lashed out again, and nicked her lip. The lip opened up and oozed a red tear. Somiela glared at Marieta. Tasting the saltiness of her own blood, she promised herself that she would make this monstrous woman pay. The first opportunity she had she would pee in her coffee, poison her food, smother her with a cushion in her sleep. Even as her mind raced with vengeance, she knew she could never do it. But her mood was violent. She was capable in that moment of causing harm.

Kananga appeared at the door.

"Take this slut outside and flog her!" Marieta ordered him.

Kananga looked at the two women. He remained standing.

"Didn't you hear what I said? I said, flog her!"

The mandoor made no move to obey.

"You black bastard, I'm talking to you!"

Kananga moved forward, his fists clenched at his side.

Rachel stepped quickly between them. "Don't be foolish, Kananga. Think!"

"What's going on?" Andries's voice sounded behind them.

Marieta turned, breathless and out of control. Her face changed colour. She hadn't expected to see her husband there, thought he had left long ago.

"This meid's insulted us! I told Kananga to teach her a lesson. He won't do it."

Andries was appalled by the scene before him. "I turn my back, and this is what goes on? Kananga takes his orders from me, and he's not here to beat women. You know that's against the law."

"The law!" Marieta snorted, aware that he was upbraiding her in front of servants. "Since when do you care about the law? You've got the maleier in chains! Where's the law? And who asked for this naai-mandje in the first place? Did I say bring this slut here?"

"Quiet! You can go, Kananga. Get back to work."

Kananga left without looking at any of them.

"What happened here?" Andries asked.

Marieta told him what Somiela had said about his children.

Andries listened without interruption. He didn't look at anyone, and kept his eyes on his hands in front of him. "Anything else?" he asked when Marieta had finished.

"You need more than that?" she asked sarcastically. "The meid defied me!"

Andries turned to the aia. "Rachel? Is there more?"

Marieta bristled at the insult. "You don't take my word?"

Andries ignored her. "Rachel?" he asked again.

Rachel thought it unfair that he should put her in this position, and knew she would answer later to Marieta. "Somiela didn't start it," she heard herself saying.

"What do you mean?"

"Nooi accused her of causing trouble in the house."

"I did not!" Marieta cut in, outraged at Rachel's disloyalty.

Andries turned to Somiela. Her doek had come off in the beating, the short hair, grown a few inches, standing wild about her face. There was an angry welt on her cheek and she had a cut lip.

"Did you say those things about my children?"

"Yes, Seur."

"Why?"

"Nooi called me a slut, Seur. She was angry about this dress. Rachel was making me a dress, it isn't finished, so I wore this one. The twins' dresses are big, and this dress is special to me, my mother made it. I didn't think I would get into trouble for wearing it. I've taken off the lace. It's the only thing I have of my mother." She wiped her hand across her face. "I didn't mean what I said about the twins, Seur. It just came out."

Andries believed her. She wasn't one to make trouble, and worked diligently at her duties, listening to Rachel and delivering some very tasty food to their table. His daughters also seemed happier to have her around. But he knew what Marieta's trouble was. She was feeling her age, and didn't much like what she saw in the mirror. The irritable mouth, the set of the jaw, the flinty eyes, the little hairs sprouting and growing darker on the stiff, upper lip – all were reminders of a body made ugly by a bitter soul. Somiela was a young apple, fresh off the tree, sun-washed, and ripe, and uncommonly handsome for a slave.

He hardened himself. "I'll take Rachel's word that you didn't start this, but you've crossed the line, and I won't tolerate rudeness. This is my house and my family, and you're a slave. Do you understand?"

"Yes, Seur."

"About your dress, you can wear it until you have another. We won't turn this house upside down over clothes." He paused to lend gravity to his next statement. "As for being rude to the nooi, you'll work for one week in the pressing house. When you've learned your lesson, you can return. If not, you'll work permanently outside." He got up. "I want to hear no more about it."

The twins, dressed and fed by this time, left with their father in the wagon for school, and Marieta and Elspeth retreated to the front of the house. Rachel sighed. It wasn't over. Marieta wouldn't forget. And there would be trouble now between husband and wife. The farmer had rebuked Marieta in front of the slaves. Somiela's punishment, also, wasn't enough. A beating was what the wife wanted, to strip the girl of her dignity. And working in close proximity with the men? Rachel didn't like that at all. There was no telling how those men, deprived so long of female company, would behave. Was that the farmer's intent? To have Somiela compromised by one of them, so that he could claim the child, and increase the numbers at Zoetewater? She didn't know any more. Couldn't think. It had been a stressful morning. Somiela's outburst. Sangora's warning. Kananga's flagrant refusal to obey. What did it bode for all of them?

She watched Somiela wash her face in a basin of water, dabbing the bruised skin with a cloth.

"I'll give you something to put on it."

Somiela put the doek on her head. Her manner was quiet, she didn't want to talk.

Rachel knew the hurt that Somiela was feeling. It wasn't the hurt of physical pain. It was the hurt of injustice, of being wronged when you were innocent.

"What happened today mustn't happen again. It was a dangerous thing that you did. Opening your mouth like that and letting everything just fall out like loose potatoes. Don't test the farmer, you don't know him. Her evil you can smell, it comes from her like goat stink. His doesn't show."

"What happened was my fault? I started it?"

Rachel sighed wearily. She was tired. "You didn't start it, but when are you going to get it through your head that you won't win? The farmer's not one to trifle with. He's swift. Look what he's got planned for Kananga. Kananga doesn't even suspect. He's putting him on the block. Just like that. He's approaching the landdrost's brother tonight to be the new overseer at Zoetewater."

"If he's anything like Martinus, he won't suit."

Rachel smiled at her spirit. "The point is, the seur doesn't talk, he acts. He gets rid of you if you're trouble. You don't want to wake up one morning and find yourself on the block. He means what he says. Don't mistake the little kindness he shows for softness."

"I didn't start it. I just wanted to keep my dress."

"It doesn't matter who started it. You want to survive. A dress isn't worth being sold for over the mountain. Then there's no chance of ever seeing your mother again."

"You mean I might see her if I stay here?" Somiela brightened slightly.

"It won't be difficult for Arend or Salie to make enquiries when they go to town on their day off." She hadn't meant to raise expectations, but there it was, she had said it. The girl needed something to give her hope.

Andries was cleaning his rifle at the kitchen table when Martinus's wagon was seen coming into the yard.

"They're here," he said, getting up.

Marieta looked up from her needlework. She hadn't forgotten her husband's treatment of her that morning, but knew that sulking would have little effect. Already he behaved as if nothing had happened. She went along with the pretence, as she would go along with it in bed later that night and for several nights. Marieta had learned the secrets of marriage: what to question, what to ignore. Constantly aware that she was older than him by several years, it wasn't lost on her that there were women only too willing to step into her boots. She didn't delude herself that Andries de Villiers had married her for her looks.

"What's his name?"

"Harman," Elspeth said, rearranging her long hair over her shoulders. "He's the first son."

"The first son will inherit," Marieta said.

"No, Ma. Not necessarily. There're two farms. One in the Cederberg, and one in the Hantam. The one in the Cederberg belongs to the grandfather. Karel, the youngest, works there."

"Martinus isn't working on either one of them, and there're three sons and a daughter."

"He's his father's favourite."

"Is Martinus the second or third son?" Andries asked.

"The second."

"And this makes him a favourite?"

"He's seen the will, he knows what's in it. His father has over five hundred merino as well as other sheep. The Kloots hire Koina to help during the shearing season. Kloot's Nek's big enough for two sons."

"What son will agree to share?"

"One who's not greedy."

Andries laughed. "You have a lot to learn about men. And I've not heard of property passed on like this. Usually, the spouse takes half, the children subdivide the rest. And what about the daughter? Have you forgotten her?"

"Maybe I'm wrong," Elspeth said. "And there's more than one daughter. A half-sister, I believe. Lives here in the Cape with her husband. Martinus doesn't see her much, they're not close."

Andries led his family outside. "Martinus! You're here. This must be the brother we've heard so much about. Welcome to Zoetewater."

"Oom Andries, Tante Marieta," Martinus greeted them. "This is my brother, Harman. Hello, Elspeth."

Harman came forward and extended his hand.

Elspeth watched. He was tall like Martinus, bronzed by the sun, with a tassel of platinum hair tied back with a leather cord. She had never seen a man with hair past his shoulders, and never one with such eyes. But it wasn't only the colour. There was a flatness to them, an oriental slant that made the greyness unnatural.

"Your brother's talked a lot about you," Andries said, leading them inside. "He says you're the expert on merino."

Harman laughed, making light of the matter. "Sheep are sheep." He took the chair with the riempie seat offered by Andries, and looked around the lofty kitchen with its beamed ceilings and highly-polished yellowwood floors. It was an impressive room with a coal stove agleam with brass pots and pans, a koskas for the storage of food, and a stinkwood dresser displaying rows of fancy plates with a green leaf design. The table at which he sat was an oval yellowwood gate-leg table with baluster-turned legs, and heavy stretchers. They had a neerslaan-tafel themselves in the voorhuis at Kloot's Nek; Harman wondered if he found something as fine as this in the kitchen, what he would find in other parts of the house. Hanging from hooks on the wall near the door was a powder horn, bullet mounds, and a rifled musket. He recognized the weapon as one used in the fight with the English in 1795, with a set trigger and twelve grooves to make the bullet spin as it was fired down the barrel to travel in a straight line. What was Andries de Villiers doing with such fancy weaponry? Was he also a hunter, and if so, of animals or human beings?

"A nice house, Oom. And a good spot for it, at the foot of this mountain. My brother's fortunate to have made the acquaintance of such a prosperous family."

Andries grinned, not sure if it was a compliment. A man didn't just come into another's home and remark upon his prosperity. Still, there was nothing in the visitor's behaviour to indicate malice.

"We thank the Lord for what we have. And Martinus is part of the family. But, tell us about Kloot's Nek. I'm sure it's equally pleasing."

"The Karoo's different, not for everyone, as I'm sure Martinus has told you. We have land and open space, but don't have the climate. Very hot, and very cold. No in-between. Dry and dusty as a mountain tortoise. We're at the mercy of the gods."

Andries laughed. "That's what I've heard. So, what brings you down to the Cape?"

The smile went slowly from his face. "I was involved with a band of Sonqua. Their children had been stolen by farmers. There was trouble. My father thought it best if I left the area."

On the other side of the table, Martinus coughed into his hand. He had asked Harman not to mention anything.

"What kind of trouble?" Marieta asked.

"I shot at one of the men."

"One of the farmers?"

"Yes. They had set a trap to attract the hunters with a slain eland, to kill them and take their children. An old ploy. They raid

74

the camps of the Sonqua and take the children to work for them. The Sonqua retaliate, and burn their farms."

"This is what happened?"

"More or less."

"And you were part of this?" Andries asked.

"I helped the Sonqua get back their children. The law's one-sided. These people have no rights. Taking back your kidnapped children, by any means, should be every man's right."

"I see."

Elspeth, seated next to Martinus, felt an unexpected thrill. She had never heard anything so irreverent and lawless. The kommando was probably out looking for him – was this the reason his father had told him to leave? There was something strangely exciting about that. And to speak so openly to her stepfather, so daringly, not caring what anyone thought. She looked at her parents. Their expressions gave nothing away, but they were shocked. Harman had struck them in the heart. The bosjesmans and hottentots were savages. The Boer was boss, and had been compromised. Harman had helped in the plot. Why had he told them? Was it to shock or to taunt? Or simply to express his concern about the treatment of the Sonqua? She wanted to look at him across the table, but didn't trust herself. Eventually, she raised her eyes and stole a glance. Her heart sank. She found him looking at the half-breed in a way totally unbecoming for a white man.

At the stove, Rachel filled the serving platters with food and handed them one by one to Somiela. "Don't look at anyone. Serve from the left."

Somiela walked slowly around the long table, serving the guests, careful to avoid eye contact with Marieta. She came to Harman and lowered the bowl. His hand accidentally brushed against hers. Her heart lurched in her chest, and for a moment, she lost her concentration and looked directly into his eyes.

Elspeth, watching from under her lashes, caught the silent exchange. "Ma, I've torn the hem in my blue pinafore. Rachel doesn't need any help in the kitchen, does she? I thought Somiela could mend it for tomorrow morning."

Marieta stopped with the fork halfway to her mouth. She found this a most unusual request, especially in front of guests. She looked at her daughter. Elspeth's face seemed unusually flushed. Marieta knew right away what was going on. She also knew the story of the cut hair, the twins had told her. Her eyes moved to Somiela. The girl had on a doek covering her hair, but it was hard to deny her beauty, and Marieta wondered for a moment at the identity of the father. German? French? She glanced at Harman. Harman's eyes had taken on a flat expression, as if he knew why the request had been made. Was there something going on between him and the girl? She returned to the food on her plate, angry with her daughter. If Harman who was a stranger sensed that Elspeth found him appealing, then Martinus who knew her, would also pick it up. Marieta didn't want her daughter jeopardizing her future with Martinus over a silly attraction for his brother.

"Rachel can mend it in the morning. I've seen the dress, it won't take long. There's much to do here." She flashed Elspeth a look. Elspeth did not miss the chill in her mother's voice. She lowered her eyes.

Harman put down his fork and poured himself a glass of water. "This is good food," he said, his eyes watering slightly. "Is it a dish particular to the Cape? We have very plain food in the Karoo."

"It's maleier food," Marieta said. "Too many chillies in it."

Andries pushed the bowl nearer. "Have more. The young one cooked it."

Marieta was irritated by the remark. Why had her husband mentioned it? There was also something in his choice of words, as if he wanted to draw attention to the girl. And on hearing that it was Somiela who had cooked the food, both brothers reacted. Martinus smiled openly at the slave, forgetting himself. With Harman there was only a trace of amusement at the corner of his mouth.

The brothers stayed overnight. After a breakfast of fried meat, fresh-baked bread, and sugared coffee the next morning, Martinus left for town to attend to his duties as a magistrate.

Harman spent the morning with Andries who showed him around the grounds.

"It's a big place you have here, Oom. Do you get lots of rain?"

"Too much sometimes. We're right in the valley. No neighbours. Very peaceful."

They walked down to the lower end of the yard, in the direction of the jongenshuis. Harman noted the bell tower in front of it. "And this?"

"It's to wake the slaves and summon them in case of an emergency. Also for dop."

Harman looked around, impressed by the immensity of the vineyards stretching down into the valley, then up into the hilly distance. "All this must take a lot of maintenance."

"It does. That's why I need a kneg. I have eleven slaves. Nine are here presently, two more will arrive from Joost van Heerden's next week. Van Heerden's a wheat farmer. I hire the slaves out to him. His grain has to be sifted and threshed before the south-easterly gales ruin the crops. In May they go back there to help with the sowing and ploughing." He stopped to remove a pinch of tobacco from a small pouch and tamped it into his pipe. "Wheat and grapes are harvested at different times. There're slow times when the heavy work's done and I can free up two or three men. It doesn't pay to have a man sitting idle when he can earn money. A slave with time on his hands has time to think."

Harman studied the lushness about him, the tall trees in the forest beyond. Table Mountain was well-wooded halfway up, its summit rocky and bold. There were mountains in the Hantam, but nothing as majestic and awesome. He noted the clouds, soft as kapok, drifting down the slope. What Tuka's people wouldn't give for some of those clouds, he thought. Clouds would bring rain, rain would bring back the animals.

"My overseer's giving me trouble," Andries continued. "He broke a man's ribs a few weeks ago, his second incident. The fiscal's issued a warning. I need someone who can work with these heathens."

"Oom's offering me a job?"

"If you're interested. What happened up north, that's between you and God. I have no problem with a man and his ideas as long as those ideas don't interfere with his work. Ideas can get a man in trouble, especially wrong ones, and ones he has little knowledge of. Knowledge can be good, and it can be bad. The Lord says too much knowledge causes grief. I don't need grief. I need to produce wine. Let's cross here," he led Harman to a narrow wooden bridge built over a lively stream. They had walked all around the property, and were now at the back of the house. "The pressing house is on the other side."

Harman waited for him to continue.

"The most important things for wine farming are the correct soil conditions and climate. Soil can have all the necessary moisture and minerals, but if the climate isn't right it can counteract the advantages obtained from the soil. A vine needs warmth and sunlight when it's in leaf and flower; it also needs rest in the winter months."

Harman listened with interest. He knew nothing about wine farming and found the farmer to be knowledgeable about his work.

"Grapes are gathered when they're perfectly ripe," Andries went on. "Or if a sweet wine is to be made, when they're overripe. They're crushed by human feet. The pressed-out must is fermented. For a red wine, the must is fermented together with the husks of a dark-berried wine. For a white wine, the husks are not permitted in the fermenting vat. Afterwards, the husks, pips, and stalks are dug into the vineyards as manure. Sometimes, the husks and the debris left after the must has been pressed out are covered with water and allowed to ferment. This provides a thin, watery wine of a very low alcoholic strength which I keep for the men on the farm." Andries stopped and drew on his pipe. "It's hard work, and there's a right time to do everything. Come, this is the pressing house where we press the grapes and ferment the wine. You'll see what I'm talking about."

"It all sounds very interesting."

"What do you think of my offer? You'll learn all about wine farming. And the slaves, too, are quite knowledgeable. Some of them have been here a very long time."

"I have no knowledge of slaves."

"You don't need knowledge. Just guts and a good sjambok."

78

"A sjambok?"

"That's right. One that delivers the message. Kananga knows how to use it. He just doesn't know when to stop."

They entered the building. Harman's eyes took a moment to adjust. They were in a long room with a high ceiling, no windows, with vents high up on the walls. There were men decanting wine from one barrel to another, others busy picking off leaves and debris from the top. But it was the spectacle in the middle of the room that caught his attention. It was the girl he'd seen in the kitchen the previous night, with a rope dangling from the ceiling tied around her waist, her dress pulled up to above her knees, trampling miserably around in a barrel of grapes raised several feet from the floor. This barrel stood on a second, larger one catching the juice. Her legs were stained purple, and she seemed humiliated by the task, conscious of the men stealing glances at her.

"Why's she up there?"

"She misbehaved."

"Those small feet surely can't have any effect on these grapes. It will take forever. One or two men would get the job done much faster."

"I know, and we usually have two pressing out the grapes, but sometimes you do things for other reasons."

Harman wanted to look up, but knew it would embarrass the girl. "She seems young to be in here with them."

"The one over there in the leg irons is the stepfather. He won't let anything happen."

"A thin guarantee, if you don't mind me saying so, Oom. What can he do if there's trouble?"

"You worry too much," Andries laughed. "And you can't stop what comes naturally to these men. We need children. There're no children here. Half-breeds like this fetch a high price."

Harman was horrified. The farmer spoke of his people as if they were nothing more to him than horses to be bought, bred, spanned in, and sold again when they'd served their purpose.

A big slave to their right suddenly leaned forward in pain.

"What's wrong?" Andries asked.

"It's his stomach, Seur," Arend said. "Kananga's been sick since last night."

"It must be something he ate." Andries raised his voice to Kananga. "Go and drink some water to flush it out."

Kananga didn't move. He was now doubled over in pain, sweat drops dripping from his brow.

"Perhaps it's something else," Harman ventured.

"No, it's the weather. Affects the slaves every year. Tomorrow he'll be up to his old tricks again. Go on, get something to drink."

Kananga went stumbling out the door.

"That's the one I was telling you about, the mandoor. A big bastard, as you can see."

Harman's attention was arrested by a scantily-clad figure climbing out of a barrel with a scrubbing brush in his hand. He moved closer to the man.

"What's your name?"

Geduld heard his language being spoken. He looked up and realized Harman was talking to him. It confused him for a moment, the strangeness of hearing the clicks and pops issuing forth from the mouth of a white man.

"Geduld, Seur."

"That's your real name?"

"No, Seur. It's Gumtsa."

"Where are you from?"

"From below the yellow river."

"Do you know Koerikei and Tuka?"

Geduld's eyes brightened. "Yes, Seur. From Toma's tribe. Toma's dead now, Tuka's the new leader."

Harman wanted to talk more, but didn't want to keep Geduld from his work and cause trouble for him with the farmer.

"You know his language," Andries said.

"I was taught !Khomani by my father as a child. He grew up with an old Sonqua tracker. They were friends. Twa taught him his language and how to track. My father taught me."

"You're a tracker also?"

"Yes."

Andries considered this new information for a moment, then clapped a hand on Harman's shoulder. "Come, we'll leave them to their work." They stepped outside and stood for a moment breathing in the fresh air. "You've seen the men, a little of what we do. Much of the work consists of planting and pruning and picking and pressing. We keep busy all year. When the hard stuff's over and things slow down, the slaves do maintenance work and repairs. The one in chains is a carpenter. He'll soon be moved to the barn where he'll be able to use the skills I bought him for."

"Why's he in chains?"

"To temper his nature. He defied me."

"I thought it was against the law to put them in chains."

"It is. But who will report it?"

"The slave?"

Andries laughed. "First, he'd have to get there to make the complaint. He'll get no day off for a while. The others wouldn't dare take the chance on his behalf."

They started walking again. Andries drew on his pipe. "The job pays thirty rix dollars a month, three meals, your own quarters. What do you think? Do you think you might be interested in being foreman here?"

Harman was thoughtful. "I would very much like the opportunity to learn about grape farming, Oom, it would be a good thing for me to know. Martinus tells me that Zoetewater produces some of the best wine, and that the farm has established quite a name for itself. And knowledge is always helpful."

Andries wished he would come to the point. He sensed a but in there somewhere.

"But I couldn't work with a man who's in chains. It would disturb me."

"You won't be working with him. He'll work on his own in the barn, with an assistant. You'll oversee the other men. But you're telling me that you're turning down such an opportunity because of his chains?"

"Yes."

Andries was dumbfounded. He hadn't expected such a response, and from someone with the law on his tail, no experience, and no prospect of work if he maintained this attitude. Andries waited to hear if there was anything else, so he could respond, but there was no more. By his silence, Harman Kloot had closed the subject. His "no" was the last word on the matter. They walked for a few minutes in silence.

"Perhaps you're right," he said after a while. "This job's not for everyone."

"I hope you understand," Harman said.

"It's better to be forthright. Although I'm disappointed that you don't understand the way things are in the Cape."

"I had built up a different picture, I can see."

"And you'll have to adjust it if you want to remain." Harman Kloot had insulted him. Spoke to him respectfully, but spoke his mind nevertheless.

Back at the house, Harman took coffee with the farmer and his wife, then collected his things and saddled his horse. The family came to see him off in the yard.

"Thank you for everything, Oom, Tante Marieta. The food was good, I slept well."

"Come soon," Andries said.

"Yes," Elspeth added. "Come with Martinus."

Harman mounted his horse and rode off.

"Insolent bastard," Andries said when he was gone. "Told me straight out he couldn't work with a slave who's in chains. Can you believe it? I tell you, if it wasn't for Elspeth, I would've thrown him off the premises."

Marieta pulled her shawl about her shoulders. She was always cold, and with the weather changing, was seldom without her woollen covering. "Be glad he refused. We can't help that he's Martinus's brother, but we don't want his kind contaminating the slaves. Helping bosjesmans against his own people. Whoever heard of such a thing? Traitorous bastard."

Galloping down the drive on his horse, Harman had mixed feelings about what he'd just done. He still had the money his father had given him, and could stay with Martinus as long as he liked, but he was also anxious to put his mind to something that would make him forget his troubles. He needed to work. And he had no doubt also, that despite his dislike for the farmer, if he was going to learn anything about wine farming, Zoetewater would be the place. He didn't like Andries de Villiers, but it didn't mean the man didn't know what he was doing.

A sudden movement to his left frightened the horse.

"Seur . . ." a voice called from behind a tree.

Harman stopped. It was the little Sonqua, who seemed almost to melt into the trunk.

"What is it, Gumtsa? Why are you hiding?"

"I have a message for Seur."

"A message?"

"Yes, Seur. The others want me to tell Seur that they hope Seur will be the new man at Zoetewater."

It was the last thing he expected to hear. "Me?"

"Yes, Seur."

"But where would they get such an idea? I can't."

The smile went out of Geduld's eyes. "Seur can't? But we thought . . . The one in chains, Sangora, he is convinced that Seur will come to Zoetewater. He also asked if Seur could enquire about his wife. She was sold to an Englishman who lives at the foot of the Table Mountain on Roeland Street. He says he'll be forever in Seur's debt if Seur could do this for him."

"He's brave in his request. What's her name?"

"Noria. From Malabar. She was sold in February."

Harman studied the little hunter for a moment: the warm, brown eyes, the small, round head with tight balls of hair. "Are the others so sure of me that they would send you to ask me?"

"Sangora can feel things. It was his decision. I also told them Seur knows my people. Only one man in the Hantam understood them. He's getting old now, but he's still friend to the Sonqua. I said perhaps Seur was related to him. Eyes of the Sky."

Harman smiled. To hear the name made him feel proud. It also conjured up memories of the old Koi-na woman, Sanna, who had washed and fed him as a child, and told him many things. It was Sanna who had filled in the pieces his father had omitted: it was she who told him of his father's enormous feeling for the spirited Zokho, who had been brought to the farm as a very young girl, of his father's attachment to the old tracker Twa, and of the soft spot he had for the Sonqua. Not that those bosjesman tendendies didn't land him in a lot of trouble with his own father, Sanna had said, but the young Roeloff Kloot always went his own way. Harman could see in the manner and voice of the one before him that his father had not lost any of the respect with which the Sonqua had favoured him.

"Eyes of the Sky is my father. He and Toma knew each other when they were young."

Geduld's face pleated into a smile. "That's what I said. I said so. I said Seur *had* to be the son. Only one man had hair like that." He heard the sound of wheels crunching down the drive and dodged behind a tree. "I must go before someone sees me talking to Seur." Before Harman could say anything, he was gone.

That night in the jongenshuis the men sat around the candle and made Geduld tell them over and over again what Harman had said. Except for Salie, who couldn't really say why he didn't like the landdrost's brother, they were deeply let down by his decision not to work at the farm.

"Are you sure you understood him?" Petroos asked.

"Yes. How many ways can someone say no? I understood it."

"What if Kananga dies?" Arend expressed a concern. "I saw him. He's in a lot of pain."

"I hope it kills him," Hanibal managed to express himself. For once his hands were not occupied with pen and paper. Hanibal was as keen as the others, if not more so, to have the inlander come as foreman to Zoetewater.

"Perhaps the little white man will reconsider," Petroos said.

"He's not little," Geduld countered. "He's the son of the great one. Did I tell you about his mother?"

"What do we care about his mother? Who's she, anyway?"

"It's not *who* she is."

"What do you mean?"

But Geduld's feelings were hurt. He picked up one of his arrowheads and started to sharpen the tip, refusing to speak.

"Geduld's talking nonsense again," Salie said. "Leave him."

"Kananga mustn't die," Sangora spoke for the first time.

"I hope he does."

"No, Hanibal. If he dies, Seur will have to do the job himself. You don't want *him* standing over you, do you?"

"That's still better than that cruel bastard."

"Kananga's cruel, but he didn't report us. With the farmer it'll be worse. We must pray for Kananga to get better, and that he doesn't get sold."

"That he doesn't get sold?" Salie asked incredulously. "I can't believe that you would say that. He put your daughter up in that grape barrel on purpose for everyone to look at. The seur said she had to work in the pressing house, he didn't say she had to press out the grapes. That ka'fir put her up there. I saw you, Sangora, you didn't like it. Why should we pray for someone like Kananga? It's better if he dies in his sleep. It'll save him from the block."

The door opened quietly behind them. Tromp entered, a weary look on his face. He had been assigned the task of checking up on the mandoor and to report any change in his condition to the farmer.

"His fever's high. The doctor said he has a diseased soul."

"His soul's always been diseased," Salie scoffed.

"If he dies, you'll all have your way, but I think you may regret it," Sangora said.

"I don't understand you, Sangora. Look what he does to Hanibal. Night after night. Is it because Kananga didn't beat your stepdaughter that you have this sympathy?"

"He didn't do it because he hates the nooi," Arend answered. "He won't take orders from her. Also because he didn't want to hurt Somiela. It's not a man he'll be flogging."

"Since when has that heathen grown a conscience?" Salie asked.

"He doesn't have a conscience, but I was there. I saw."

"Who asked you? I asked Sangora."

"I don't have to have a reason to feel sorry for someone," Sangora came back into the conversation. "Anyway, if everyone is so hard-hearted, I'll make an azeemaat for Kananga."

"What?" Salie got up. "For goodness sake, let him go."

"Where's your spirit of forgiveness?"

"I have none for him."

"What's an azeemaat?" Arend asked.

Sangora got up and removed a small box he had hidden in a hollow behind one of the loose bricks in the wall. He took a sheet of paper and placed the box on his lap, smoothing the sheet on top of it. He took the pen, and touching it lightly to his tongue to wet the tip, drew a neat, square box on one side of the page. In the square he sectioned off nine little squares, and in each of them, scribbled a sign. Next to the square, he wrote a few lines in Arabic. The men watched closely, fascinated by the squiggles, dashes and dots of this strange language, and the ease with which his hand flowed over the page.

"It's a verse for healing the sick." He put the last flourishing touches to the paper, and folded it into a tiny square. When this was done, he tore a strip of cloth from the end of his shirt, and wrapped it around the azeemaat. He handed the thick little pellet to Tromp. "Give it to him, Tromp. He must wear it close to his chest."

"I don't want to go back there," Tromp said. "And why do you think it'll work? Your God's not listening. If He exists at all, pray to Him from this side of the wall, He'll hear you."

"*I'll* do it, Sangora," Arend said.

"You want to curry favour with Sangora for his stepdaughter?" Salie charged. "You're a convert."

"Stop it," Sangora said angrily. "I'll go myself."

"What if they see you?"

"What if? You're all wearing me down with this bickering."

The leg irons were on the floor and they watched in silence as he put them back on and shuffled from the room.

Out in the dark, Sangora listened for sounds. He couldn't hear anything and walked slowly along the wall to the mandoor's quarters. He reached the door and put his ear to it. Everything was quiet. He knocked. No one answered. He pushed on the door. It opened slightly.

He stepped inside and stood in the doorway waiting for his eyes to adjust to the dark. He made out the coir mattress on the floor, the huge body of Kananga curled up on top of it. It was his first time in the mandoor's room. There was little difference between the dinginess of this room and the one next door except for a small table in the corner.

"Kananga . . ."

There was no response.

He stepped closer. "It's me. Sangora."

Kananga's eyes opened slightly.

86

"I brought you something. Here," he said, daring to touch the big slave's chest, "I'll put it under your shirt."

Kananga groaned.

Sangora watched him drift back into the agony that had claimed him, vulnerable as a fish washed up on shore. He pinned the azeemaat to the inside of the shirt, then smoothed it back in place and stood for a few moments, quietly reciting a prayer. *O God, I ask You to heal Kananga, to make him better, and to lift him out of his darkness and to put light in his heart.* He ended with a few words in Arabic, then blew his breath three times in a circle over the mandoor. Sangora left the room as quietly as he had entered, slipping out into the darkness of the deep Cape night.

. . . the master, however independent he may have wished to be in his slave, needed his community to both confirm and support his power. The community, through its agents, wanted this support reciprocated if only to safeguard the interests of its members . . . the relationship between the master and his community was never a static one. The master wanted to influence public attitudes and deflect attempts to interfere with his proprietary claims on his slaves.

(O. Patterson, *Slavery and Social Death: A Comparative Study*, Cambridge, Mass. 1982)

Harman sat on the edge of the bed and watched Martinus in front of the hall mirror adjusting his clothes and combing his hair in preparation for his visit to Zoetewater. He marvelled at how much his brother resembled Neeltje, his mother: the high forehead, the open eyes, the unassuming manner. But Martinus was rigid in his thinking and cared too much what people thought, finding it difficult to venture outside social formality or convention. Harman was therefore pleasantly surprised when he had asked his brother if he could make some enquiries on his behalf, and Martinus had done so without asking questions. Martinus tended to be a cross-examiner on and off the job. It was in his nature to probe.

"Was it difficult to find the address?" Harman asked him, admiring his fine clothes. Martinus didn't dress like his father, or any of them. He had a tailor, he said, on Loop Street, who measured him once a year. Martinus had grown thick around the waist from sitting all day long listening to people's complaints, so he frequently had occasion to visit his tailor who would show him a piece of imported cloth and impress upon him how well it would suit him, in his important position, to have a pants or jacket, or both, made up of the same cloth. Martinus was wearing a pair of black trousers with a matching jacket reaching almost to his knees, and had a gold watch in an inner pocket which he kept taking out every so often to check on the time. Harman wondered when he might be able to afford to dress himself up like this. But then where would he go, he wondered. In the Karoo a man only got out his suit for nagmaal or a wedding or a funeral – Harman wasn't planning on attending anyone's wedding other than his brother's, and didn't expect to have anyone die.

Martinus handed Harman a piece of paper with the address scribbled on it. "My clerk made the enquiries. There're not many English doctors of women's complaints living in the Cape." He changed the subject. "Is there anything you want me to tell Andries? I'm leaving in a few minutes."

Harman knew what he meant. Martinus wanted him to reconsider the job on the farm. And he'd thought about it. Hard. He understood better from Martinus why Andries de Villiers did some of the things he did. Andries hated the English, Martinus said. The last ten years had seen a series of changes giving slaves increased protection under the law. De Villiers kept just within a hair's breadth of that law. The appointment of a Protector of Slaves was perhaps the hardest thing to accept: for many farmers this was tantamount to appointing an outsider to interfere in their affairs. Slaves could lodge complaints with this Protector who was then obliged to investigate and represent them in criminal actions against their masters.

The present government wanted to promote stable family units by allowing slaves to marry and by forbidding the sale in separate lots of husbands, wives, and children under the age of ten. Slaves could also not be compelled to work on Sundays except for domestic work and work of necessity. The slaves at Zoetewater were given Sunday off, but from what Martinus told him, De Villiers frequently took away this day to punish a slave, which was presently the case with Sangora. Then there was the matter of Sangora's leg irons – something which was blatantly against the law.

"I can't go back on my decision."

"Why not? I can present it so he thinks it's his idea." Martinus put on his hat and smoothed the sleeves of his jacket. "Wine farming's a good thing for you to learn. It's prosperous, and the climate's good for it in the Cape."

"I'm not planning to spend my whole life in the Cape, Martinus."

Martinus laughed. "I also said that when I came. We'll see. It takes you, this place. Anyway, I must go. Do you want me to raise it, yes or no?"

Harman walked with him to the door. "If I go back on this, I'll go back on other things."

"Who says?"

"Better not."

"Sometimes, I swear, you're just like Pa."

Harman smiled. Martinus was always likened to their mother, Karel to Oupa Wynand, and he to his father. "Don't you miss home, even a little?"

"Sometimes, but you get used to it here. The first year's the hardest. Then you get used to it and find you can't do without some of the things." He opened the door and stepped out. "Sure you don't want to come?"

"Sure."

Harman watched him ride off and stared at the piece of paper in his hand. He was tempted to go and see where the house was. Perhaps he would catch a glimpse of the woman. He couldn't understand why Andries de Villiers hadn't bought the whole family, or at least, mother and daughter. And why hadn't the slaves asked his brother long ago to determine Noria's whereabouts? But he knew why. Martinus was betrothed to the daughter. He was also a magistrate. It was strange, thinking of his brother as upholding the law. It didn't seem to fit with where they came from. And with a father like Roeloff Kloot. There was *his* law, which was simple, then there was the law of the bush where you made your decision the instant it was required, on the spot, sometimes to save your own life, sometimes to minimise the suffering of others. The law Martinus embraced stood for a whole lot of paper and little else.

An hour later he stood in front of the doctor's house at the foot of the hill on Roeland Street, not far from Martinus's house on Keizersgragt. The house had a high gable, a large garden in front, and a tree with branches heavy with yellow lemons. Sitting on the stoep was a fair-haired girl with an infant on her lap. A young slave was on his knees in a flowerbed, pulling weeds.

"Good afternoon," he greeted the girl. "I'm wondering if this is the house of the English doctor."

The boy stood up and dusted the soil off his knees. "She doesn't understand the language, Seur. This is the house, but the doctor's not here."

"Is there a woman working here, called Noria?"

"Yes, Seur. She's the nurse for the baby."

"Could I speak to her? Is that possible?" He didn't know why he had asked it. It hadn't been his intention to speak to the woman.

"I'll call her." The boy disappeared around the side of the house. Moments later a handsome woman in a full skirt and a yellow shawl opened the front door. She stood for a moment looking at him at the gate, then came out.

Harman was surprised by her looks. She was dark, with hair knotted in a bun at the back of her head, and didn't look at all like Somiela except for the upward slant of the eyes. An attractive woman with sharp features, exceptionally well-dressed for a slave.

"Your husband asked me to find your address. I thought – "

"Sangora?" Her hand flew to her mouth. "You're coming from him? You know where he is? And my daughter?"

"They're on a farm at the foot of the Wynberg mountains."

"Oh," she moaned, unable to believe it. "A farm? What kind of farm? Are they well?"

"I didn't speak to them. They appear so. It's a wine farm."

Noria's eyes filled with tears. "I think so much about them, if they're with good people. How's my daughter, do you know?"

"She helps in the kitchen. She's made a friend there, I think. An older woman."

"Oh . . . that's good news. I'm so grateful. You don't know what this means to me, to know where they are. I've thought of nothing else. Thank you."

Harman was touched. She was an honest woman. Like his own mother, the one who had raised him from birth, and the only one he considered. But his mother's children had all chosen their own paths. This woman's destiny was out of her hands. "I must let you get back to your work. I only came to see where you were, if this was the right place."

"It is. And I'm so glad you came. The doctor and his wife are very kind. They won't mind."

"Do you have a message you want me to take?"

"I could give you something to give to my daughter?"

"Yes."

Noria took off the yellow shawl and folded it. "It's not much, but it will keep her warm. I made it."

Harman took the shawl from her. "I'll make sure she gets it."

"Tell them I'm with good people. The doctor will return to his country in five years. He's promised to give me my freedom. I'll not go back in the slave book."

Harman said nothing. With talk of emancipation in 1834, the slaves would be free long before then, if they didn't have to serve the four extra years.

"And tell Somiela not a day goes by when I don't think of her. She's in my heart. She mustn't forget God."

"I'll tell her." He extended his hand.

Noria took it. "What's your name?"

"Harman. Harman Kloot."

"Why did you come here, Seur?"

He didn't answer immediately. "I don't know."

Noria studied him. She could see far. Her instincts were never wrong. Harman Kloot had come all the way from Wynberg to bring her a message. People didn't do things like that just for nothing, especially not for slaves. "Thank you for taking the trouble to come and see me, and please tell Sangora five years is a long time. I'll understand if he finds someone."

"Excuse, please?"

"Tell him, God allows it. I won't mind."

He waited to hear if she would explain herself. She didn't. He said goodbye and walked slowly down the hill. He would walk through town, take his meal at one of those drinking places on Long Street, and think. From Noria's demeanour and from the liberties she seemed to have – she could talk to visitors and had been informed that she would be set free in five years – he could tell that a slave fared better at the Englishman's house than at the farmer's. Somiela would've greatly benefited from living with her mother in the doctor's house.

The next morning Martinus brought him up to date on events at Zoetewater while they ate breakfast. "The mandoor's still sick, but there's improvement," he said. "Oom Andries hinted that he wouldn't mind you helping out for a few days."

"Really. He didn't strike me as someone who begged. I wasn't kind to him when I rejected his offer."

"You don't like him?"

"Do you? He's cruel – keeping a man in chains – not like Pa."

Martinus laughed suddenly. "No one's like Pa, and thank God for that. You must stop comparing everyone with Pa. Pa lives in the bush. You're here, you need work. Forget his manner. If I considered his manner, I would stay away. But I don't go there for him."

"So you know what he's made of."

"Of course. That's how people are here in the Cape. He's not very different from anyone else who has slaves. But I look past it. It's not him I want."

Harman liked this new side of his brother. But in fact he'd made up his mind after talking to Noria and thinking it all out. He thought also about what his father had said in the past. *Sometimes you cut your nose to spite your face, and the pain's worth it. Other times, you bite hard on your teeth because there're not always explanations for things when you need them, but something tells you that it will be better for you in the end.* Harman didn't know what that end was, but admitted to himself that the slave girl had something to do with it.

"Well, I've thought about the situation. You're right. It won't hurt to learn the wine-making business."

"I promise you, Harman, De Villiers knows what he's doing. He got Zoetewater through marriage – it was Marieta's, left to her by her late husband. I checked into the farm's history. It wasn't doing too well before Andries came. He doesn't have a head for people, but he knows grapes. He makes a fine wine, he's successful. You don't have to like the people you learn from. I found that out long ago. Zoetewater speaks for itself. Forget the chains and forget his manner – he's a damn sight kinder than his wife. Yes, yes, I go there, and I sit the seat warm, and I make pleasant conversation. It doesn't mean I share their views. I want the daughter. I have my own needs. So do you. Make some money, and take what knowledge you can."

Harman nodded. He felt he was doing the right thing. "I'll do it until his man recovers. Not longer."

"You're doing the right thing. When will you go?"

"This afternoon. What do you know about Mohametans?"

Martinus looked up at him curiously. "Very little. Good craftsmen. Not all of them are slaves. Some of them are political exiles, with religious knowledge. They're having a lot of success with the heathens, converting them. They don't believe in the Lord."

"What do they believe in?"

"A prophet called Mohamet."

"Mohamet is their god?"

"I don't know. One thing I do know, a man can have more than one wife. Can you imagine me having two like Elspeth?"

Harman couldn't imagine it. "The slave in the leg irons, and the girl, they're Mohametans, then."

Martinus wiped his mouth with the back of his hand and got up. "You're not getting yourself involved with these people, are you? I know you, when you start asking these questions. You think you can save people. You can't."

Torn from his home, his family, and relations . . . brought to the Cape, and bound to serve fourteen years without wages, in a strange country, among people of a strange language, professing an unknown religion, and exhibiting customs and manners which to him are utterly unintelligible. At the end of this strange process he is told he is free. Free to do what? . . . He has no pride of nation or tribe . . . no family . . .

(*South African Commercial Advertiser*, 1831)

Sangora and Salie were washing themselves at the water barrel behind the jongenshuis when Arend came running up excitedly. "Have you heard? The inlander arrived this afternoon!"

Sangora shook the drops from his face, and stared at him. "Soemba," he asked Arend to swear an oath.

"I swear. He's come here to work."

"Making that azeemaat was a bad idea," Salie said, taking off his shirt. "That ka'fir's recovering."

"They've decided to sell him, so it doesn't matter. They're just waiting for him to get better, they can't sell a sick slave. The inlander will stay until a new man's hired."

"Perhaps he'll stay permanently," Sangora said. "Whatever it is, he's decided to come. We won't have another mandoor, or the seur watching over us."

Salie threw him a look. "I don't know why his being here's so important to everyone. It doesn't mean he'll be any better than the others. You think he's coming to work here out of the goodness of his heart?"

"You know, you don't know what you want. You don't want Kananga, you don't want the inlander."

"There're things here that he wants."

"Like what?"

"Maybe the farmer's daughter. Maybe yours."

Sangora laughed. "Now I know you've lost your mind."

Salie wrung out his shirt and slung it over his shoulder. "Hope you're right. Rather my mind than her virtue. You know what they all want. Just one thing, Sangora. Don't say I didn't warn you."

At dawn the next day the slave bell summoned the men from their beds. They got up and gathered under the bell tower where Andries de Villiers and Harman Kloot waited. Harman was in brown working clothes, his long hair pulled back and held together with a leather strip. In the greyness of morning, he looked more like a foreigner than a ward of the bush.

"Kananga's going on the block this morning," Andries started, looking in the direction of the wagon house where the mandoor sat on a rock, head down, staring at his feet. Kananga was dressed in his customary waistcoat which now seemed too big for his decreased frame. "This is Mijnheer Kloot. Mijnheer will help out until a new man is hired."

The men stood silent. They glanced briefly at the dejected figure on the other side of the yard. Kananga was going the same way he'd come, with no words of introduction, no words of farewell. He was waiting at the wagon house because the farmer was leaving with him the moment he was through instructing the slaves.

"With Kananga sick all this time, and the rain, we've fallen behind," Andries continued. "There's lots to be done. You'll listen to mijnheer and do as he says. I want no complaints. July and November have returned, and will work where mijnheer tells them. Now that they're back here, February can start his carpentry work in the barn. Arend will be his assistant."

"Seur?"

Andries turned to Salie. "Yes?"

"I've worked before as a carpenter's assistant. Arend has no knowledge of wood. Perhaps I can be of better assistance to Sangora."

"Sangora?" Andries asked caustically. "Don't you know what his name is?"

"February, Seur. I'm sorry."

"Next time, don't speak unless I ask you to. I know what you can do, but I want Arend to learn. That way I'll always have

96

carpenters." He turned to Harman. "You want to say something to them now?"

Harman looked at the men. It had rained during the night, the morning was cold, and three of them stood shivering before him in nothing more than pantaloons and a shirt.

"I don't know your names. Only Gumtsa's. Perhaps you can tell me who you are."

"Tell mijnheer your names," Andries ordered. "This one here, in the jacket, he's the oldest. He looks after the sheep. Step forward and say who you are."

Tromp, a thin, dark-skinned slave with tight, wiry hair, grey at the temples, muttered something under his breath that no one could hear. He did as he was told, and one by one, the others gave their names. They reached the end of the line and it was Sangora's turn. Sangora stepped forward and tripped over his chains.

"Sangora Salamah. From Java," he announced in a calm tone.

Andries stepped up to him. "What did you say?"

"Sangora Salamah. From Java."

"Didn't I change your name?"

"Sangora Salamah's my name, Seur."

Andries smacked his fist into the dark face before him. The blow was so unexpected that Sangora lost his balance and fell backwards. But it didn't stop him. He struggled up. "The name I was born with," he persisted.

Andries grabbed him by his long hair. "You will show me-"

"Oom . . ." Harman said, daring to intervene. "Let me talk to him. I don't want to start my first day like this. Let me, please. You said I would have a free hand. This is where I'd like to start."

Andries was swelled up with rage. "I was mad to buy this maleier! Don't know why I did it. Any more trouble, and he goes on the block! Straight to the Bokkeveld! Let someone up there tame him! Or maybe he wants to go with Kananga right now!"

The men stood silent. They knew these rages. A fly fiddling with the farmer's nosehairs right now would set him off louder than the twelve o'clock gun in Waalendorp. They didn't stir a muscle. Those who dared, glanced over at Kananga without moving their heads. Kananga had heard the commotion, and looked their way. Then his head dropped again, and he waited, more concerned about his own fate, not knowing himself where the night might find him.

"Arend!" Rachel's voice cut across the yard, breaking the tension. "Pap's ready!"

Andries released Sangora with a shove and turned to the men who stood waiting. "Go. Get your pap, and don't take all morning about it. Talk to this maleier," he said to Harman. "I don't trust myself with him."

"I will."

Andries strode off towards the house, the men following silently at a safe distance. Sangora didn't go with them. He shuffled over to the apricot tree and sat down with his back to the trunk, touching his cheek where the farmer had struck him.

Harman walked up to him. "You're not going with them?"

"Arend brings me my food."

Harman studied him for a moment. He'd been humiliated, but hadn't acted the submissive slave. He'd shown his teeth and challenged the farmer. Slaves didn't usually own this kind of strength.

"I found your wife."

Sangora looked up. He was too surprised to respond.

"She's at 22 Roeland Street."

The carpenter got to his feet. "Mijnheer looked her up for me? Mijnheer *went* there?"

"Yes. The owners are treating her well. Her appearance says it. She has some freedoms. She says she'll be released in five years. They've told her."

"Released?"

"The doctor and his wife will return to their country and give her her freedom." He waited for Sangora to digest this. "She also had a message she wanted me to give you. She said five years is a long time. She would understand if you made the acquaintance of someone else."

The import of the message dawned on Sangora. He sank back down on his heels. "She would think such a thing? Five years is nothing if there's something waiting for you at the end of it. But what good would it do if I'm here and she's free?"

"You'll be free also when the new law's passed."

"There's still the four-year apprenticeship. It'll be 1838 before we can leave. Unless the farmer lets us go, but why would he, if he can squeeze more work out of us and pay us goat snot for it?"

Harman saw the men approach with their plates. "Your food's coming. I'll be back when you're all done."

Sangora closed his eyes. The inlander's words had restored his faith, given him hope for a future. God hadn't forsaken them. Noria was close. She was well-treated. Safe.

"We saw you talking to him, Sangora. What did you talk about?" Arend asked, handing him his plate.

"I like him," Petroos giggled.

"Get your head out of his pants," said Arend dismissively. "What did he say, Sangora? Did he say anything?"

"He found my wife."

"What? He actually did you this favour you asked?"

"I was shocked myself when he told me, but he did it."

"Did he say where she was?"

"Yes. He spoke to her."

"Really? What did she say?"

Sangora was aware of the newcomers sitting a few feet away. He'd only met July and November the previous day, and didn't know them well enough to speak in front of them. There were slaves who reported to masters on the sly. Already he'd said too much. He saw Harman striding through the vineyards towards them.

"Not much. She's well. The people are good to her. Did you have a chance to say anything to Kananga?"

"Who wants to say anything to him?" Hanibal asked.

"I did," Arend said ruefully, wiping his bread around his tin plate to soak up the last of the porridge. "I feel sorry for him. He'll be sold up country this time."

"I thought it was only Sangora who felt sorry for Kananga."

"I didn't before, but did you see how thin he looked? That sickness took his wind. And no one's even said goodbye to him."

"I would've said goodbye to him," Salie said. "We just didn't get a chance."

Sangora believed Salie, despite what he'd said earlier about letting the mandoor die. Salie wasn't as heartless as he wanted others to believe, and Sangora had seen the change in all of them except Hanibal. But he understood Hanibal also.

"Here's the inlander," Sangora said, getting to his feet.

Harman arrived and saw that they had finished eating. "You all understand the language I speak?"

"Yes, Mijnheer," Arend said. "Hanibal speaks Portuguese, but understands if we speak slowly."

"First, I want you all to know that I'm not here to change the rituals and procedures on Zoetewater. I'm used to working with people. I've never used a sjambok, and don't intend to. I have allegiance only to those who don't make it difficult for me to execute what I've come here to do. I'm not much older than you, and some of you are older than me. I came here to help out, and expect that you'll be as fair with me as I'll be with you. I've placed my faith in you and promised the farmer results. I wouldn't like any of you to disappoint me. Does everyone understand?"

The men looked at one another, and nodded or said yes.

"We'll meet here in the mornings to discuss the day's work. If there're questions or suggestions or anyone has a complaint, that's the time to air it."

Sangora listened to every word. What overseer took slaves into his confidence and spoke with such fairness? There was disbelief on many of the faces. They'd never heard utterings like this from a white man.

"Anyone has any questions now? No? Then we'll start. Sangora and Arend, you two in the barn. Hanibal and Petroos and Gumtsa in the pressing house. The rest of you, in the vineyards. You all know more than me about the work that needs to be done. So I'm learning from you also. And if there's anything anyone wants to bring to my attention, that I need to know, I'd appreciate your doing so. I understand from your seur that there's rust on some of the vines and that the leaves need sulphuring. July or November, I believe, are best at this."

There was a mumbling from the group.

"What is it?"

Hanibal turned to Arend and said something in his own language.

"Hanibal doesn't want to work with Petroos, Mijnheer," Arend said. "He says Petroos pesters him."

"Pesters him?"

"He's touchy."

Harman didn't understand.

Hanibal made a gesture with his hand. Everyone burst out laughing.

Harman realized what he was saying. He turned red. "You and July, then," he said.

"November's flat face will guarantee his safety," a voice sniggered from the back. "He's too ugly for 'Troos."

November picked up his plate and pretended to throw it at Tromp.

"All right, that's enough," Harman said. "If everyone understands, we'll start."

The men split up and went off to their different posts. Harman watched them for a moment; a strange mix of people thrown together by circumstance. He wondered how they had all ended up here. How did he know so little of what went on in the Cape?

The day started high and was productive, and it ended without incident when Harman announced, just on sunset, that they'd reached their goal and would stop for the day. The men picked up their bottles of water and belongings and headed for the water barrel behind the jongenshuis.

"So? What do you think?" Arend asked the old shepherd. "The day was easy or hard?"

Tromp looked at him with hooded eyes. "You're asking the wrong person."

"You don't like the inlander?"

"He's still one of them."

Arend dipped his hands in the barrel to wash his face. He saw Harman come round the corner towards them, his shirt slung over his shoulder.

Arend realized with some amazement why he was there. "Mijnheer can wash first, the water's clean." He wasn't sure why a white man should want to wash in the communal water, especially when there were facilities for him in the house.

Harman dipped his head into the water and soaped himself with a piece of carbolic that Arend handed to him.

The men looked at each other. Petroos giggled. November thumped Petroos on the head. A movement at the far end of the jongenshuis made them turn.

"Somiela!" Salie went up to her. "What are you doing here? And what happened to your hair?"

"I have to call Mijnheer Kloot to come and eat."

"I'll tell him. What happened to your hair? It was growing so nicely."

"Seur!" she called out.

"I said I would tell him. Now go back to the house."

Somiela made no move to turn away.

Sangora watched from where he was sitting a few feet away, astounded by his stepdaughter's appearance. She was wearing an old calico dress that had probably belonged to one of the women in the house. The dress was too big over the shoulders and hips, and hung clumsily at her bare feet. But this wasn't what shocked him. Her hair which had been ruthlessly cut off by the farmer's daughter, had undergone a further drastic change, and was now cropped close to the scalp, making her look like a boy. It wasn't at all what a girl would choose to do to herself. Had *she* done it? He had lived with Noria and Somiela long enough to know that Somiela had a streak which made her do strange things. He remembered well the incident when she was ten years old: one of the master's children had taunted her, and Somiela had peed on the girl's dress, dried it, and given it to her the next day to wear. Had she cut her hair deliberately to make herself ugly? If so, she hadn't succeeded. There was less than a fingertip's length of hair – yet strangely, the look, lean and mean as it was, didn't diminish her appearance, but instead accentuated the fine lines of her face. There was also something different in her manner; she seemed almost provocative, waiting for the inlander to respond. He remembered what Salie had told him. Was Salie right?

Harman also had heard her voice and seen Salie separate himself from the group and go up to her. He had already noted the Mohametan's sullen reaction towards him. Harman drew his fingers through his wet hair and approached her. "You called me?"

"Seur said Seur must come and eat."

He smiled at her use of the many seurs. "I'm not Seur. I'm Harman."

She blushed. "I'm sorry. Seur said the food's waiting." She turned to go back to the house.

"Wait there. I've a message for you from your mother."

"From my mother?" She stopped to look at him curiously, thinking he was playing with her. "How does Seur know her?"

Some of the men sniggered.

Somiela didn't want to look at them, but looked shyly at Harman, who was naked from the waist up. "Seur's seen my mother?"

Harman wiped himself with his wet shirt, wrung it out, and threw it over the branch of a tree. "Yes. I went to see her. She lives at 22 Roeland Street."

"Really?" She was astounded by this news.

"I want to get a clean shirt. Come with me. We'll talk on the way to the house."

Somiela was unsure. The men were laughing. Salie had a dark look on his face. And he had said, Harman, not seur. She was to call him by his name. What did that mean? It wasn't proper. And it wasn't proper to be walking with him. She glanced at her stepfather sitting under the tree. Sangora never said much, but big things went on in his head. What was he thinking? His expression didn't give anything away. Was he thinking she was forgetting her place? That she was interested in the Afrikander? She hoped he wouldn't think ill of her and that the men didn't take it into their heads that she was playing herself up to a white man. They reached the buitekamer where she waited outside the door, facing away from it, while he went inside for a clean shirt.

At the kitchen window, Marieta watched Harman and Somiela walk up the path and cross the yard. Her first reaction was a sense of outrage. She didn't care much for the traitorous Harman Kloot, but didn't want to see a white man with a maleier either. She watched them approach; the girl listening, Harman doing all the talking. Then suddenly they stopped and Somiela grasped his hands. What had he told her? And why were they walking together in the first place?

A sound behind her made her turn.

"What is it, Ma?" Elspeth came into the kitchen.

Marieta pretended to wipe the window sill. "Where are the girls? Food's ready."

"They're coming." She came to stand next to her mother and looked out the window. Her breath caught in her throat. "My goodness!"

"Don't bother yourself over it," Marieta said.

"What's he doing walking around with a slave?"

"There're men who like that sort of thing."

"What sort of thing?"

"Slave women. They come easy."

Elspeth looked at her mother in surprise. "You're saying he's like that?"

"He likes bosjesman and hottentot. Betrayed his own people for them."

"Let them be," Andries said, coming up behind them. "We need slaves. If there's a child, whose is it?"

Marieta's eyes narrowed. It was crude, but it was one way to ensure an ongoing slave population. Van Heerden had three basters running around on his farm. Everyone knew they were the son's. At least Andries didn't seed the help at Zoetewater himself.

"Maybe you're right," said Marieta slowly.

Elspeth glared at her mother. "Ma! You don't mean it." She didn't know if she was upset with the cunningness of the idea of reproducing slave children, or the thought of Harman doing the propagating. She went to sit at the table and stared at the ring on her hand, the ring Martinus had put there just a few months ago. Elspeth wondered why she was feeling so upset. Was she jealous of a common slave? Or was it that *she* did not have Harman's attention? What did the slave girl have that she didn't, and why did it disturb her? I'm betrothed, thought Elspeth. And Harman wasn't half as refined as Martinus. He was uncivilized, a law breaker. Still, there was something about him that made her think about and want things. She had seen him that first day and wanted to touch him. The thought disturbed her that she could be attracted to one man while attached to another. It disturbed her even more than that he should completely overlook her for a slave.

The twins came to sit at the table and rattled on about a new child that had joined their school. Elspeth was grateful for the distraction, but stopped listening when Harman and Somiela entered the kitchen. She wanted to believe that it was only a kindness he showed the half-breed, but then she'd seen the look between them that first night. She watched him sit down on the other side of the table, his wet hair leaving damp patches on his shirt.

"How was the first day?" Andries asked when a platter of fried meat, boiled potatoes and carrots had been placed before them.

"Productive. We finished what we set out to do."

"And the carpenter?"

"Sangora and Arend spent most of the day sorting through the mallets and hammers and other tools, and sawing wood. They need new tools. Sangora's made a list."

"A list?" Andries was aware that Harman had used the carpenter's original name. "I didn't know he could write."

"He does. In his own language."

Andries looked at his wife. "No wonder he has this opinion of himself."

"A slave with a little knowledge is a dangerous thing," Marieta said. "But it shouldn't be any wonder. The half-breed reads to the children. She can write also."

"Seeing as we're talking about Sangora, Oom, I was wondering – and I ask you to consider it before saying no – I was wondering if we could take off his chains. He'll work much better without them."

Andries looked at Harman as if he'd asked for the hiding place of his money. "Out of the question," he said immediately, and gave a list of reasons why he couldn't entertain the idea. "He's insolent. You saw for yourself how he defied me."

"We don't want trouble here," Marieta added.

"He'll work with them on or suffer the consequences," Andries stabbed viciously at the meat on his plate. "You give these people your finger, they rip out your arm."

Harman said nothing. He was aware of Somiela a few feet away, listening to them discuss her stepfather. In the silence that followed Andries realized that Harman wasn't arguing back. "Harman?"

Harman knew it was his last chance. "You're right, Oom."

"You agree with me, then."

"I agree that he's insolent. And I know if you take off his chains it'll seem like he's won, but you'll be the winner in the end. Sangora will feel better disposed towards you. The others will see this. He's an important slave. They look up to him. You want loyalty."

Andries put down his fork in irritation. "I don't need a slave to feel kindly towards me, and don't care to impress him. I feed him and clothe him and put a roof over his head. That's quite enough."

"Removing his chains will lighten his spirit."

"His spirit?" Andries laughed. "Who cares about that?"

"A contented worker is one who performs well."

"No slave is ever content."

Harman said nothing. His father had taught him when to make a point, and when to keep quiet.

Andries saw that Harman had given up. He forked a piece of meat into his mouth and chewed thoughtfully. "I tell you what. I'm not saying I will, but I'll consider it. It makes sense what you say. If it makes for better work, it's worth a try. But don't let me raise your hopes. I'll think on it and see how I feel." He turned to Rachel standing at the stove. "Rachel, bring me that bottle over there on the dresser. And some glasses. What is your experience with wine, Harman?"

"Not much. Pa sometimes brews an apricot brandy for a special event, and no one can remember anything afterwards. Other than that, there's not too much drinking."

Andries had finished eating. He pushed back his plate, and drew the bottle and glasses towards him. "The day deserves some kind of reward. Try this and tell me what you think. Natural wine, when it's just been refined, can be drunk at once, but it's young, immature, and doesn't possess the virtues that time alone gives it. It may show promise and blossom into splendour, but you don't know whether it will or not. All wines mature. They have their period of growth, reach their peak when the chemical compounds within them change. No one, not even the best expert, can tell when that stage will be reached. Some wines don't live to see it. They grow grey before having had a chance to mellow. Others may take years, and then rapidly decline. There's no rule you can apply. But all wine should be given a chance. It should stay in the cask, in wood, for months, and in the bottle for some years to shed whatever it may have to drop, and to be undisturbed by the oxygen in the air around it, resting peacefully to develop those qualities that only time and the slow chemical reaction can achieve."

Harman listened with interest. It was hard to believe that this was Andries de Villiers speaking, and that he could both dislike and admire the man at the same time. Knowledge was a thing he respected; when it was put into practice, even more so. He could listen to Andries forever when he spoke like this. His voice was different, his speech more elaborate, even the meanness in his eyes disappeared.

"This is a Madeira," the older man continued. "One of my best. I have only a few dozen bottles left. And three vats, which won't be ready for some time."

Harman had seen the vats. Made of mahogany, or a wood very much resembling it, they were very thick, highly polished, and bound round with great brass hoops, the edges secured by the same metal to prevent damage. The bung holes were covered with plates of brass hasped down and locked, and the cocks had locks and keys so the slaves couldn't get to the wine. Many people came directly to the farm with their own bottles to buy wine, and the vats were never opened by anyone other than the overseer or Andries de Villiers himself.

Harman took the glass offered to him, and drank of it. But he was not a connoisseur, and drank too quickly, not doing full justice to the deep violet wine. He allowed his glass to be filled three times, and when he found his head feeling heavy and his thoughts drifting to things other than what the farmer was saying, Harman got up, thanked the couple for a good meal and said he would take an early night.

On a cold morning in July, Andries came out of the kitchen pulling his jacket tightly about him. He was pleased to see Arend already on the wagon, getting ready to go to the market.

"Morning, Seur," Arend greeted.

"Everything's loaded?"

"Just three more, Seur," Arend said, clambering over the barrels of apples, trying to find place.

"We can't leave them behind." Andries was a wine farmer, but a small orchard in the back had produced a good harvest of apples he wanted to sell.

Arend shook his head. "I don't know, Seur. We're quite overloaded."

Andries rubbed his hands together vigorously, trying to warm them up. "Just see what you can do, and hurry. There'll be wagons on the road, all going to the same place."

Arend started to move the barrels around. A few apples fell out as he did so. Finally, he jumped off the wagon shaking his head. "There's no place, Seur. Not even for me."

"We have to find room."

"Does Seur see how it's sagging at the back?"

Andries moved to the rear of the wagon and looked under it. It was still grey at that hour of the morning and he squinted his eyes to get a good look.

Harman, crossing from the buitekamer to the house, saw the farmer peering under the wagon. Everything had been put ready the previous night and he was surprised to see him still there.

"Morning. Is anything wrong?"

"I can't get these on," Andries pointed to the three barrels on the ground.

Harman walked around the wagon slowly. "The right wheel's under pressure. I can't get a good look at the axle, but it's my feeling it's not going to hold."

"Are you sure?"

"I'm not sure, but I wouldn't chance it. And I would take off a few more barrels."

"I can't do that. Come, Arend, it's getting light."

Harman watched Arend climb up and perch precariously on one of the barrels. Andries stepped up after him and sat down on the seat in front. There was a complaining creak, then a loud crack as the back of the wagon dropped suddenly, and lurched sideways. Barrels and apples toppled over and rolled to the ground.

"Aiee!" Arend exclaimed, landing with a bump on his behind, trying to scramble up under the slide of apples swirling about his feet. Andries had just time to jump off as the seat gave way under him.

Harman watched in horror as everything collapsed.

Andries looked anxiously about him. "Now what?"

Harman examined the wood where the axle had broken. "I'll get Sangora to take a look at it."

"You think he can fix it? It's in half."

"I don't know. The best thing is a new axle, but perhaps he can think of a way, even if only to get you to the market and back."

Andries said nothing. He had already discovered Sangora's ability for detailed work and craftmanship when the slave had made a small jewellery box for his stepdaughter's eighteenth birthday; polished and carved with little chips of glossy shell inlaid all around the edge.

Harman strode off and arrived at the jongenshuis, preoccupied with his thoughts. He knocked and opened the door without thinking, coming upon the men in various states of undress. The first thing he saw was Sangora pulling on his pants. At first Harman couldn't say what it was that was different about the man, then realized that there were no chains on his legs.

"Sangora . . ." He was confused. He and Sangora often talked on Sunday afternoons, and he'd learned much about the carpenter's country, his beliefs, how he'd met Noria and her daughter. Sangora had shared many things, but not this.

"I can explain."

Harman shook his head. "It's not necessary. I don't want to know. I didn't see anything. Just put them back on before he sees." Then he said, "The axle broke on the wagon. I need you to fix it. Salie, you and Hanibal come and help. There're apples all over the place."

"Before breakfast?" Salie asked.

Harman turned to him. He was tiring of the antagonism. "Yes."

Harman left with Hanibal. He still couldn't believe what he'd seen. And for the slaves to keep such a secret. But then he wasn't surprised any more. Their keepers knew little about who their slaves were. The De Villiers family knew Sangora was a carpenter and could read and write. They didn't know that he came from a line of caliphs and sheikhs and had a high religious background. They knew Salie had woodworking skills. They didn't know he was also a tailor, and made men's vests in his spare time which Arend sold in town on market day. They didn't know Hanibal could draw – well enough to get himself work as a sketcher of human events.

Sangora came shuffling up in his leg irons to where Harman and Andries stood.

"The axle broke on this wagon," Andries addressed him. "Do you think you can fix it?"

Sangora examined the axle, then gave his opinion. "I can lay a piece of wood alongside the axle and nail it together. If we had a piece of iron, we could try to bolt it to the wood to make it extra secure." He turned to Arend. "Get some bolts from the tin we keep the long nails in, and a piece of wood of the same thickness and length. And see if you can find a suitable piece of iron. Don't forget the big hammer."

Andries looked up at the sky. It was getting light. "I'll be inside for a few minutes. See what you can do."

Hanibal and Salie filled the barrels with apples, and lined them up. When Andries returned, Sangora had secured a length of wood to the broken axle, joining the two pieces neatly together, but couldn't get the bolts to penetrate the iron bar.

"Is there no other way?" Andries asked.

"It's not going through," Harman said. "We can tie it with rieme. I can knot it so it doesn't come loose." He would've liked to suggest that they use the cuffs around Sangora's ankles – the iron wasn't too thick and there were holes in them – but knew what the farmer would say.

"The load will have to be lighter," Sangora warned.

"You won't be able to take all this, Oom," Harman agreed.

"Tie it up, then," Andries said, desperate to get away. Harman laid the long iron bar alongside the repaired axle and secured the whole thing with leather rieme, wrapping them several times around it. When he was done, he pulled vigorously on it. "It's safe, but perhaps Sangora should go with you, just in case."

Andries hadn't thought of the risk which he ran, going to town in a wagon with makeshift repairs, and studied the men waiting anxiously for his instructions. "Arend, run up to the house and get Sangora's pap. He's coming with us."

Everyone stared at the farmer. He had just used Sangora's real name.

"And ask the nooi for the keys."

"The keys, Seur? What keys?" Arend asked.

"The keys to take off these chains."

Harman couldn't believe his ears, and didn't want to look at the farmer for fear he would change his mind. He noticed that Sangora, shocked by the announcement, had turned his back, not trusting his emotions to be seen by others.

"There're no keys, Seur. Remember? There were no keys with them when I brought Seur the chains." Arend couldn't tell the farmer that the keys were hidden in the jongenshuis. But he was overjoyed to hear that the farmer was finally relenting, and couldn't think how to suggest a way for the chains to come off without arousing suspicion.

"I can get them off," Harman said suddenly.

They all looked at him. "How?" Andries asked.

"I think I might have something in my room. I have my own tools. Come with me, Sangora."

Sangora shuffled off behind him. When they were out of earshot, he said, "You really have something that will unlock these irons?"

"No, but you have. I had to say something before he changed his mind. Where're the keys?"

"Under my mattress."

Harman turned to see what Andries was doing. The farmer was busy talking to Arend and Salie. "Let's go," he said, and instead of heading for the buitekamer, they dodged into the jongenshuis. A few minutes later, they returned.

Andries nodded his approval, pleased that Harman had managed to remove the leg irons. "You can eat on the wagon," he said to Sangora. "Get on."

The rieme held, and the wagon made it to the market and back without incident. When Harman saw it roll up the gravel drive later that evening, he walked over to the wagon house where Arend and Sangora had outspanned the horses and were leading them back to the stable.

"Was everything all right?" he asked the farmer. "The wagon looks in one piece still."

"We got there. The axle held. I had some other matters holding me up. How were things here?"

"Good. We can start with the pruning next week." He paused to consider his next words. "About my decision to stay a bit longer. You wanted me to tell you as soon as I could. I've thought it over. I'll stay the extra month or so, until a new man's hired."

Andries looked at him. "It might take several months."

"I understand."

"Well, this is a relief, and it should all be settled before December. Perhaps even at the time of the wedding next month. There'll be many farmers here, and word gets around. People know people who know people to hire. Your family also will attend as you know."

"I know."

They walked up to the house. Andries stopped and faced Harman under the overhead lamp just before opening the back door. "I was approached by two men at the market today. I know one of them. Helped him out in a crisis once when he was accused of beating a slave half to death. I'd been a visitor at his farm when the whole thing happened, testified for him in front of the landdrost." Andries paused for a moment. "They'd heard there was someone from the Hantam working here on the farm. They're on the lookout for a man involved in the shooting of a farmer."

Harman stiffened.

"I told them, yes, I had such a man. The brother of a landdrost. This landdrost was soon to become my son-in-law. A visit to Zoetewater wouldn't conceal this. But I challenged anyone who said this man had committed a crime. Yes, they were welcome to come and look. There were no secrets at Zoetewater."

Harman could hear the pumping in his own chest. "What did they say?"

Andries kicked his boot against the step to rid it of dirt before stepping inside the house. "They bought a barrel of apples and wished my daughter happiness. I don't think we have to worry about unwelcome visitors to the farm. I'll say goodnight to you now."

At breakfast the following morning, Harman sat quietly drinking his coffee while waiting for the meal to be served. It was to be eggs that morning, made a special way with tomatoes and chillies. He liked the flavoursome food he ate at Zoetewater, and had learned to tell the difference between Rachel and Somiela's cooking. Both women used spice in the food to liven it up, but Somiela's dishes, he noticed, had a sharper taste. "She'll learn," Rachel had once said when he asked for water after a particularly strong-tasting meal. "Somiela uses too much garlic and chillies." He didn't know if he wanted Somiela to learn. The sadistic green chillies brought tears to his eyes, but added a real bite to the food.

His thoughts returned to his conversation with Andries de Villiers the previous night. There was no mistaking what he'd been told and the import of it. The farmer had called in the note on an old favour, and in so doing, given him another chance. He didn't have to worry about anyone coming to look for him at Zoetewater. But was he exchanging an old liability for a new one – was he now indebted to the farmer instead?

Rachel left the kitchen, and Somiela served Harman four poached eggs steamed on braised tomatoes with chillies, and several thick slices of hot bread oozing chunks of melting butter.

"Thank you, Somiela."

Hearing him say her name sounded strange to her ears. "More coffee?"

He looked up and smiled. "Yes, please."

She fetched the kettle from the stove and refilled his mug.

"You have a day off on Sunday?"

The question caught her off guard. "Me?" She was surprised that he would be interested in her routine.

"I could take you to see your mother."

The kettle felt heavy in her hand and she put it down on the table. "My mother? You mean you'll take me to her?"

"Yes."

"Why?"

"You ask so many questions. Don't you want to see her?"

"Rachel and I have to alternate on Sundays. One of us always has to be here. And for two Sundays coming I have things to do. But I'll be free the week before the wedding."

"Would you like to go then?"

She looked at him nervously. "They won't like it if they found out."

"Who's they?"

"The seur and the nooi."

"Will *you* like it?"

It was as if he had touched her. "Yes."

"Then that's it. And they won't have to find out. I'll tell them. I'll ask if I can borrow the wagon."

Somiela didn't want to think what that meant. She had welcomed the attentions of Arend and Salie when she first came and even thought her fate would lie somewhere between them, but it had all changed with Harman's arrival. She was thinking dangerous things, things a slave had no business considering. Was this trip going to inflame her fantasies and lead her further astray?

Rachel came into the kitchen and immediately sensed that something had happened. She looked from one to the other, but nothing seemed out of place. Somiela was at the working table slicing bread, Harman concentrating on the food on his plate. It was all too contained. She knew something had passed between them. The girl was too attractive for her own good. Harman Kloot was easy to like, but one still had to remember who he was.

The Sunday before the wedding finally arrived and dawned with a torrent of rain and gale force winds rattling at the windows and doors. Somiela, snuggled up behind Rachel's back on a mattress in front of the fireplace, listened to the storm raging outside. It was warm under the blankets, but she couldn't linger. Everyone had big appetites on Sunday mornings and there was much to do before she could leave. It was growing lighter in the cavernous kitchen. She had to get up, light the stove, put the bread in the oven. A day off meant only from noon until sunset. There was breakfast and dishes and dusting and ironing before she could think of going anywhere. She hoped the storm wouldn't make

Harman change his mind about taking her to her mother. Why was he really doing it? Was it out of concern for a miserable slave? He was good natured, they said, but was it really just a good heart, or was there something he was looking for in return? Dare she think it? That he might have just the slightest interest in her? That question went round and round in her head. He couldn't just be taking her to her mother out of the goodness of his heart. But what exactly was it that he wanted? There were other white men who went after slave women, and there were slave women who trusted them, like Rachel had done and ended up with Arend, and there were women like her own mother who'd been brutally taken against their will and also ended up with child. Did she fall somewhere between these two kinds of women – one who trusted too easily, and one who rejected a man outright? Or was Harman's interest in her born out of curiosity? He was certainly curious about things, and interested in the ways of the men. She had dreamed of being with him, and today she would be with him for some hours. She would sit next to him on the small bench behind the horses as they travelled to town. They would talk. What questions could she ask? What if he asked things she didn't understand?

She listened to Rachel's soft snoring. Rachel could give hard looks and scold you till you cried, but under the gruffness was a soft heart. The aia always made sure there was enough on Somiela's plate, and saw to it that her clothes were adequate and warm. She was fond of Rachel, and last night watched her lovingly mend an old coat for Somiela to wear. During their little coffee talk, alone in front of the kitchen fire, Rachel had revealed a part of her past. "Arend's father was a Frenchman. He cared for me, or so he said. We were to marry. But nothing happened. In the end, he went away. White men are full of promises." She knew why Rachel had told her, and it hurt her that she didn't understand.

"Rachel, wake up. It's getting late."

Rachel stirred heavily, and opened her eyes. They got up, put away the bed things, and started breakfast. A short while later, the kitchen was pleasant with a bright fire crackling in the stove. Somiela felt cheered. Despite the rain and the storm raging outside, it was a day of anticipation. Her spirits were high. The kitchen was warm. There was the smell of hot bread baking and meat and eggs frying. And she was going out.

The family arrived and seated themselves at the table, and shortly after, Harman entered through the back door, letting in a cold blast of air. He greeted everyone and sat down.

"The weather looks miserable out there," Andries said.

"Yes, it's still raining fiercely. And there's a leak in my room. I have a bucket catching the water. I'll have a look at it tomorrow."

"You're still going out, I take it," Andries asked.

"Yes."

Somiela brought the coffee. She didn't look at him directly and was glad that he paid her no attention. There was nothing to indicate that they had plans for the day. She arrived at Elspeth's side with the kettle. Elspeth looked up.

"We can start with the ironing and packing of my trousseau today, Somiela. We'll be very busy during the week."

"I'll do it," Rachel said. "It's Somiela's day off."

"Can't she have a day off next week?"

"Next week's your wedding, Kleinnooi. Everyone's working."

"But we have guests coming tonight."

"She'll be back before then."

"Back from where? She's going somewhere?"

"To see her mother," Harman intervened.

Everyone looked at him. He was the last person they had expected to say anything.

"What're you talking about?" Marieta asked.

"I'm taking Somiela to see her mother."

"Her mother?" Marieta turned to Andries. "Is this true?"

"Yes."

"But you don't mean to say – "

"It can't hurt. Harman's taking her. He's promised to be back by nightfall. Arend and Salie are also going. It's Sunday. I said they could go with the wagon. No use having everyone get sick in the rain."

"You're making a mistake allowing all these liberties. And why does Harman have to get himself involved? I thought no one knew where this woman was."

"I got the address from Martinus," Harman said. "I went there."

"You went there? Why?"

"I wanted to see who she was."

"That seems a bit unnatural, doesn't it?"

Harman laughed. "I don't think so. I'm always curious about people. Who they are, where they come from. I know the nomads and hunters, their habits, their beliefs. Somiela and her people are interesting to me. I don't know much about them. I want to know more."

Marieta didn't know how to respond, and was sure he was laughing at her behind those flat eyes. She pushed back her chair so that it grated along the floor.

"I think my appetite has quite left me." She got up and left the kitchen.

Andries looked at Harman. Harman buttered a slice of bread. Somiela didn't dare to look at anyone.

The meal continued in silence. When it was over and everything had been washed and put away, the family departed for the voorkamer where Rachel sat on a chair close by and Andries conducted the Sunday morning prayers. Somiela stood for a few minutes in the doorway listening to the farmer preach the words of the Lord, then went quietly back to the kitchen, took the brown coat Rachel had darned from the hook behind the door, and put it on. She looked at the jars of watermelon konfyt on the top shelf of the dresser. Would they miss one? She looked around to make sure she was alone, then stole up to the dresser, reached for a small jar at the back, and stuffed it into her pocket. She stood for a moment listening to the voice of Andries de Villiers drifting out to the kitchen, then opened the back door and stepped out into the rain.

The ride into town was not how she had envisioned it. Arend and Salie were travelling with them and Harman told her to sit out of the rain in the back. She didn't mind. It gave her time to consider things. She could observe him from where she sat, talking to Arend who had joined him in front. She listened to their talk, dulled by the rain against the canvas roof of the wagon, and paid little attention to Salie who was staring morosely at her.

"He will not want you like I do," she heard him say. She didn't expect he would bring up the subject, and was glad no one could hear them in front.

"You're a slave," Salie continued. "What's he doing this for?"

Somiela closed her eyes and leaned back. She didn't want him to read her thoughts, and to respond to him now would start a whole argument that she didn't want.

Salie gave up and huddled in a corner, the swinging motion of the wagon rocking him to sleep. She opened her eyes and studied him. He was a handsome man, and had made himself fancy in a white shirt and coloured vest for the merang at the house in Dorp Street. She liked him, despite the nasty things he sometimes said, and understood his frustration. He had met her first, and they were both Mohametan. Perhaps if she hadn't met Harman she would've allowed things to develop between them in a natural way, but things hadn't worked out like that.

The wagon rolled along at an easy pace, and eventually slowed. She felt the climb, and looked out the back. They were in Strand Street, going slowly up the hill to Dorp Street. They passed the church, the houses, flat-roofed and white-washed, some with high terraces running along the front where families sat and drank coffee, deserted today because of the rain. The familiarity of the ride reminded her of her last visit there with her mother. Soon she would see Noria, see where she lived, if she was all right. She put her hand out. The drizzle had stopped, but there were a few people about, two wagons in front of the Lutheran Church, a stray dog scratching in the mud.

Salie woke up and drew his knees close under his chin.

"You should've worn something warmer," she said. "You're shivering."

He looked at her, bundled up in the big coat. "What do you care?"

"I care, even though you don't think so."

Salie folded his arms about his legs and rested his chin on his knees. "Anyway, I'm sorry for what I said earlier. About him."

"Don't be sorry. Perhaps you are right."

"If I'm right, then why, Somiela? We won't be on Zoetewater forever. One day we'll be free. You'll need a husband, I'll need a wife. We're the same. He'll not understand you. How can he? Or is it that I'm not good enough?"

"You *are* good enough. And I like you. It's not that."

"What then?"

She couldn't answer.

"We're here," Arend said from the front.

The wagon stopped. Salie jumped off through the opening in the back, and came round to the front to talk to Harman. "We'll wait here at this corner. What time will you return?"

"An hour before sunset."

Two men, the older one with a toding on his head, separated themselves from a group in front of the house and came towards them. "Boeta Mai! Salaam aleikoem," Salie greeted them. He turned to Harman. "This is Boeta Mai, and his son, Soleiman – we call him Sollie. Boeta Mai, this is Harman Kloot, the overseer on the farm where we work. He was good enough to bring us."

"Kloot?"

"Yes," Harman said, raising his hat in greeting. "You know the name?"

"Yes," Boeta Mai said hesitantly.

Harman looked at the two men. They didn't look like father and son. One appeared to be in his late forties, dark, with tight hair sitting close to his head, and light grey eyes. The other was honey-complexioned, about Harman's age.

"My brother's a landdrost in the Cape. Perhaps that's where you've heard it. Maybe there're other Kloots. I must ask Martinus about it."

Boeta Mai didn't say anything.

"Well, we must be on our way. Nice to make your acquaintance," and turning to Arend and Salie, "I'll see you two later. Don't let me wait for you. Be here."

"We will," Arend said.

Harman watched as they walked off.

Somiela waited anxiously in the back of the wagon to see what he would do next.

"Come, sit up here in the front, Somiela. It's stopped raining."

Somiela climbed over the seat and sat down next to him, looking for a place to put her feet. There was a voorkis in front of them, tapered to allow additional space for the driver's feet, with a ridge of wood along the upper surface of the lid to prevent them from sliding off when going down or uphill. She manoeuvred her feet gently behind it where there was a little space. Somiela wondered what there was in the chest. Things for Martinus, where Harman was going? Perhaps for his sister who lived near the docks? Did he take anything when he visited? The gereedskapkis hanging under the wagon contained tools, in case a wagon broke down, and one never travelled without it. There would be no personal things in there.

"What do they do inside there?" he asked her about the house they had just left.

"It's where we come to pray. People feel strong when they pray together. The ones who are free, come on Fridays also, for the midday prayers. But today there's a merang. Merangs are usually on Thursdays, but there's one today. People will talk to each other and make new friends. Afterwards, there'll be fish and rice, followed by cake and tea."

"All of them are Mohametans?"

"Almost all of them. Some of them have no faith. They've heard that the imam converts people, you can have God if you become Mohametan. You can't be nothing, my mother says. You have to have something to believe in."

"You take this belief seriously then."

"Yes. But I'm not as good as my mother, or Sangora. They pray five times a day."

"Five times seems like a lot."

She laughed for the first time. "God wanted us to pray fifty times, but Mohamet talked to God and God reduced it to five."

Harman looked at her. "How did Mohamet talk to God?"

"You won't believe me if I tell you."

"I will."

"Mohamet was at the holy shrine where he went in the middle of the night to pray. He fell asleep and was awoken by the angel, Jibriel, and lifted onto his horse and flown miraculously through the night to Jerusalem. They came to this place where they climbed a ladder through the seven heavens to get to God. Moses was in one of the heavens. When Mohamet reached the place where God was, God told him that the Muslims must make salat fifty times a day. On his way down, Moses told Mohamet he must go back to God and get the number reduced. Moses kept sending Mohamet back until the number of prayers was reduced to five. Moses thought five times was still too much, but Mohamet didn't want to go back and ask God to reduce it more."

Harman looked at her. She had said it all so seriously. "I don't know what to say."

"I told you you wouldn't believe me."

"Are you saying Mohamet saw God? Maybe it was a dream."

Somiela pulled her coat tightly about her. "Sangora can tell you more," she said stiffly. "That's all I know."

"Mohamet isn't God, then."

"No. Only a messenger. What is your belief?"

"I don't know. My mother always talked about God. How He allowed his son to die on the cross for our sins. She would read to us from the Bible. Not my father. He believes, but not the way she does."

"What does he believe?"

"He says God's in your heart. If a man reads from the Bible all day, but steals your sheep, he doesn't know God. If you have a conscience, you have God. I think that makes sense."

Somiela looked at him sideways. "It makes sense, but I think you still need to pray."

"Come, we must go. We'll go down Keizersgragt, I'll show you the house where my brother lives. Roeland Street's just a few minutes from there."

Somiela knew where it was. They had come along it, perhaps even passed the English doctor's house before turning down Buitenkant Street. Harman could easily have dropped her off first. Why didn't he? She thought she knew why. There had been other people with them in the wagon. He wanted to spend a few minutes alone with her.

"Are you excited about seeing your mother?" he asked.

"Yes."

"I'll leave you there for the afternoon, then come back for you. I'll go to Martinus to pick up some clothes, then stop in at my sister Bessie's house."

"Oh."

"You wanted me to come with you?"

"I don't know these people."

"You're going to see your mother."

"My mother's a servant."

"That's the only reason you want me to come?"

"What other reason could there be?"

He looked at her. "Maybe I was hoping for another."

Her face reddened. "Like what?"

"That you might like me."

"Of course I like you. Just as I like Salie, or Arend, or Rachel."

He smiled. "I thought you only spoke the truth, Somiela. Shame on you."

Noria was at the window when she saw the wagon pull up. She wouldn't cry, she told herself. She didn't cry any more. She'd cried her last tears when the hammer fell, separating her from her husband and daughter. Suddenly the memory was before her: she was ten years old, standing on the harbour with her mother at dawn. Her mother handing her over to the captain of a ship, her mother's figure disappearing in the fog. That day was etched in her mind. "Lieda", the captain renamed her. At night she had slept in a hold, crying for a mother who'd sold her; during the day she peeled potatoes and scrubbed floors. Three years later she was sold to a crew member for ten silver rupees. The crew member changed her name and sold her to another for a handful of pagodas. At sixteen she was sold to the captain of a Portuguese slaver and renamed for a third time. The slaver was invaded by a Dutch ship, who brought them all to the Cape. She was put on the block and was told that her new owner would own the baby growing in her belly. She was brought to a farm where she slept in the kitchen in front of the stove, and Somiela was born two months later. The rules were clear, the work never-ending. Punishment followed any disobedient act. But she had a child to lose herself in at night when they lay cuddled together on the small mattress. After two years, she and Somiela were sold to a widow who had no children for Klaratje to look after – Noria was called Klaratje then – but who had hired her for her dressmaking skills. Noria spent her days cutting patterns and sewing clothes for the widow who sold what she made. The widow made no claim on the child.

Then the widow married and everything changed. The new husband sold the house and brought them to a farm where people worked long hours ploughing fields and harvesting wheat. It was here she met Sangora, and trusted a man for the first time. Sangora wanted to live by God's law. The widow allowed Noria to use her original name, and to marry. When the widow died, the farmer married a younger woman who came with her own house servant and put her and Somiela out in the field. It was at this time that Noria had found herself pregnant. Her son was born weeks before he was due, had not been strong enough, and died. Sangora blamed the punishing hours in the field for the poor condition of his wife and the death of his child, and refused to work. The other workers – many of whom had been converted by Sangora – supported him, said their religion forbade them to do certain things, and stood up to the owner. They were all given twenty-five strokes, put in chains, and a few days later, sold on the block.

Noria stood for a few moments watching Somiela come through the gate, and noticed the hair cut close to the head, the ugly coat. What had happened to her hair? The coat didn't hide the gauntness of her frame. And there was something else, a look, one such as she'd seen on the face of a man who'd been told he had a strange sickness and was trying to keep it from others. Was her daughter suffering where she was? What would be her fate, God? Where would life take her? And what was Harman Kloot's real interest in her?

Noria couldn't complain about her new life. Except for being separated from her family, she had settled in, and her situation was vastly improved from where they'd been before. The doctor's wife was young, the house had a pleasant atmosphere. Noria had never been in a place with music and laughter and where all the rooms had names. The servants ate in a servant's hall, the baby slept in a room called a nursery, and the wife had a small space called a boudoir for her correspondence and the handling of household affairs. The English wife had an agreeable disposition, although a slave woman she knew on Keerom Street said her English master treated her no differently from the Dutch one she'd had before.

She went to the front door and opened it. "Somiela . . ."

Somiela threw her arms around her.

Harman stood at the gate and watched them embrace. He waved, then got up on the wagon and rode off.

"You look grand, Mama, look at your clothes." Somiela stood back and admired the black dress with the long sleeves and cuffs, tracing the tips of her fingers over the cloth.

"It's one of the madam's old dresses. We're the same size." She led Somiela into the drawing room. "Are you happy where you are, Somiela? You look thin."

Somiela recognized the concern in her mother's voice. Her mother herself looked like she'd lost weight, and might worry more if Somiela told her the truth. Still, she couldn't make it unbelievable either, and have her mother suspect things that weren't true. If her mother was content in her surroundings, that at least was one thing she and Sangora could feel pleased about.

"I'm not happy that we are away from each other, and wish we were together, but I'm glad Mama's all right. We didn't know what to think, Sangora and I – we were so glad when we got the message." Somiela looked at the books and glasses and decanters displayed in the cabinet. The De Villiers family also had fine furniture in their voorkamer – riempie chairs, a hanging lamp, a teetafel which would be laid with a white tablecloth at three o'clock on Sunday afternoons when the farmer's wife presided over tea – but no glass cabinet, and no books. There were books here on history, voyages, and travel, and on subjects Somiela did not recognize. She touched the spine of one with a title about theology gingerly with her fingers, and turned to her mother.

"What's this about, Mama?"

"It's about religion," Noria said. "Of other people."

"Not ours?"

"No."

Somiela looked at it for a few moments. "Mama's allowed to read them?"

"Yes."

Somiela put down the book and looked at the other pieces around the room. There was a storage chest with a star inlay in the wood, with a surround of stinkwood and yellowwood blocks, both in front of the chest and on the lid. A half-moon table against the wall with glass items on it. Curtains on the windows. Carpets under their feet.

"This is a nice house. Harman said Mama liked it here."

"They're good people. And I don't work too hard. I look after the baby and help Cook. Besides Cook, there's a coachman, a housemaid, and a garden boy. In the afternoons, when madam has her nap with the baby, we all have an hour off."

"Mama's lucky. We only get Sundays. And Mama's allowed to sit with me in this room?"

"Yes. It's a room for visitors, like a voorkamer, but they don't mind. They're different from the people in the house where we were." Noria took her daughter's hands. "Now tell me about Sangora. He's well? Behaving himself?"

"Sangora will never behave. Mama knows his nature. He doesn't keep quiet."

"Like you," Noria smiled.

"I'm like that?"

"Yes. But go on."

"They put him in chains the first day we arrived. But the chains are off now. He works in the barn, making furniture. The men like him. They look up to him. They'd found a key and unlocked his irons at night. No one found out. Now they're off permanently."

"Why'd they put him in chains?"

"He stood up for me in an argument."

"Is that how you lost your hair?"

Somiela covered her face with her hands. "No, I cut it myself, so I don't have to wash it so often. It was something stupid I did. It's all over now, Mama." She fumbled with the buttons on her coat. "Sangora says I must give Mama this azeemaat. He'll find his way here when he's allowed a day off."

"He mustn't do it if it will get him in trouble."

"He won't. He made a tea table for the daughter's wedding. They're pleased with his work."

Noria took the azeemaat. Touching it briefly to her nose for any lingering fragrance, she put it lovingly down the front of her dress. "And you? They're treating you well?"

"There's a woman there, Rachel. She looks after me."

"So the inlander said. I'm glad there's someone. You're not so alone. But the woman of the house, the family – they're good to you?"

"Yes."

Noria looked at her curiously. "You've made friends?"

"Yes. Rachel's son, Arend. He's a convert. There's also a Mohametan, Salie, from Celebes."

"You like this Salie?"

"He likes me."

"But you like the inlander."

Somiela blushed. "What does Mama mean?"

"I mean, you like the inlander."

"Yes."

Noria nodded. "He *is* handsome, yes. And I was surprised when he came here, bringing me a message from Sangora. And today, he brings you all the way to see me." She took her daughter's hands into hers. "A man doesn't do that for nothing. "

"What does he do it for?"

"You know what for."

Somiela looked at her mother, trying to read her eyes. Her mother's opinion was important to her.

"He's good to me."

"How is he good?"

"He protects me."

Noria nodded her head slowly. "You must forget it."

"Why, Mama?"

"It is obvious, child. He is what he is, and you are what you are."

"I don't care if he's white."

"Do you care that he's not of your faith?"

Somiela stared down at her hands. Her mother had said the words that had nagged at her own heart. She couldn't argue with that.

"There," Noria said, stroking her hair. "Don't look so sad. It's good to have friends. Everyone needs a friend, and he seems genuine. But don't take it further than that." She put her arms around Somiela. "Come, we'll go to the kitchen and meet Cook. She's made a nice pot of barley soup."

Somiela slipped her hand into her pocket and took out the jar of watermelon konfyt. "For you, Mama."

"Where did you get it?"

"The nooi. I told her you liked watermelon konfyt. She said I could bring you a jar."

Noria looked at her. "So. You have a good madam, also."

"Yes," Somiela lied.

... he not having any slaves had not once inquired about it . . . my master replied that although he had not any slaves, he must nevertheless stand up for his country, further saying that he would shoot the first Commissioner, Englishman, or landdrost who should come to his place to make the slaves free ...

(overheard by slave, name unknown, in 1830s)

The day of the wedding dawned bright and clear after the heavy rain, and by noon there was no trace of the storm which had gripped them all week. There were days like this in the Cape. In the middle of the wettest months of the year, the skies would suddenly clear. The sun would be generous, puddles would evaporate, and it would be hot enough for a few hours to remind you that summer was poking out its head. Geduld called this the teasing of the gods. The rest of the men were only too grateful to warm up again. Weather was everything for a man with too few clothes on his back working bare-footed in the rain and the wind. The sun took the chill out of their bones. Restored their spirits. Warmed their souls. Some of the men, taking advantage of the good weather, had brought out their coir mattresses and laid them behind the jongenshuis, where they hoped to rid them of fleas and dry out the dampness.

It wasn't only the weather that lifted their spirits – it was also that they didn't have to work. The wedding afforded them a full day's respite, and some of them lay stretched out, asleep in the sun while others sat under the tree watching the activity up at the house. Wagons lined the drive, and several guests stood about in their best clothes – the men with long-tailed coats, the women in bonnets and colourful shawls over their long dresses – enjoying the natural heat of the day, their laughter drifting down to the apricot tree. Arend, looking smart in a clean shirt and pantaloons and the hat which he had brushed vigorously the previous night, emerged from the house where he had acted all morning as interpreter for some of the guests, and came to sit with his friends.

"It's a big party inside," he said excitedly, taking a handful of Rachel's hot biscuits from his pocket. "You've never seen so many people. Farmers from Stellenbosch, Paarl; merchants from overseas; that thief, Van Heerden, and his whole family; his cripple son playing the fiddle. They're just waiting for the landdrost's family to arrive."

"What about food?" Hanibal asked. He had learned several words and expressions in Dutch, and could express himself reasonably well. "There's a lot?" He had a flat board with a sheet of paper on his lap, drawing a picture of Tromp.

"Too much. My mother says they're not paying attention to servants today, so she'll send out some food later on. Can't you smell that meat roasting on the spit? They've got enough there to feed the military."

"Let's hope we get some of it," Hanibal said.

Sangora's attention shifted to the dusty wagon rolling up to the back of the house. "Maybe this is the landdrost's family coming now. The wagon doesn't look as new as the others."

Geduld looked up from working on his bow. He twitched his nostrils. "It's not from these parts. I can smell the horses from here. They've come a long way."

"There's another wagon, pulling up alongside. They must be together."

"They may have come together, but not from the same place. The second one's from here."

They watched as a tall, long-haired man in a black coat got off the first wagon.

Geduld whistled softly through his teeth. "Look how big he is. It's him."

"Who?"

"Eyes of the Sky. The inlander's father."

Sangora studied the figure silently. A big, strong man, helping two women off the wagon. A younger man, shorter, also dressed in a black coat, got off last. Sangora didn't know who the young couple was in the second wagon, but they were acquainted with the people in the first.

"There's Harman coming out of the house to greet them,"

Arend said. "Look at him all feathered out like a peacock in that jacket. He looks grand enough to be the groom himself."

Salie looked up briefly from the vest he was stitching. "He looks ordinary to me."

"You're just jealous," Arend said, teasing him.

"Why should I be?"

"He's got what you want."

"He's got nothing."

Sangora listened. He felt sorry for Salie. Salie was wounded in a silent, secret place. Harman Kloot had come from nowhere and won over the men, and spirited Somiela away with his manners and looks. Salie's grief was understandable. He was being passed over for a Christian. The Christian had freedoms he didn't have.

"I want to ask your advice," he heard Salie say.

"My advice? What advice can I give you?" He was surprised. Salie never came to him for anything.

"I won't speak in front of this imbecile."

"He's talking about you, Arend," Geduld laughed.

"Now he calls me an imbecile. Tomorrow he'll ask me to sell his goods. Come, let's go." He got up, dusting off his pantaloons. He looked at Geduld. "You're still leaving at the end of the month?"

"Yes," Geduld said, picking up his quiver and following Arend to a spot further away.

"You too, Hanibal," Salie prompted. "Go with them."

Hanibal got up reluctantly and went to sit closer to Tromp, who was still sitting stiffly under the tree.

Salie waited until he and Sangora were alone. "Somiela's changed towards me. He's complicated things."

"Who?"

"You know who."

"You think it would be different if he wasn't here?"

"It was different before. His coming here changed her. She liked me well enough. Now she's cheeky with me, ignores me, has clever answers. You must talk to her, Sangora. You're good at making people understand things. Tell her it's wrong. A snoek cannot be with a whale. They'll swim together for a while, but eventually the tide will work against them."

Sangora smiled at this insight. He couldn't have put it better himself. "Yes. A fish must be with a fish, it's easier. But who said they're going swimming? And why do you think she will listen to me?"

"You are frustrating me, Sangora. You know you agree with me, why are you being difficult?"

"Because I'm only Sangora, not God. Somiela has her own mind, she will do what she wants. And no man can stop a tide. Do tahajud for forty nights. Break your sleep and get up and pray."

"What if it doesn't work?"

"Then that's your answer. You accept it."

"Accept, accept. I'm tired of accepting. Accept what they give us. Accept how they treat us. Accept that I'm a slave. How can you be so charitable, Sangora? Aren't you even the least bit angry about what's happened to you?"

"Of course, I'm angry, and you've seen how angry, but what will it change?"

"Nothing, but you always walk around accepting and understanding, like nothing's too hard for you. You always forgive. It makes me sick sometimes."

"I'm sorry."

"What about an azeemaat?"

"An azeemaat for what?"

"To make her, you know, come towards me. Or make him go away."

"Azeemaats are not for that, and I don't do doekoem work. But tell me, you'll be satisfied to get her that way? To know she didn't come on her own?"

Salie sank back against the tree. "Of course I don't want her that way. What do you think of me? You think I have no pride? I hate him."

"You don't hate him. Hate's a strong word. You're upset. You can't understand it."

"And you understand, right? You're very understanding. I still can't stomach his guts."

"And he knows it."

"How?"

"You're always challenging him in front of the others."

"And you like him, right?"

"His heart's clean. He's not bad."

"He also located Noria, and took Somiela to see her," Salie continued sarcastically.

"That's true."

"And that makes it all alright?"

Sangora saw where he was going. "You know it doesn't. And now it's you who's frustrating me. I'm not God. And God says to love those who love to do good. He does good."

"He's Christian."

"He's of the people of the Book."

Salie got up angrily. "Who do you think locks us up at night? Don't be so naive, Sangora. It's the people of the Book!"

Roeloff Kloot stood in the yard with his sons Harman and Karel, listening to his host and a neighbour discuss their respective crops. He listened with interest while his eyes looked around, smiling inwardly at the competitiveness of the two men. When De Villiers talked of how hard the year had been, the neighbour emphasized how much worse it had been for him. Roeloff had already formed his own opinion of the wine farmer and concluded that Andries de Villiers stood too close to his own shit to recognize how rotten it was. There was an arrogance about the man that irked him.

"It was money well spent. He really was a good buy, an excellent craftsman. That table in the voorkamer with the flower inlay, that's for Elspeth. He made it. I couldn't believe when I saw what he did."

"It's a good piece of work."

"He's very skilled, and works well by himself. Needs no supervision, he likes his work. I just tell him what I want done, and he does it. I pretend I don't see the coffee mug. The aia sends him coffee twice during the day. And I don't interfere when I see him with his head on the ground praying to his god. He doesn't waste time like the others." De Villiers smirked. "But he wasn't like this when he came. He was trouble, and I put him in chains and set him to work in the field."

"You didn't," Joost van Heerden said in astonishment.

"I did. Had to, to tame him. But there's no problem now. He's settled down, and Harman works well with them. I don't interfere."

"I didn't know chains were allowed," Karel said.

"They're not," Andries answered. "And your brother asked me to take them off." Andries looked at Harman. "I didn't immediately, but eventually I gave in. It turned out Harman was right. The maleier worked better without them."

Everyone looked at Harman. Harman felt a little embarrassed by the sudden attention. "It just made sense to me," he said, a little dismissively, not wanting to say what he really thought and embarrass the farmer.

"I could use someone like him," Joost said.

Andries smiled. "You should've bought him when you had the chance." He turned to Roeloff. "Joost was with me when I bought the maleier."

Joost rocked back on his heels. "I'll give you double what you paid for him."

"You're not serious, man," Andries laughed. "There's no money that can buy him. I know his value. He does excellent work. No, no, he's not for sale. I'm using him just to make tables now. I've already got two orders." He turned to Roeloff. "I'm sorry, I'm being inattentive to my guests."

Joost van Heerden grunted an acknowledgment. He was a bigger man than Andries de Villiers, tall, and his prosperity as a wheat farmer showed in the new pair of boots on his feet. "We hear things going on up north," he said to Roeloff. "Trouble with the Xhosa."

"Not where I am. But that doesn't mean others aren't having their troubles further east."

"What about the missionaries? Are they still trying to sell God to the hottentots up there?"

Roeloff grinned. "Of course. Wherever you find people who appear to be a little different from you, you'll find the man with his Bible trying to convert them. But then we all have a bit of the missionary in us. We had this old Sonqua tracker on the farm when I was young. In my eagerness to show him the right way, believing myself to have all the answers, I talked to him about

God. He talked to me about how to kill an animal without causing it pain. How to divide and subdivide a carcass until every member of the clan had his share. He talked to me of the value of silence. He said silence was the voice of the soul, and that one should pay every attention to it. It seems he was a missionary also."

The two men looked at each other. Their expressions said that they didn't know whether they had just shared in a joke or had been the joke.

Roeloff pointed to a long, low-roofed building down by the vineyards. "Harman?"

"That's the jongenshuis where the men sleep," Harman answered.

"Aah." Roeloff turned to his host. "Mind if we take a look?"

"No, no. Please do. Harman can show you around. I should go back inside. I've been neglecting some of my other guests."

"I don't like him," Karel said to his father when they were out of earshot.

"Martinus is the one we have to feel sorry for," Roeloff agreed.

"Martinus has changed, Pa, have you noticed?"

Roeloff laughed. "Martinus was born with a pen in his hand. You wanted to farm. Every man gets what he wants." His sons were all different. Karel was not his Oupa Wynand's favourite – Harman would always hold that place as the first grandson – but Oupa Wynand got along with him best. Shorter in stature than the others, Karel looked like his mother's side of the family, with his grandfather's brown eyes and curly hair. Roeloff turned to Harman. "How'd you end up working here?"

"They had difficulty with a mandoor and asked me to help."

"What the devil's a mandoor?" Karel asked.

"A black overseer. He'd beaten a slave senseless for losing a cow, and broken his ribs. The slave died."

"Damn ridiculous," Roeloff said.

"De Villiers is a cruel bastard, Pa. Don't be fooled by his Sunday manner."

"I'm not."

"And he knows why I'm down here."

"What do you mean?"

"I told him."

"Why'd you do that?"

"I don't know. But it turned out to be the best thing. He was approached by some men at the market who'd heard there was someone from the Hantam working here, someone who might've been involved in a shooting. He told them there was, but challenged anyone to say that that person had done anything."

"And that was enough to put them off?"

"No. He'd testified as a witness for one of them in the past when he was a visitor at the man's farm and there was an incident with a female slave. He lied on the man's behalf in court and spared him embarrassment and a fine. The man owed him."

Roeloff was silent for a moment. "So Andries de Villiers saved your neck."

"Yes."

"Nothing's for nothing, you know that."

"I know."

They stopped near the orchard to look around. "It's a good place, this. Well situated."

"Wine farming's a lucrative business, Pa. It's to my advantage being here. I'm learning. The man's hard to like, but he knows his work. And like Martinus says, you don't have to like someone to learn from them."

Roeloff looked at him. "Martinus is right. But it sounds like you're thinking of staying in the Cape."

"No. I'll return to the Hantam, but not now."

"Your mother will want you at Kloot's Nek, remember that. Karel will inherit from Oupa Wynand, and be in the Cederberg. He and Martinus will still have something from Kloot's Nek, but Kloot's Nek will one day be yours. Bessie has a husband. Beatrix doesn't have one yet, and will live at Kloot's Nek until she does. She will be your responsibility. She and your mother."

"Why are you talking about such things, Pa?"

"Because I have to. I want you to know. If your heart's set on the Cape, then you must stay. If not, when it's safe for you to return and you've done what you've had to do here, you must come back."

"Harman . . ." a girl's voice sounded behind them.

They turned.

It was Somiela. She was wearing a grey woollen dress Harman had once seen on Elspeth, plain, with long sleeves, the cut of the fabric emphasizing the narrowness of her waist.

Harman left his father and Karel and walked up to her.

"They're asking for everyone to come and eat."

"You look beautiful, Somiela," he said under his breath.

She blushed, and looked over his shoulder at the two men with him.

He smiled. "Come, I want you to meet my brother and father."

She was hesitant.

"Pa, Karel, this is Somiela, the carpenter's stepdaughter."

Roeloff smiled at the girl. He had noticed that she had called Harman by his first name.

Somiela stood awkwardly, not knowing what to say.

"They want us up at the house," Harman said. "It's all right, Somiela. We'll come now."

Somiela was only too glad to escape.

They stood for a moment watching her walk away.

"She's handsome for a slave," Karel said.

"She's a half-breed. She's had some trouble in the house, but there's a good woman with her in the kitchen who looks after her."

Roeloff said nothing. He had seen the way his son had reacted to the girl. And then to introduce her. But if he was surprised at that, Harman's next words startled him.

"One day I'll speak to De Villiers about buying her freedom."

"Whatever for?" Karel asked. "I mean, why would you want to do such a thing?"

Harman turned to his father. "I didn't mean to tell you this way, Pa, but I will marry her."

Roeloff felt a stab to his heart, and was plunged back to the carelessness of his own youth. He had never married Zokho. Instead, he had used her crime to forget her, and found solace in Neeltje's arms. History was repeating itself. Children paid for the sins of the past. But the son would tread where the father hadn't dared. What could he say? He loved his wife, but had never forgotten the Sonqua girl he'd loved first. Their union had produced a son. That son was trudging the same path now, taking it further.

"Did you hear what I said, Pa?"

"I heard."

They walked for a few minutes in silence.

"How much does a slave like that cost?" Karel asked, too stunned to say anything else.

"A lot. The half-breeds cost the most."

"You have money for such a purchase?"

"No. And even if I had, it doesn't mean he'd agree to sell. I'll have to find something to bargain with."

At the back door Roeloff stopped and turned to both of them. "There's no point your mother knowing any of this now."

"Ma won't hear anything from me," Karel said.

"There's nothing to tell," Harman agreed. "Not yet. I know I've shocked you, Pa, but I'd rather you heard it from me. I didn't even know until now how I felt."

"Then perhaps you should think it over."

"What do you mean?"

"Don't complicate life for yourself."

"Will it complicate things with my father?"

Roeloff looked at him. "Your father will not live forever. Your children will carry your name."

"I didn't suffer," he looked his father in the eye.

"You look like a Kloot. People accepted that you were Neeltje's." He looked at Harman hard. "Black blood's a funny thing. You never know when it'll surface."

"Then it doesn't matter who I marry. And it's not important to me. I'll think about what you said, Pa, but it won't change how I feel. I don't care at all what people think."

"Then that's it. We'd better go in and not keep everyone waiting." He turned to Karel. "And don't look at me with your mouth hanging open like that, catching flies. It's true. You two don't have the same mother. Just as Bessie is different also. But there's no difference to me."

Night came early in August, and despite the warmth of the winter's day, the mist came curling down the slope, bringing with it a clinging dampness and cold. Guests started to put on their coats and say goodbye, and by sunset all the wagons except two had cleared from the drive.

Inside the house, Harman sat with his family and Andries and Marieta in the voorkamer. The music had stopped, the people had gone, and the bride and groom would soon retire to a bedroom allocated to them for the night. In the morning they would leave with Elspeth's belongings for the new home next to the music master on Waterkant Street into which Martinus had recently moved. It was the first moment that the Kloots had been able to sit down together and catch up uninterrupted with family news.

"You're welcome to stay a few days," Andries said to Roeloff. "You all must be very tired from being so long on the road."

"Thank you, but we're staying with Bessie and Braam near the harbour. They've insisted that we stay with them. Bessie's lived with her mother, Soela, all her life, got married, then moved here. We're making up for lost time. And this is only Beatrix's second time in the Cape, so we want to go and see a few places before we head back. But you must come up to the Hantam and visit. It's quite different from what you have here."

"So Harman says. Still, I think the Cape's working its magic on him."

"Harman's heart's in the Karoo," Neeltje said. "He would never stay here for good."

"I agree," Beatrix added. "Harman likes it out in the veld. Same as Pa."

"You're all talking about me as if I'm not here," Harman laughed.

"Well, tell them then," Neeltje said. "Which is it, the Karoo or the Cape?"

"Don't worry, Ma," he said, putting his arm around her. "I wouldn't stay here even if – "

Somiela came into the voorkamer carrying a tray with several cups of coffee. The tray seemed heavy, and Beatrix got up to help her.

"It's not necessary," Marieta said. "Sit."

"It's all right, Tante." Beatrix took two of the cups off the tray and gave one each to her mother and father. "Pa likes a lot of sugar if he can get it. Right, Pa?" She stirred three teaspoons of sugar into the black coffee.

"You were saying," Marieta said, returning to Harman, "that you wouldn't stay in the Cape even if?"

Harman was aware of his mother on one side and Somiela leaning over him with the tray. "Even if there was everything in the world to keep me here," he continued. "Ma's right. Beatrix also. We don't have the luxuries you have here in the Cape, but we have other things." He turned to his mother, and touched her shoulder gently. "They know, Ma. About the incident."

"Oh." The colour rose to her cheeks. She hadn't expected that he would speak so freely about it.

"An unfortunate thing," Andries said. "But there's no cause for alarm. The matter's settled."

"Settled?" Neeltje looked at her husband.

"That's right," Roeloff said, and related what Harman had told him.

Neeltje turned to Harman. "So you can come back then. There's no need for you to stay on."

"It's not a good idea now," Roeloff said. "They may not come after him here, but the Hantam's open territory. People have long memories when it comes to clashes with the Sonqua. Two or three years isn't such a long time to let the dust settle."

"Two or three years! I could be a grandmother by then."

"Let's hope so," Roeloff laughed. "Let's hope we see the first Cape-born Kloot by this time next year."

Harman listened with interest. His father knew how to turn things around. He watched his brother, Martinus, a little red in the neck, get up from his chair to announce that he and Elspeth would go to their room now as they wanted to be on their way early the next morning. Martinus looked handsome in his black clothes and high hat, and Elspeth too was flattered by her white dress with the lace that reached high up her neck. She was all softness and golden curls, and watching the dominee giving his blessings after he had married them that afternoon, Harman thought that perhaps she suited Martinus after all. Watching his brother get married had made him feel strange. The whole family was there to join in Martinus's happiness. He had chosen a woman that pleased everyone – a woman that suited not only his heart and sensibility, but also one that solidified his position in the community. Martinus had everything stacked the right way. He could go to bed and know that every man there wished for his happiness. And no one more than Harman wanted Martinus to have a happy life. He had never felt threatened by this brother in any way, despite his success and the name he was making for himself as a landdrost in the Cape, although Harman felt now that he would not receive the same outpouring of jubilation when his turn came.

He turned to his sister, Bessie, next to him. He had grown up with Beatrix, but had always felt something different for Bessie. The first child, she was the only one of all Roeloff Kloot's children who looked exactly like him, her clear and discerning eyes her strongest feature. People said Harman had the hair and the manner, Karel the jaw, Martinus the height, Beatrix the blue eyes. But Bessie had everything. And when she looked at you, without speaking, you knew that she knew what went on in your head. He had found out early that she was his sister. She came only on weekends. His father didn't treat her with the same strictness as he did the younger children. When Tante Soela died, Harman had heard the story for the first time. He didn't know yet that his own mother was Sonqua, but already identified with the strange girl who for years wouldn't speak.

"I'll come and see you next week, Bessie," he whispered. "I want to talk to you."

"You've only visited twice since you're here. Braam said the other day that he wished you came more often. He's got a new pastime, and wants to take you fishing with him. What do you want to talk to me about?"

"I just want your opinion on some things."

Bessie studied him. "Is it about a woman?"

His expression changed. "Well . . ."

"The girl who served the coffee?"

Harman was astounded by the question. "How do you know?"

"I know my brother."

He looked at her. "You're not shocked?"

"No. I know things you don't," she lowered her voice. "But Braam doesn't. I don't tell him everything."

Harman nodded. "I knew I could talk to you. Do you know anything about Mohametans?"

"No."

"Until next week then. We'll talk more." Martinus had said good night to everyone, and Harman got up and shook his hand. "I'll see you at breakfast. I'll be up long before you leave."

Harman waited a few minutes after the newly-married couple had gone to their room, then excused himself for a few minutes and left the voorkamer. He found Somiela in the kitchen, packing away the dishes. Rachel was at the stove dishing chunks of meat from the roast pan onto a plate. He knew where that plate was headed.

"Something to eat?" she looked up.

"No, thank you, Rachel. I don't think I can eat another thing."

"Take this out to them, Somiela," Rachel handed her the plate. "No use having good food go to waste."

Somiela took it and headed for the door. Harman followed her out.

The mist was heavy, the yard in darkness except for the dull glow of the lamp hanging near the back door.

"You don't have to walk so quickly. I'll come with you," Harman said.

Somiela said nothing, but slowed down a little. The mist touched their skin as they walked.

"Is anything wrong?" he asked.

"No."

"It doesn't sound so from your voice. Is it what you heard me say inside?"

She didn't answer.

"It's true," he continued. "I'll not stay here forever. When the time's right, I'll take what's mine, and that could include a wife, and return to the Hantam."

Somiela dropped the plate and the meat scattered to the ground. She looked down helplessly. There was no moon, the mist was thick and engulfing, and Harman was standing very close. She kneeled down to feel for the pieces, then felt his hands on her waist.

"Somiela . . ." He drew her up towards him.

Somiela's heart fluttered wildly in her chest. He was holding her. He had his arms around her waist. And then it all happened at once. One moment he was looking into her eyes, the next he was kissing her. She had never kissed a man, and it thrilled her, the hardness of his mouth, the feel of his body against hers. How long they stood there, she didn't know. When she felt his hand at the buttons on her dress, she pulled away.

"You're so beautiful . . ."

Somiela trembled. She couldn't think. "I have to go."

He caught her hand and pulled her back. "I thought you liked me, Somiela."

"I do."

"What then?"

"I know what white men want with slave girls."

He let go of her hand as if she'd bit it. "Is that what you think?"

"What else can it be? I won't have a white man's baby – like my mother did, or like Rachel."

"Even if you are married to him?"

Somiela was stopped by his words. "I don't know of any white man who has married a slave. I'm a slave, and a Mohametan."

"And I'm a baster."

She didn't understand.

"Look closely. My eyes are not theirs. They're blue, but shaped like those of the mountain men of the north."

"What are you talking about?"

"The woman you served coffee to is not my mother."

"What?"

"My mother was Sonqua. I found out when I was sixteen years old. My father told me."

"You are – you're a – "

"Yes. I'm like you. Not one, not the other. In the middle somewhere."

She was silent for a moment. "Your father shouldn't have told you."

"Why not?"

"Some things are better not to know. They confuse you. Perhaps if you didn't know, you wouldn't waste your time with someone like me. Perhaps you think you are tainted."

"Tainted?" He laughed. "I'm proud of my mother's people, and I'd pick you out no matter who I was. You're not common, Somiela. I don't like common. Andries de Villiers is common. His

142

wife's common. His stepdaughter's common. You're different from others. You have spirit. You appeal to me."

Somiela was struck by his words. This was Harman Kloot speaking to her. Whatever he considered himself, to her he was still a white man. To the men in the jongenshuis he was mijnheer. To the people in the house he was the brother of the landdrost, and now a relative.

"What happened to your mother?"

"She was eaten by lions."

Her eyes rounded with horror. "Lions? How?"

"Her spirit was diseased, she'd lost her powers, and couldn't smell them. But that's a story for another time." He put his arms around her again and drew her close. "I want you, Somiela. Not just to play with. I don't know what that means exactly, I just know that I want you around me. I like how you make me feel. Now you'd better get back to the house before I forget myself."

"What about this?" she pointed to the meat at her feet.

"Leave it for the dogs."

"What do I tell Rachel?"

"The truth. Rachel knows about us."

"I don't think she approves."

"God does."

"Whose God?"

"*Our* God."

She was silent for a while, standing close to him, aware of his maleness. Then she took a step away. "Good night, then."

"Good night, Somiela. Think of me when you fall asleep." He squeezed her hand and let her go.

Somiela walked quickly up to the house. She had much to think about, to savour later on when the occupants of the house were asleep and she was alone with her thoughts on the little mattress behind Rachel's back. Harman Kloot had held her in his arms. Kissed her. Told her she was different from others. Told her he wanted her for himself. Told her he liked how she made her feel. How was that? The same way she felt when she looked into his eyes, or spotted him with the men outside in the yard, or waited on him at the table? She just had to think of him to feel the sharp little tremors inside her. She thought of the other things he had

143

said, and wondered what the De Villiers family would say if they knew their daughter had married into a family with mixed blood. A Sonqua mother? It was hard to believe. She turned to take one last look at him, but he had been swallowed up by the mist and she couldn't see anything.

She neared the back door and saw the dim outline of a man's figure in the yard.

"Somiela . . ."

She was startled by the tone of the voice. Andries de Villiers hardly ever addressed her by name, and she was surprised to see him standing there in the dark. Something in his manner made her feel suddenly uncomfortable.

"Yes, Seur?"

"Where were you just now?"

"I took some food to the men, Seur." It was dark, but she could see the crooked smile on his lips as he steadied himself against the wall. He was drunk.

"You mustn't give it away like that."

"What, Seur?" She looked nervously towards the back door.

He came towards her, reached out and touched her breast.

Somiela recoiled from him in horror. He had never done such a thing before. She was so unprepared, she didn't know whether to run or scream. But even as she stood there, transfixed, she knew that to raise the alarm was to invite trouble. No one in the house would believe her.

"Things can be much easier for you here," he continued. "I can arrange for you to sleep in one of the rooms." He touched her again, this time squeezing her breast.

"No!" she pushed him away. His face was close and she could smell the foulness of his breath.

There was a shadow in the doorway and Marieta's figure appeared. Andries darted back into the dark.

"What's going on out here?" Marieta asked, her voice shrill with suspicion.

"Nothing's going on," he said. "What should be going on? The girl took food to the back. I was out checking the horses, and asked her what she was doing out at this hour."

"Why is she taking food to the back?"

144

"Why should it go to waste? There's plenty left over."

"There's tomorrow. The slaves have had their supper."

Roeloff Kloot and his family appeared behind Marieta and stepped into the yard. "We must thank you for everything. We're ready to leave for Bessie's house now."

"So soon?" Andries asked.

"Yes. There's mist, it'll be slow going. We're all tired."

"Quite so. Well, the horses are spanned in. Everything's ready."

"Thank you. It was a wonderful wedding. We don't have such grand affairs in the Hantam. And as I said, you must visit us soon. Aah, here's Harman."

"You're leaving, Pa?"

"Yes."

"I'll see you at Bessie's before you head back."

Somiela watched Andries and Harman accompany the Kloots to the wagon, and slipped quietly into the kitchen. She went looking for Rachel and found the aia in the twins' room, picking up clothes from the floor.

"Rachel, something terrible's happened. It's the seur. He tried something with me."

"What are you talking about?"

"It happened as I was coming back to the kitchen. Seur was waiting for me outside in the dark. He touched me here," she looked down at her breast, "and told me that he could make things easy for me, he could arrange for me to sleep in one of the rooms."

Rachel's face turned a dark colour. She turned her back and continued picking up clothes and straightening things.

"Rachel, you're not listening."

"I'm thinking. This is bad. Oh, oh, oh, this is bad."

"And the nooi came out. I don't think she saw anything. She asked what was going on. He said he'd checked on the horses. I don't know if she believed him."

"When that woman gets something into her head, a doekoem can't chase it out. It was a mistake to send you outside with the food."

"It's not your fault."

"Maybe, but maybe it also wouldn't have happened. I should have thought about it. There was a lot of drinking going on."

"You don't think it will happen again?"

"If the seur hadn't said those things, maybe, but what he said – oh, oh, oh. I have to think. You must stay out of his way, not be alone with him under any circumstances. I'll clean their bedroom from now on. I don't want you going in there unless the nooi specifically orders you."

"What about taking in his water in the mornings?"

"I'll have to do it. We'll work out a new way to do things."

"And when you're not there, or the nooi isn't? The kleinnooi also won't be here. What will I do? If he tries again?"

Rachel had no answer to give. Then she said grimly, "Pray."

"Praying won't help, Rachel. What will I do? I'm scared."

Rachel's bottom lip curled. "You'll raise the roof of this house if you have to, and do everything to stop it, even if it means he beats you afterwards. It's better than giving in. Once that happens, it's over. It'll be easier the second time. After a while you'll accept it."

"Never! Is that what happened to you?"

"A lot of things happened to me, but we're talking about you now. I wouldn't mention any of this to the inlander."

"Why not? If he knew, he would surely do something. The seur wouldn't dare try anything. Harman would leave. There would be no foreman."

"Get that thought right out of your head," Rachel said impatiently. "You're too young to be causing this kind of trouble. Do you know what that would do? This whole house will be turned upside down." Rachel paused to look at her. "And you seem very sure of things. Of him. Calling him Harman. He's Harman to you now, not mijnheer?"

Somiela blushed. "He told me to call him that, and he's just my friend."

"Your friend? Don't make me laugh. No man is just your friend. There're men who are obvious in their intentions and don't care if you know it, and there're those who come at you a whole different way. I'm not saying he's one of them, but you must ask yourself: what does a white man really want with a slave?"

Somiela was hurt, and perhaps because she'd asked the same question herself, retorted more harshly than usual. "It's so hard to believe that someone could care for me, Rachel? I'm so ugly and miserable? Sangora isn't such a man. Your son isn't such a man. There're eight men in the jongenshuis. Are you saying they're all bad?" And she would've liked to tell Rachel that Harman was a baster, but that secret would never spring from her mouth.

Rachel bent down to pick up a pair of shoes. This was what she liked most about the girl. A bag full of troubles, but no shortage of fire. She had no doubt that Somiela was right, and that the inlander had honourable intentions. But that wasn't going to stop her from keeping the girl's head in the right place. The more pressing problem was what to do about Andries de Villiers.

August in the Cape was often the wintriest month of the year with gale force winds and heavy storms, and the August of 1832 was no different. But the month wasn't all thunder and gloom, and on those days when the skies cleared and the sun scuttled out, spring made a determined approach. By September, the rose buds as well as the apricot and plum trees had burst into bloom and Zoetewater was awash in the fresh colours of the new season.

Sangora, working quietly by himself in the barn, smiled when he saw the tall figure of the inlander in the doorway.

"I have good news, Sangora. The farmer's so pleased with that new dresser you've made, he's giving you the whole day off on Sunday. You don't have to work in the morning any more. Not only that, you'll be allowed to go into town."

Sangora put down his measuring stick. "Please?"

"I'm serious."

"You mean, he just came out and said Sangora can go into town if he wants to on Sunday?"

"Of course not. I told him I was visiting Martinus. If he would allow me to take the wagon, I could take Arend and Salie and make sure everyone got back on time. I sort of brought it up."

"You sort of brought it up. You're too good to be true. Will I have every Sunday off like the others, or just this one?"

"Every Sunday. I thought I could take you to see your wife."

Sangora looked at him in amazement. "My wife? Why would you do this for me?"

Harman took off his hat and hit it against the side of his leg. A puff of dust punctuated the air. "It's not only for you, Sangora. It's for me, too."

"So, we come to the truth."

Harman looked him in the eye. "The truth was always there, Sangora. I never hid it. My feelings have always been out there."

"What're your feelings?" Sangora asked, knowing that Harman was referring to his friendship with Somiela.

"You know what they are. Right now, I don't have money, but I will, and then I'll purchase her freedom."

Sangora's brows shot up in surprise. "Somiela's freedom?"

"Yes."

"And when you've purchased it?"

Harman responded with confidence, "I'll marry her."

Sangora leaned forward to measure a piece of wood to mask his shock. He needed to think. Harman Kloot was letting him know his intentions. He wanted Sangora's stepdaughter. And if Harman said the words, it was as good as done.

"And Somiela? What does she say?"

"She doesn't know."

Sangora looked up, a faint smile on his face. "She doesn't? You're planning to do this all by yourself?"

"Of course not, but it's pointless telling her now, isn't it? I don't even know why I told you."

"You told me because you wanted to see my response. Marriage is a serious affair, and we're Mohametan, don't forget."

"I haven't forgotten. But, you have your own God, Sangora, is that it? God is exclusive to Mohametans? *That* God doesn't allow you to love others?"

Sangora noticed the testiness. "A Mohametan cannot step outside of his faith."

"Who said he has to? And you didn't answer my question."

"No answer I give will be the right one. You have your way of understanding things, we have ours. But there's only one God. The same one for you as for us. It's the white man who believes God put him in charge."

148

Harman smarted under the insult. "You're religious, Sangora, how old are you?"

"Thirty, I think. Younger than my wife. And I'm not religious. Not in the way you think."

"I didn't mean to imply anything."

"And I didn't mean to be rude. It's just that with you, I find myself saying things, trusting you. And yet – "

Harman sensed what he wanted to say. "And yet we're not supposed to be friends?" Harman concluded for him. "But we are, Sangora. It's written out there. On the wind. In the heavens. We have something in common, maybe a spirit. I knew that first day that we would be friends. And you're right about white men thinking God's there only for them. But not all white men, Sangora, and you're not always right."

Sangora saw that he had been arrogant. "Agreed." He extended his hand. "Friends?"

"Friends," Harman shook his hand. "And call me Harman, please."

Sangora considered this. "It will be strange calling you by your first name. I will not do it in front of the others."

"As you wish. Salie says there's a ratiep at the house in Dorp Street on Sunday. He said I might find it interesting."

"Salie told you this?" Sangora found this unusual behaviour on Salie's part. Salie, after all, considered Harman a rival and competitor.

"Yes."

"He's right. You should come. Better for you to see for yourself."

Harman walked to the door. "I'll see. Well, I must let you get back to work. How's that table coming along? Those people who ordered it are coming on Saturday to pick it up."

"I've stained it, it's done," Sangora pointed to an elegant stinkwood tea table in the corner.

Harman looked at it. "You do good work, Sangora. Maybe one day you'll make something like this for me."

Sangora smiled. "Of course. God willing, everything will work out, and I'm not dead yet. About Somiela," he paused. "You know the farmer will never sell. She's too valuable. He's hoping for what every slaveholder hopes."

"What's that?"

"Little ones."

Harman's eyes became slits. "Well, there's no harm in dreaming. I have dreams of my own."

On Sunday morning, Sangora stood with Arend, Salie, and Petroos in front of the wagon house. Arend had already hitched the horses to the wagon, and waited for Harman to emerge from the house where he was having breakfast. Dressed in an old jacket Harman had given him, Sangora was both nervous and excited at the prospect of seeing his wife. It was six months since they had been together. Would she be at the house when they got there? Would she be allowed to talk to him? Would she have met someone else during their long separation? There were far more slaves in the heart of town than on an isolated farm, far more opportunities to meet them. Would she be happy to see him, shocked, surprised, changed in her feelings? All these things raced through his mind as he listened to the excited chatter of the men around him.

"Here he comes," Salie said.

Harman arrived and handed a food bundle to Arend. "Your mother made this for everyone to share. She wants the jar back. Ready?"

They nodded.

"Good. First, we'll go to Sangora's wife, and wait for him, then to Dorp Street where I'll leave you. I'll come back an hour before sunset. I took responsibility for all of you. I don't want to get there and find that I have to wait. Understood?"

"Understood," Sangora said.

"Who put you in charge, Sangora?" Salie asked "Arend and I are used to going to town. We don't need anyone vouching for us."

"Don't start," Harman intervened. "Anyone who wants to be difficult, can walk." He climbed up onto the wagon and waited for everyone to get on.

"Idiot," Arend elbowed Salie in the ribs.

Salie elbowed him back, but got on.

Sangora got on last and sat with Salie and Petroos in the back.

Arend took his customary position on the bench next to the driver.

"Where's the food, Arend?" Petroos asked. "We're hungry here in the back. Are you eating it all by yourself?"

Arend handed it to him. "We're not even out the gate yet."

Petroos took the parcel and unwrapped it. It was a loaf of bread, still hot from the oven, with a small jar half-filled with apricot jam. He broke the bread in four, spread the thick jam in equal portions, and handed everyone his share. They ate in silence, rocking back and forth as the wagon rolled and jigged along the stony road, past houses and businesses and shops, a stretch of open fields, the Claremont House at the seventh milestone, on through the village of De Drie Koppen where Harman sometimes stopped at the inn when he went visiting his brother or sister on Sundays. The road was clear, the horses well-rested, and Harman rode quickly, taking every opportunity to build up a sweat in the mares. Eventually they passed out of the shade of the trees and saw the old fort in the distance.

"Almost there, Sangora," Harman said from the front.

Sangora felt his heart speed up in his chest. Was he really going to see her? What would she look like, and how was she going to receive him? Would he be allowed to speak a few minutes to her? Somiela had told him after her visit with her mother that Noria was happy in her new place, but one didn't always know with Somiela. She could've left out things which she thought might disturb him. He felt the others in the wagon watching him, and picked at an imaginary piece of lint on his jacket, keeping his gaze down.

"You're lucky," Salie said. "You start out in chains, and here you're going to see your wife. We've been on Zoetewater since Eve bit into the apple and nothing like this has happened to us."

"And now he has a woman also," Petroos lamented. "But look at us. We'll die virgins on Zoetewater."

"Virgins?" Salie scoffed. "Look who's talking. You wouldn't know what to do with a woman if she fell from the sky and landed on doelie."

The wagon came to a halt. "We're here," Harman said, turning around.

Sangora looked out. The house was close to the road and he saw that the windows were open. People were home. "I should just go up and knock on the door?" he asked Harman. "No one's expecting me."

"Yes."

Sangora jumped out the back and stood for a moment looking up at the house. It was one of the bigger ones on Roeland Street, white, with many windows, a high gable, four steps raised in front of it, a garden with a few rosebushes and two fruit trees, behind all of which Table Mountain reared a few thousand feet above its head.

He swept his dark hair out of his face to make himself look more presentable, then walked steadily up to the iron gate.

"Good luck, Sangora," Arend shouted after him.

At the door, Sangora gave four short knocks and waited. His heart was jumping in his chest and he rehearsed what he was going to say. Harman had told him the doctor and his wife spoke very little Dutch and Sangora was preparing the easiest words he could think of. The door opened, and expecting to see the master of the house, his mouth fell open when he saw that it was Noria. She was thinner than before, looking younger than her years. When she saw who it was, she gave a little cry and flew into his arms.

"Sangora!"

Sangora felt all his fears melt away. Nothing had changed. Her feelings were still the same. And so were his.

From the wagon, four men watched anxiously as Sangora wrapped his arms around a handsome woman in a black dress. Harman flicked the reins and the wagon moved a short distance down the road where it stopped.

An hour later, Sangora returned to the wagon. In his right hand was a parcel, in his left, a small book. He was quiet and seemed reluctant to speak. The others left him alone, respecting his wish to be silent. The wagon pulled away and they travelled along Roeland Street as far as Plein, turned right all the way to Keizersgragt where they turned left, continued for a few minutes, turned right, then left again all the way up Strand Street to Dorp Street. They arrived at the house where the Mohametans came to pray, against a background of a rattling of musical instruments and drum beats.

"The ratiep's started. Can you hear?" Arend asked.

"You can hear it at the bottom of the hill," Harman said. "And so many people. I didn't know there were so many Mohametans."

"They're not all Mohametans," Sangora said, hearing the exchange and leaning close to the driver in front. "Some of them are curious about our faith and want to learn more about it. Leave the wagon here and come with us."

"I promised my brother I would visit him."

"Come for a short while," Sangora insisted. "You'll find it interesting. We'll try and get in through the back. You don't have to stay long if you don't want to."

Harman stopped the wagon a little further along the street where he found a suitable place. He got off and followed the men. He saw immediately that he was the only white person in this environment. The people there were mostly men, some with shoes, and coverings on their heads, some wearing robes over their pantaloons, some very scantily dressed. One or two of them stared at him openly.

"Will I be allowed into the house?"

"Anyone's allowed," Salie said. "The three of us are going over there, to some friends. We'll see you later."

Harman followed Sangora through the crowd, around the side of the house, to the door of the small kitchen. Here the music was much louder, and he heard the voices of men chanting, tinkling bells, drums; an exotic music he'd never heard before.

"What's the instrument making that music? It's new to my ears."

"It's a rabanas, a small round instrument with a skin pulled tightly over it, and clappers that sound like tinkling bells. You shake it, and strike the middle of the skin at the same time."

They stepped into the kitchen where a tall man dressed in a white robe, white pantaloons, and a turban stood with several other men near a doorway. They were looking into a room where the ratiep was taking place.

"Sangora! We thought you'd gone away. It must be almost a year since we've seen you."

"Salaam, Imam. How is Imam? It's almost that, yes. I'm at a new place with my stepdaughter, in Wynberg. They separated my wife and I. Noria's with English people in Roeland Street."

153

The imam listened sympathetically above the din of the music. "I'm sorry to hear that. You're all right?" he asked, looking at the man standing awkwardly beside Sangora. "And Noria also?"

"Yes. I've just seen her. She's well-treated where she is." Sangora turned slightly. "This is Harman Kloot, a friend. He brought us all here. Harman, this is the imam I was telling you about."

The imam extended his hand. Harman took it, overwhelmed by the appearance of the man and the faint smell of scent flowing from his clothes. He greeted the other men he was introduced to, then moved with Sangora to the doorway leading into the front room.

This room was small, the floor covered with green baize, on which was spread a large white sheet. Twelve men sat on the sheet facing each other. Behind the men was a bench with an array of swords, skewers, and knives, and behind the bench, the kalipha, an older man with a turban on his head, leading the recital. The twelve men were dressed in black pants and turbans, their naked chests glistening from their exertions. Six of them had rabanas which they rattled and tapped, producing an evocative, mystical beat, and all of them swayed in a choppy motion, shoulders touching – right, left, right, left – in time to the rhythm.

"They look like they're in a trance," Harman whispered to Sangora.

"In tariq. They have to pass various levels of piety to get to that state. They cannot be distracted, even for a moment. Watch the kalipha. They take their cue from him. There're no women here, as you can see. They're invoking the name of a saint to give them strength."

The reciting got faster, the rabanases louder. Then one of the twelve men got to his feet, and with a studied movement, took a sword from the collection. He positioned the sharp edge of the sword over his left arm, then taking it away again, made short, choppy movements in time to the music, moving it towards and away from his arm. The reciting became more frenetic, louder. Then, the sword poised over his bicep, he cut into it.

Harman saw the knife sink into the flesh and heard a swell of voices behind him. He looked at the performer's face. There was no grimace of pain, no blood. The performer stopped to take a short breath which he did by inhaling noisily through his nose, then put down the sword and picked up a skewer. He pinched together some flesh above his navel, and pierced the skewer through the muscle.

Harman sucked in his breath. It wasn't a hoax. The skewer was locked in the flesh. He could see everything. It was real, the weapons, the incisions, the atmosphere. The performer removed the skewer. Except for an indentation in the flesh, this wound, like the arm, didn't bleed. The man sat down. There was no applause.

The chanting built to a new crescendo, and a second, younger man, got up. He selected a knife, and in one leap, had his right leg out in front of him, the knee bent, the knife poised. In an emphatic, breathless display, he swept the edge of the knife across his thigh. The leg of his pants opened up like a slit, revealing an angry gash in the flesh.

Harman looked away. He couldn't take any more. The intoxicating beat, the uninhibited faith, the intensity. It touched him in a way that made him feel suddenly afraid. He'd seen trance dances where Sonqua, in an hypnotic state, stuck their heads in a bed of coals, but nothing like this. He felt that the chanting was so inextricably linked to everything, that if it were suddenly to stop, the ritual would have disastrous results.

He turned to Sangora and whispered that he needed to go outside and catch his breath for a few minutes. Sangora didn't question him. He could tell by Harman's face that he was overwhelmed, and let him go. After two more performances by different men, the ratiep ended and Sangora went outside. He found Harman leaning against the side of the wagon in the street.

"The ratiep's over," Sangora said, not wanting to ask Harman immediately what he thought of the proceedings. "They'll clear the room now for prayers, then have something to eat. Come inside with me, and you can see what we do."

"I'm allowed to stay for prayers?" Harman asked, already resigned to the fact that he would be late for Martinus. And he needn't explain to Martinus. Martinus was so wrapped up in his work that even Elspeth, when she could catch his attention, complained. Martinus wouldn't notice that he was late.

"Of course, you're allowed to stay. It's God's house. Every-one's allowed. This is the bilal coming in now. He'll give the call for prayer. Stand next to me. Just follow me. We'll talk afterwards."

Harman watched the room fill up slowly. Somewhere at the back, he saw Salie, Arend, and Petroos with the father and son he'd met the last time. There was no talking. A quietness had come over the room. The bilal raised his hands to his ears and gave a long, melodious chant in a language Harman had heard uttered by the men before, then the imam took his place in front and started prayers.

Harman noticed the solemnity around him. The men were concentrated on their prayers, some with their eyes closed, some whispering under their breaths. He was standing close to Sangora – there were several rows packed in the small room – and without turning his head, Harman was able to follow him in raising his hands, folding them, bowing down, putting them to his knees, coming up, then going all the way down and touching his forehead to the ground. At several points in the proceedings, the imam said something out loud, and the men echoed, *Allah hu Akbar*. Harman had come upon Sangora and Salie praying at the farm once, but he had come upon them unexpectedly, felt that he was intruding, and hadn't stayed to watch. He didn't know there were so many prostrations, and wondered whether every man said what he wanted to God or whether there were set prayers. He was still reeling from his experience with the ratiep performance, and was amazed by the rituals of a people he had not known of before his arrival in the Cape. He didn't know what they were saying, didn't know them, their origins – and they were a strange mix, of all colours and manner of dress and manner – but Harman somehow understood the importance of their worshipping together in that room. No one was doing anything different. All were following the imam up front. At last the prayers ended, and men turned to one another, embracing. He found himself doing this naturally with Sangora.

"You've stood in front of God," Sangora said, releasing him. "How do you feel?"

"I feel good. What have I said to God?"

"You've asked him to keep you on the path. To keep faith."

The others came up to them, and they embraced one another.

"You have prayed with us, mijnheer," Arend said, smiling proudly. "All these things in one day. A ratiep. Salat. What did you think of the ratiep?"

"I haven't had time to digest it yet. I've seen trance dances with the Sonqua, but I'll have to think about this. It's interesting."

"Petroos doesn't think those weapons were real. You were in the room with Sangora. Tell him. Were they real?"

"They were real. I don't understand what I saw, but I know what I saw, if you know what I mean. If someone had told me about it, I wouldn't have believed him. We have nothing like this in our religion."

"It's not part of our religion," Sangora said. "It's a display of faith, a tradition. Brought here from overseas by the slaves. It's good for people who don't have a belief system to see what you can do if you have faith. A normal man needs his God. Now what about a slave? As a slave you have to have faith or you'll give up. You don't have anything else."

"That's a lot of faith, Sangora, to stick knives into your body to see if it will bleed. Would *you* do it?"

"Me? I'm a sinner," Sangora laughed. "I'm not as brave as you think, and I don't have to be convinced there's a God. I know there is. Some people have to have proof."

"If I were looking for God, I wouldn't need more proof than that."

"You *have* God then?" Salie asked.

"I don't think about it. It's just so."

There was a brief silence of mutual understanding, of respect for the other's beliefs.

"There're some new faces here," Salie continued. "They've heard of this place from others, and come here for the first time. Maybe the performance will've touched them. Maybe it will make them think. If they go away from here with some kind of faith, then the ratiep's served its purpose."

Harman looked at Salie. He liked this Salie a whole lot better than the cynical one. Suddenly, he laughed. "You're not all trying to convert me, are you?"

157

"No one can convert you," Salie said.

"What do you mean?"

"What he means," Sangora responded, "is that only God can do that."

Harman thought about it. "You're right. And maybe I'm one of you already and don't know it."

They all laughed at the incredulity of such a thought.

"We have to sit down now," Sangora said. "They're going to serve food."

Harman watched the men form two rows, and took his place between Sangora and Salie on the white sheets. He would have to think of something to tell Martinus. He had been invited there for the midday meal, but this was too good an opportunity to pass up. He had already witnessed the ratiep, and stayed for prayers. He was curious to know the rest.

A few minutes later, several boys entered the room with plates, big platters of rice, and bowls containing some kind of stew with meat and small potatoes, which they set down on the floor.

"I didn't see any cooking when we arrived," he said to Sangora.

"Sometimes they do it here, but usually people make the food at home and bring it with them. Later, there'll also be cake. Everyone will take a small parcel home, a barakat. This is denningvleis. Chunks of meat braised with onions and cloves. You put it over the rice. Very tasty."

Harman felt guilty that he would have to disappoint his brother, but as he sat there, intensely curious about his surroundings, the strange languages of some of the people, their manner, the wonderful aroma of the food, he knew that he didn't want to leave. The people had got used to his presence and some of them even smiled at him now.

"You will eat with your hand," Arend said.

"I'm used to eating with my hand. You forget where I come from."

"Ah, but you're not sitting around a fire and roasting a pigeon and pulling the meat from the bones," Sangora smiled. "You'll be eating rice and meat with your hands. We eat with our hands even when there are forks. It tastes better."

Harman noticed the father and son whom Salie had introduced

158

him to the last time. They crossed over from where they were sitting, and Salie made space for them to sit down.

"Come," Sangora said to Harman. "Serve yourself before it gets cold."

"You go first," he said, wanting to see how it was done.

Sangora laughed. He moved his plate closer to the food, and helped himself to two scoops of rice, topping it with the meat and thick gravy and one potato. Harman was surprised to see the conservative portions taken by the men. They were big men, hungry, and some looked like they were famished. Still, they didn't load up their plates, unlike the burly Steenkamps and Retiefs and the men he knew in the Karoo who could eat and drink a man under the table. Harman himself ate more than the portion Sangora dished for himself. But he soon saw the reason for their moderate behaviour. Everyone helped themselves twice. There was enough for everyone. You didn't take the last piece of meat from the bowl – you always left it for someone else, even if it went back to the kitchen in the end.

The meal ended and Harman was introduced to several people in the room. After a yellow bread pudding served with stewed fruit, and a cup of hot tea, he followed everyone out to the front of the house where there were pockets of men and women in conversation.

Salie tapped him on the elbow. Next to him were Boeta Mai and his son, Soleiman. "You won't believe this," he began. "When I told Boeta Mai where you came from, he said his late grandfather had a brother who'd lived in the Hantam. Boeta Mai's name was Pieter before he changed it to Ismail. His surname's Cornelius, but his grandfather, Krisjan, was a Kloot."

Harman felt his heart pick up a beat.

"From the Hantam? We're the only Kloots in the area."

"I know," Boeta Mai agreed. "I was up there with my grandfather when I was about sixteen. His brother had already died, but the son was there, Willem Kloot."

"Willem Kloot?"

"Yes. I met a young girl there also. I don't remember her name, but she talked endlessly, and was very fond of her brother. I gave her a book to give to him. She said he was fond of reading. I didn't meet him then, but met him years later. He was married when he came down to the Cape with his wife, and looked us up. We were surprised. There had been such rifts in the family with other members. A few years later he came down on sheep business and came to visit us and stayed for supper. His sister was with him that time. She'd married a farmer in the Koue Bokkeveld who'd died under mysterious circumstances, leaving her grieving and confused, and he was bringing her along to rouse her out of her sorrow and to show her the Cape. I didn't hear from him again until just a few weeks ago when he came to the town for a wedding."

Harman stood looking at him.

Boeta Mai wiped his forehead with a white handkerchief. "Look, I can see I've disturbed you."

"The man you are talking about is Roeloff Kloot. He's my father."

But Boeta Mai seemed uncomfortable now, like one who'd just realized how foolish he'd been to open his mouth. He said nothing, nodding only slightly to acknowledge the statement. It was clear from his expression and the hurried glance at his son that Boeta Mai felt he had said something that would cause the young man before him serious concern. Why had he done it? Was it to let Harman Kloot know that he, Boeta Mai, had white relatives, or that the Kloots, who had hurt his mother, had slave blood? In either case, it was born out of arrogance, and he was not such a man. He would have to pray two extra rak'ahs that night to beg God's mercy. There had been no need to disturb the peace of mind of Harman Kloot.

"Where do you live?" Harman asked.

"Not far from here. On Pepper Street. Number sixteen. A white house with a fanlight in the door."

Just then they heard the bilal give the call for late afternoon prayers.

"The time's flown," Sangora said. "It's as'r already."

"Well, we must go in," Boeta Mai said. "I'm deeply sorry if I've disturbed you."

Harman watched Boeta Mai and Soleiman walk away and re-enter the house. He turned to the men next to him who seemed uncomfortable that they had been there to hear it all. "Well, that's that. I don't think I'll forget this day."

"He could be wrong," Salie said. "What does he know? He could've heard of those Kloots and made up the whole thing."

"He's not wrong."

There was a moment's awkwardness.

"Well, let's not stand around looking so sad. We've all had our moments," Sangora said, alluding to his own meeting with his wife. "We'll go in now, for as'r. Are you coming with us, Harman, or will you go to your brother?"

"It's too late now to go there and come back for you all. I'll wait for you out here and drop in there on our way home." He didn't want to go back into the house with the men. He needed a few minutes alone in the wagon to think. He was disturbed. He didn't know why. The day had turned out completely differently from the one he'd had in mind. It was too early to tell yet whether he regretted any of it.

When Harman returned to the farm that night with the men, he went straight to his quarters. His mood was dark, his thoughts as muddied as the water at the bottom of a well. Boeta Mai's words went round and round in his head. A chance encounter in a place he would never have visited on his own. The afternoon had changed him in a way that wasn't yet clear, but he knew that things would not be the same again. Had he gone to Martinus as originally planned, he might never have known. It certainly wasn't his father's intention to tell him about these relatives. Why had he kept it from Harman? His father had told him about his real mother, how she had walked away from her new-born son, left him under a tree for the jackals; why not this? Was it a greater shame than having a half-breed son? But Harman knew what it was. A half-breed son spoke of a father's carelessness – he could be forgiven the indiscretions of his youth – not of slave blood running through the veins of the family.

There was a knock on the door.

"Yes?"

The door creaked open. "You didn't come to eat supper," Somiela said, standing just outside the door.

"Come in. I didn't feel like it. I ate something this afternoon at the house in Dorp Street."

Somiela stepped inside. She had never been in his room before and looked around. It was a small room, about half the size of the twins' room, with a bed against the wall, a small table, a bench, and a long, narrow storage chest on the floor that she recognized as a geweerkis. There was nothing else in the room except for a sweat-stained shirt on the bed, his rifle, a small leather pouch, a few metal trinkets, and his hat, on the table.

"They sent me to find out if you wanted to eat. We heard you come back."

Harman noticed something different about her. "Oh, my word. You're wearing shoes!"

Somiela looked down proudly at her feet. "The seur gave them to me."

"He did?"

"Yes. I got them this morning. They're not new, but at least my feet are not cold. Rachel lined them with paper so my feet don't slip in and out."

"So he's been good to you."

"Yes," she said, the smile going slowly out of her eyes.

"Is something wrong?"

"No. Tell me what happened this afternoon. You went inside the masjied?"

"Arend said something to you?"

"No. Has something happened? You just said yourself that you ate at the masjied."

Harman leaned wearily back against the wall. "Sit down. I'll tell you."

Somiela looked around. There was only the bed where he was, or the bench. She chose the bench.

"I met some men this afternoon, a father and son. I had met them before, but this was the first time we spoke. It turns out they're relatives."

"What do you mean, relatives?"

"His grandfather and my great-grandfather were brothers. I think that makes my father and him cousins. The thing is, his name at the time was Pieter Cornelius. Now it's Ismail. He's Mohametan."

162

"You're saying that – "

"Yes. And my father has known about this side of the family for years. He told me about my own mother, but never told me this. It would've been better if I'd heard it from him."

Somiela sensed that he was hurt. She didn't know what to say. "Were you shocked?"

"I think so. I didn't expect it. I mean . . . well, I don't know what I mean, I'm confused. This Boeta Mai had actually been to Kloot's Nek when he was younger, and met my grandfather, Willem. And my father, after he married my stepmother, came down to the Cape and looked him up. It's hard for me to believe, but Boeta Mai knew things about our family, even of my father's sister, Tante Vinkie, who's remarried, living far away in Graaff Reinet. My father never mentioned anything to me. And he's told me many things, things he's not told my brothers or sisters. I'm disappointed that he kept something so relevant from me."

"Maybe he thought the information too hard for you to accept, that you might not be able to live with the truth." She did not say what she really thought, that perhaps his father did not want him to know that there were Mohametans in the family, for to say so to his son would be to admit it to himself.

"Maybe."

They sat for a minute or so in silence. "What were they like, Boeta Mai and his son?" asked Somiela.

"Oh, very nice people. Friendly. The father looked to be a prosperous man. Not by his clothes, but by his manner. We kept staring at each other, not knowing what to say. If you could've seen how I just stood there, looking foolishly at him. And all this in front of Sangora and the others. What they must've thought. Salie actually tried to make me feel better about it."

Somiela was surprised to hear this about Salie, and wanted to go and sit next to Harman and console him, but remained on the bench where she was. "I know what you're thinking."

"What am I thinking?"

"You're thinking of going to see this family."

"I have to."

"By staying away, you don't have to acknowledge anything. People don't have to know."

"*I* know, Somiela. I can't ignore it. And how does it make it go away? Anyway, it doesn't matter to me who knows. It's all bird shit to me what other people think."

Somiela smiled. It was what she liked best about him. She felt uncomfortable being in his room for so long, and got up. "Will you come and eat something then?"

"No. Just tell them I've eaten at my brother's."

The following Sunday after breakfast, Harman dragged a wet comb through his hair, asked Sangora for directions to Pepper Street, saddled his mare, and rode off. All the slaves had decided to spend their day off on the farm taking advantage of the good weather to wash their clothes and hang them out on the line they had rigged up behind the jongenshuis.

"He's stupid," Salie said.

"Perhaps. But brave also. You should know him by now," Sangora remarked.

"And you do, right?"

"He doesn't hide what he feels."

"He's also your friend, I forgot. Next thing, he'll be a relative."

"You should control your resentment, Salie. It turns you into something you're not. After all, you're the one who introduced him to Boeta Mai and started the whole thing. Why did you? Because you wanted him to know he had Mohametan relatives?"

"He's got wild blood anyway."

"What're you talking about?"

"Geduld told us."

"I never heard such nonsense."

"You don't hear everything, Sangora. His mother's bosjesman. Geduld told Arend. Arend told me. His father played in the bush a lot when he was young."

"Don't talk nonsense!" Sangora didn't like what he was hearing. "This is bad talk. If it gets around and it's not true . . ."

"It's true. Come on, Sangora, even you know in your heart. Look at his eyes. There're no white people with eyes like that. The inlander's not pure. He's not what you think."

Sangora shook his head sadly. "You're bitter, Salie. You have to accept things. Somiela wants him. Don't blame him for it."

Harman arrived at Pepper Street with his shirt sticking to his back. He found the house with the fanlight easily, tied the reins of his horse to a post, and knocked on the door. It was opened almost immediately by Soleiman who couldn't get over seeing him there.

"Is this an inconvenient time? I know it's Sunday."

"No, no, come in, please," Soleiman said, opening the door wide. "Sunday's no different to us from any other day. We always have visitors. My father will be so happy to see you."

Harman followed him into the house. Stepping into the narrow passage, the first thing he became aware of was the aroma. Someone was cooking food and Harman could hear dishes and utensils being moved about at the back of the house. He looked around. He had only been in the homes of farmers or white people, and was curious to see what a Mohametan home would look like. He noticed the high ceilings, the chalky white walls, the wooden floor shining like polished glass under his feet. Except for the diffused light coming through the fanlight in the door, the passage was dark with a curtain at the far end to prevent prying eyes from looking straight into what he imagined would be the kitchen.

"Take a seat, please," Soleiman directed him to a small sitting room off the passage. "Booia! Come, see who's here."

Ismail Cornelius came into the room. He stopped in astonishment at seeing Harman Kloot in his house. "What a surprise!"

"I'm sorry to burst in on you like this, Mijnheer Cornelius."

"Boeta Mai, please." He turned to his son, "Call your mother. I'm so glad you came. We spoke so much about you. I was worrying all the time that I'd upset you. Make yourself at home, please. We're not fancy people. It's hot outside?"

"I'm used to the heat. At least there's rain in the Cape."

"I know. We can thank God for the weather we have here." Maryam Cornelius came into the room, a fine-featured, olive-skinned woman with a scarf on her head, under which a long braid of black hair hung down her back. She was much younger than her husband.

"This is Harman Kloot," Boeta Mai said. "Roeloff's son. He came to visit."

Maryam wiped her hands on her apron. "Excuse my hands, I'm

frying fish," she said coming towards him, smiling. "You look like your father, the same hair. Which son are you?"

"The eldest. My brother, Martinus, is a landdrost here in the Cape."

"We've seen him," Boeta Mai said. "A friend had some trouble with the law. The landdrost on the case was a Kloot."

"We also have a younger brother, Karel, who works on our grandfather's farm in the Cederberg."

Maryam turned her head towards the kitchen. "I have something in the pan which I must see to. I'm sorry. You will eat with us?"

"Of course," Boeta Mai said. "Sit down, Harman."

Harman took a seat in a chair with a hard back, and noted the furnishings: a round oak table with a high shine, a lace doily on which a glass vase with wildflowers stood. On one wall was a mirror over a mantelpiece, and on the mantelpiece, two candles and a book. On the floor, against the other wall, there was a wooden chest on top of which was a glass bowl with six oranges. A prosperous family, he thought. But, even more than the furnishings in the room, he was fascinated by the wooden things on Boeta Mai's feet.

Boeta Mai saw where he was looking. "They're kaparangs. We have a small shop in Long Street where we make them." He took one off and held it up. It was a thick piece of wood the length of the foot, with a little knob rising out of it to go between the large and second toes. Underneath the kaparang was a strip of wood at the toe and the heel, giving it height.

Harman couldn't imagine how anyone could walk in them. "Don't they fall off when you walk?"

Boeta Mai laughed. "When you first try them, yes. We wear them when we take abdas, the wash before prayer. They keep the feet clean."

"I know about this ritual. I've seen Sangora and Salie and Arend do it, and Sangora, I know, would like these things."

"Sangora?"

"Yes. I was with him at the ratiep. He's quite religious although he will argue with you that he isn't. He's originally from Java. His wife's from Malabar. They met on a farm here in the Cape."

"My wife's from Malaya. Seventeen when I first saw her. I was twenty-six. We're together twenty-two years now." Boeta Mai stood up. "Come, I can hear everything's ready. Let's go into the kitchen. I hope you're hungry."

Harman was always hungry, but did not say so to his host. He had found the bredies and boboties and spicy dishes of Somiela and Rachel far more interesting than the bland food he was used to eating up north, and had no doubt from the pungent smells tantalizing his nostrils that he was in for something exotic. Boeta Mai's wife had said fish. He'd only had fish twice in his life.

Harman followed Boeta Mai and Soleiman into the small kitchen where there was a square table with a bench on either side. A black coal stove stood swathed in steam from a water kettle, the frying pan, and two smaller pots on top of it. There was also a cupboard for the storage of food, the top part of which had two racks with cups and saucers and plates. The table itself was laid with a cream tablecloth. Four plates were laid on the table, together with four glasses filled with water, and in the middle, dishes containing fried fish, fried potatoes, rice, something that looked like braised tomatoes and onions, and a saucer with a yellow-green condiment that Harman didn't recognize.

"Sit down, please. Don't be shy. I hope you like fish. This was bought fresh this morning."

"I've only had fish twice in my life. I enjoyed it very much."

"This is snoek dipped in several spices, then fried. Please, help yourself. Let me pass you the rice."

"I'll dish up for him," Maryam said. "He'll be too shy to help himself properly." She took his plate and placed on it a good portion of rice, over which she put two spoonsful of the tomato gravy, two pieces of fish, and some fried potatoes on the side. The fish was moist, heavily spiced, and made a bright yellow stain on the rice.

"*Bismillah*," Boeta Mai said. With his thumb and the tips of four fingers, he grouped some rice together on his plate, took a small piece of fish with it, and put it into his mouth. He saw Harman trying to do the same. "You're not used to eating with your hands. Let me get you a fork."

"No, please, I'll eat with my hands. I did so at the masjied the other day."

"The food tastes much better if you eat it this way," Maryam said. "And try some of this mango atjar. Do you know mango atjar? We pickle the mango in spices and chillies and eat it with our food. Put a little on the side of your plate."

"And drink plenty of water," Soleiman laughed. "It's strong."

For a few minutes there was silence as everyone concentrated on the food before them. Harman felt comfortable in this family's presence. They were easy to be with, generous of spirit, and spoke freely of the things that went on in their lives. They seemed even more religious than Sangora, living so close to the masjied, and were roused five times a day from whatever they were doing, they said, to attend to their devotions to God.

Boeta Mai saw that Harman had finished the food on his plate and pushed the fish platter towards him. "Have more, please."

"I've had two pieces already."

"Only two? Come, just one more, and a little rice and tomato. When will you eat such food again?"

"My father won't let you leave this table," Soleiman said.

"A small piece then. It's very good, this spice on the fish."

"It's several spices mixed together," Maryam said. "I make up the blend myself. Curry leaf, coriander, jeera, green chillies."

"Somiela also uses spices and green chillies, and lots of garlic."

"Who's Somiela?" Soleiman asked.

"Sangora's stepdaughter. She works in the kitchen. Her food's very good."

Soleiman looked up from his plate. "What does she look like?"

Harman realized that he had said too much. "A thin kind of girl. With green eyes. Not ordinary."

There was a few moments of silence. Maryam got up and cleared the table. Soleiman brought a bowl of hot water and a cloth, and offered it to Harman.

"Boeta Mai," Harman said after he had washed his hands and the other man was settled back on the bench with his back to the wall, "when we spoke last week, Salie said that your name was Pieter before, and that it was changed to Ismail. For how long was it Pieter? I'm curious."

"It was Pieter until about twenty years ago. My grandmother was a slave girl from Ceylon who used to work for my grandfather. She was Mohametan. My grandfather didn't change his religion when he married her, and gave the children Christian names. My mother's name was Maria. She married Stefan Cornelius, a baster. I have one sister. The two of us changed things. We married Mohametans, changed our names – she's Latiefa now – and returned to our grandmother's faith."

"That took courage."

"We were always curious about our grandmother's faith. We also knew other Mohametans. Not converts, but ones from Ceylon. We learned about the faith from them."

"Your grandfather is my grandfather's uncle then."

"Yes. Krisjan Kloot. He wrote books. It was one of his books that I left for your father when I was up there with Oupa Krisjan. Your father mentioned that book the first time we met – he still had it after all those years. I think it's what made him look us up in the first place. Like you, he wanted to know more about us, who we were, how it all started. We thought we would never see him again, but we did."

Harman nodded. He was finding out many things. "I don't think any of us know there was a writer in the family. Maybe that's where Martinus gets his talent for words. He loves words, knows how to use them. He and my father, give them a book, and they're happy as ants on sugar. But Boeta Mai mentioned also that the children were given Christian names. There were other children besides Boeta Mai's mother, Maria?"

"Two brothers, Albert and Reijnhardt Kloot. They looked different from my mother, more like the Kloots, white. They married the daughters of wine farmers in Stellenbosch, moved away, and never visited. My mother longed to see them. There were marriages, births, but she was never invited to their homes. My mother lived with that rejection all her life. Six years ago, she became ill and we sent word to her brothers that she was dying. No one came."

The kitchen grew quiet. Maryam set out cups for tea.

"Will you stay long in the Cape?" she asked Harman, changing the subject.

"For some time still, yes. I have things to sort out before I can return to the Karoo. But eventually I will go back to my family. I can see the attraction of this wonderful place – it really is the fairest Cape – but it's suffocating for one who's used to breathing clean air. People are too involved in other people's business here. Better your nearest neighbour lives twenty miles away."

They laughed. "I know what you mean," Boeta Mai said. "Your father said the same thing. Tell me," Boeta Mai continued, his eyes becoming serious, "this place where you are, they are good to the slaves?"

Harman took a moment before he replied. He had to be careful. Boeta Mai may be a relative, and one esteemed by his father, but he was also friends with Salie and the others. People talked.

"It depends what Boeta Mai means by good. They sleep warm, they eat well, and from what I understand, get a small sum of money and clothes once a year. But they're still forced into labour against their will."

Boeta Mai nodded. "So you are not in agreement with slavery."

"No. There're laws affecting the Koi-na also, binding them into service for a great many years. My father pays no attention to those laws. He pays the people who work for him, and when they want to go, he lets them. You can't force an animal to have affection for you. It's the same with people, he says. If a man wants to leave, you must let him do so. There're Koi-na living on Kloot's Nek for more than fifteen years now, they don't want to leave. They have huts and a patch of ground to grow a few vegetables, but if they should take it into their heads to leave, they're free to do so. I believe in a man working and earning respect by the sweat of his hands, but not belonging to another human being."

"They must not like the English very much, where you are."

Harman smiled. "I don't believe so."

Boeta Mai sipped on his tea. "Well, they can say what they want about the English, and of course, the Englishman works his slave as hard as the Dutch, but if it weren't for them coming here, a slave would never have been able to make a complaint against his own master. That caused a huge uproar. The slaveholder doesn't want to be complained about. He has his good name to protect. He doesn't want the whole world to know what goes on at his farm. Of course, a slave's word is seldom believed over his master's, but with enough witnesses and previous complaints against the owner, a slave can come out the winner. I know one who got his freedom that way."

Harman nodded. Sangora had told him a similar story.

"There's this whole argument now," Boeta Mai continued, "about whether they should set the slaves free all at once rather than hold them to a four-year apprenticeship to teach them skills to prepare them for the outside world. What rubbish! What was the slave doing all that time then, if not learning the work that he was doing? What would he learn after 1834 that he hasn't learned by this time? I agree that it's better to be skilled, but why aren't they being prepared now? A lot of them could continue to do what they're presently doing. Farmers are still going to need workers, and slaves are still going to need work. They're still going to need each other. The difference would be that the slaves would have choices. They wouldn't have to put up with the bastards if they were ill-treated."

Harman smiled behind his teacup. Boeta Mai was no different from his father when his father got worked up over ordinances and laws. He listened to Boeta Mai for some time, impressed by how much the older man knew of the situation. After a second cup of tea, Harman got up reluctantly from his chair.

"This was a very good afternoon. I did not think I would stay so long and take up so much of Boeta Mai's time. Thank you. The food was good, and Boeta Mai answered a lot of my questions. I'm sure I'll have more, but it's getting late, and I must go."

"I'm glad you came," Boeta Mai shook his hand. "Give my regards to your father when you see him." Then he remembered something, and sent his son, Soleiman, into the bedroom. Soleiman came out a few minutes later with a pair of wooden kaparangs. "This is for you. For your friend."

Harman looked at the kaparangs in wonder. "Boeta Mai didn't have to do this. I didn't mean – "

"No, no, take them, please. It's just a little something to mark your visit."

Harman took them from him and turned them over in his hands. It was a new pair, not yet worn, the wood still fresh-smelling. "Thank you very much. I don't know what to say. I'm not used to receiving gifts."

"It's nothing," Boeta Mai said, walking him to the door.

"You must come again," Maryam added.

"I will. I promise." He got on his horse, waved at them, and rode off. He had meant what he said. He would visit again. Harman felt a kinship with the Cornelius family; ordinary people with ordinary concerns and a fierce devotion to God, and he wanted to get to know them. He would ride over to Bessie next Sunday and share his news.

When Harman returned to Zoetewater, he found the slaves sitting outside in front of the jongenshuis. There was a full moon, and the yard was bathed in a silver light; a warm evening for September, with strong indications that the season was changing. Salie still hadn't returned from his excursions, but the others were all there, some of them eating butter pits which they cracked expertly between their front teeth, spitting out the shells. They seemed to be very proficient at this – cracking, spitting, chewing – all without using their fingers to separate the shell from the hard nut inside.

"Mijnheer . . ." they greeted.

"You're enjoying the evening outside?"

"Yes," they chorused. Harman noticed a mischievious look on some of the faces, as if they knew something he didn't.

Sangora got up and walked with him to the stable.

"I put something in your room."

"What?" Harman asked. He didn't believe it could be the storage chest. He had so much admired the one that Sangora had made for the De Villiers voorkamer, the carpenter had said that if Harman supplied the wood, he would make one for him in his spare time. Harman had bought the wood from a woodcutter in town, and given it to Sangora. Sangora had to do his regular work during the day, and Harman didn't expect that he would see the chest much before the end of the year, if then.

"How was your visit with those people?" Sangora asked.

They had reached the stable where Harman unsaddled his mare and led it to the water trough. "Very good. They're friendly people. They invited me to eat with them. Fried fish and fried potatoes and tomatoes and onions, and rice. Boeta Mai's wife uses a very powerful spice."

Sangora laughed. "Your mouth was burning."

"A little, but I didn't say anything. Here, I have something for you."

"For me?" Sangora raised his brows.

Harman took the kaparangs out of his saddle bag, and handed them to him.

Sangora's mouth fell open in surprise. "Kaparangs!"

Harman smiled. "They're for you to wear after you wash your feet."

"How did you know? He gave these to you?"

"Boeta Mai was wearing a pair. I admired them. I said you would like such a thing for your feet, you're always at the barrel washing yourself. When I left, he gave these to me. He makes them in a shop he has on Long Street."

Sangora didn't know what to say. They had left the stable and now walked back, past the men. He held up the kaparangs to show them.

"You're lucky," Petroos said.

"Yes, Sangora," Hanibal lamented. "We don't get anything."

Harman and Sangora reached the buitekamer. The door was closed, although never locked.

Harman opened the door and stepped inside. He took four steps to the table and lit the lamp. The chest was on his bed.

"Sangora! It's beautiful!" He had given Sangora a few yellowwood planks and some hinges, nothing else. What was on his bed, covering almost the length of it, was a magnificent chest, with a lid that had a red tinge to it, and three panels with flower paintings in the front. He couldn't believe the chest before him.

"I didn't do it by myself," Sangora said. "Hanibal painted the flowers. And look closely, under the third panel."

Harman kneeled down in front of the chest. The initials H.K. and the date, September 1832, were painted in black letters in the right-hand corner.

"We tried to keep it a surprise. We primed the wood with lead paint first, which gives it this red background. Hanibal worked on that front panel almost a month by candle light in the jongenshuis, and on Sunday afternoons when there was no one around. He only had one brush, and had to do all the greens first for the stems and the leaves, clean the brush overnight, then do the red heads on the stems, clean it again, then the gold border. Arend got the paint cheap from someone in town, just small amounts. Salie helped with the dovetailing of the joints. Not a single nail in the whole chest. Remember, he has woodworking skills also."

Harman shook his head in amazement, marvelling at the workmanship, and the way they had all managed to keep it a secret from him. And they had used their own money for the paint.

"It is the handsomest thing I've seen, Sangora. I don't know what to say. Thank you. I'll treasure it always."

"It's from all of us. You gave the wood. I only gave my time. And Hanibal, and Arend, and Salie. We carried it in here just an hour before you came."

Harman didn't say more. Sangora wasn't one who liked to be complimented effusively. The carpenter knew how Harman felt. Time was something a slave had very little of, and to give of it to someone else was a precious, precious thing.

. . . are condemned to a perpetual state of servitude, nor have they the power, by any exertion, however great and praiseworthy, of liberating themselves from the bondage; for, no sooner is the period of their contract for serving one inhabitant expired, but it becomes necessary for them to enter into service again; and the only option left to the Hottentot, is, whether he will engage himself to the same master, or to another. Their condition, therefore, is, in this respect, more deplorable even than that of the slaves, for the latter have generally a hope, however faint, that they may possibly one day obtain their freedom.

(John Philip, leader of the critical wing of the missionary faction)

The weeks passed, and soon the days got longer, the nights shorter, and it was summer again. Christmas came and went, the new year followed with some festivity, and Somiela was at the ironing table folding sheets exactly a year after her arrival at the Zoetewater farm. She was thinking of her meeting with Harman later on in the afternoon when the sound of a wagon in the backyard disrupted her thoughts. The De Villiers family had gone to pay their respects to a neighbour whose husband had died during the night, and she and Rachel were alone. The house was quiet with no one there, Somiela's work almost done, and she hoped it wasn't some relative or visitor coming to spoil her plans. She walked to the door and looked out. Her spirit sank when she saw the family wagon.

Andries came into the kitchen and threw his hat on the bench. "I need to wash. Is there hot water?"

"Yes, Seur."

"Where's Rachel?"

"She's at the jongenshuis tending to Hanibal's fever."

"He's sick again?"

"Yes, Seur."

Andries looked at her standing at the ironing table. "Bring some water. Make sure it's hot. Bring it into the bedroom."

Somiela waited for him to leave, then walked back to the door. There was no wife and children. Andries de Villiers had come back by himself. She saw Arend outspanning the horses.

"Arend!"

Arend walked up, kicking the dirt in front of him. He seemed preoccupied with his thoughts, as if something was troubling him.

"Where's the rest of the family?"

"They're still there, at the neighbour's."

"Are you to go back for them?"

"The seur didn't say. He just told me to take him home. But it's not far for them to walk, if they have to. Someone there will probably bring them home." He looked up from the hole he was gouging in the ground with his toe. "Where's my mother?"

"Checking on Hanibal. Is something wrong?"

"I don't want to live here any more."

It was the last thing she expected to hear. Not Arend. He and his mother were part of the mortar and stone.

"Did something happen?"

"No."

"What then?"

"I don't like it here any more. The seur talked strange in the wagon. He never talked like that before."

"Like what?"

"Doesn't matter."

"Things about you?"

"No."

"About your mother?"

"About you."

Somiela put her hand to her mouth. "Me? What did he say?"

Arend hesitated. "Well . . ."

"I want to know. Tell me," she prompted.

"He wanted to know if you – if any of us had been with the half-breed."

Somiela felt a pang of dismay. It wasn't at all what she'd expected to hear. Even though she despised the farmer, it hurt her that people could think of her in this way.

"I have to go, he's waiting. Tell your mother to come." She went inside and removed the tin tub from a nail on the bathroom wall, and a clean towel from the cupboard. It was quiet in the house and she carried the tub down the hall, stopping for a moment to compose herself before knocking on the door.

"It's open," the voice came from within.

She opened the door and saw Andries in front of the bed wearing only a shirt, his pants in a crumpled pile in the middle of the floor. She was shocked to see that he had already started to undress. He wasn't a tall man, and his legs, spindly under the weight of his protruding belly, seemed grossly out of proportion. She felt uneasy, and knew suddenly that he had worked this out before. Andries had waited for the right moment, then purposely left his wife behind at the neighbour's. Giving no outward sign of her fear, Somiela put the tub on the floor and set the towel and wash cloth over the edge.

"I'll get the water," she said, half-expecting him to detain her. He didn't. Out in the passage, she stood for a moment and leaned against the wall. Had she imagined it? Were Arend's words putting things in her head, making her over-react? She went into the kitchen and looked out the back door. There was no sign of Rachel, and no sign of any of the men. Somiela looked at the kettle on the stove. The steam was pumping out of the spout in fast bursts, much like the thumping in her chest, and she wondered how long she could stand there before he grew restless and called. She took a cloth to protect her hand from the heat of the handle, and lifted the kettle. The kettle was heavy and she used both hands to carry it down the passage where she set it down in front of the door, returning to the kitchen for the cold water. When she had everything, she knocked on the door, waited, and went in.

She caught her breath in shock. Andries was where she'd left him in front of the bed, but was completely naked.

"I'm sorry, Seur. I didn't know."

"No, no, come in. Pour in the water."

Somiela tried not to look at him. She poured in half of the hot water, then the cold, and put her hand in the tub to see if the temperature was right.

"It's ready, Seur," she got up, waiting for him to dismiss her. "There's more hot water in the kettle if Seur needs it."

"Take the cloth and wash my back. I've hurt my arm."

"Seur?"

"Wash my back."

It was an order which she daren't disobey. She watched him lower his porcine figure into the tub, a layer of fat pushing against the edge. To wet the cloth, she had to put it into the water, and the only water visible was the small pool between his legs. Somiela got down on her knees, took the cloth and dipped it gingerly into the water. She rubbed soap onto it, then applied it vigorously to his back.

"The front now."

"Seur?"

He got up, making a squishing sound as his body came unglued from the sides of the tub, and hovered over her, his eager little penis inches from her face. "The front. Wash the front."

She didn't know what to do.

"What are you waiting for?" he laughed.

She took the cloth to his knees.

"Higher."

"Seur?"

"Come, come, don't let me stand here shivering."

Somiela dipped the cloth back in the water, grimy now with his dirt, and washed him above the knees. She didn't want to look up, dared not for fear she would knock her face into him. Her heart raced. She wanted to flee from the room. She wanted to scream. A noise at the door made them both turn.

"Marieta!" Andries turned red with shock.

"What's going on here?" Marieta screeched, the bags dropping from her hands onto the floor.

Andries leaned down to pick up the towel. "She came in here without knocking."

"It's not true, Seur."

Marieta gave her a resounding slap. "Shut your mouth!" She didn't know what to believe. Her husband told her one thing, her eyes another. "I saw her hands on you!" she accused Andries.

"She came in here uninvited, I tell you. Don't you believe me?"

"You forced me to do this!" Somiela blurted, unable to contain herself any longer. "I didn't want to do any of this!"

Marieta turned on her. "Didn't I tell you to shut your trap?" She grabbed the first thing she could lay her hands on and hurled it. Somiela cried out as a hairbrush smacked into her head.

Outside in the hallway, Rachel had her ear to the door. She had returned to the house and rushed down the passage, only to see Marieta beating her to the bedroom. Listening to the shouting going on, she knew something terrible was going to happen.

"Rachel, what's going on?" Annie asked tearfully, standing next to Leentje at the end of the passage.

"Nothing. Go play outside." Rachel didn't know what to do, and ran past them into the yard. She didn't know who she wanted, what anyone could do, but Sangora coming out of the barn certainly wasn't the one she wanted to see right at that moment.

"What is it, Rachel? Is something wrong?" he asked, looking at the aia as she crossed the yard.

It stopped her. She had been foolish to run outside. Oh, oh, oh, she pulled at the edge of her apron. What was she going to do? To tell Sangora about his stepdaughter's predicament was to show him the rope with which they would drag him down the street. Sangora would tear De Villiers apart, there would be no mercy for him. Rachel saw Harman come round the corner and was tempted to tell him, but that would not help matters either. She ran back to the house, past the twins who were still standing there, crying. She was about to knock and go in, when she heard a chilling cry. Seconds later, the door flew open and Somiela burst into the hallway, clutching her shoulder. Her dress was wet and steam seemed to be rising out of her clothes. Rachel looked at the kettle lying on its side on the floor and ran down the passage after Somiela.

"Somiela!" But Somiela ran screaming through the house into the yard.

Rachel thought her heart would burst from the exertion. Her breath was coming in gasps, and there was a knife-like pain in her chest. "Somiela!" she called again, trying to stop her. But it was too late. The men in the yard had heard the screams, and got to her first.

"What happened?" Sangora stopped her.

"The nooi threw boiling water at me!"

"What?"

"She burned me!"

"Calm down and tell me what happened. I want to know everything. Everything."

The whole story came out.

"Bastards!" Sangora balled his fists. "I'll get them!" he swore. "They won't get away with this."

"Let me take a look," Harman said.

Rachel watched him trying to calm Somiela down, examining the swollen flesh which extended from the neck, halfway down the right side of her back and arm. His jaw was clenched, his eyes cold. Rachel didn't know who was the more dangerous at that moment; he or Sangora.

"We have to get something on it right away," she said.

"It's a bad burn, Rachel. What do they have in the house?"

"I know what to do. Come, Somiela. Basta! We're going inside. And don't open your mouth, you hear me? Stop that now. Here, wipe your face with this rag."

"How are they allowed to do this?" Sangora asked. "Tell me. I don't understand. How? I thought we had rights. Protection. That pig! What was he trying to do to her? And that bitch! I'll get them!"

Harman was too angry to respond.

"There he is!" Salie spat. "Moerneuker! Still has the nerve to come out. Someone should stick a knife in his gut."

Harman looked at Andries de Villiers in the kitchen doorway. "Wait here," he said, and strode up to the farmer.

"I'm going to report this," he said flatly when he reached him. "Your wife threw a kettle of boiling water at Somiela. Her whole shoulder's burned."

Andries was surprised to hear Harman Kloot speak to him this way. "Are you showing me your strength? Threatening me?"

"I'm telling you."

"It was an accident, and shouldn't have happened. I couldn't stop it."

"And what *you* were trying to do, was *that* an accident also?"

"What was I trying to do? She's a liar if she said I did anything."

"So it's your word against hers, is it? Well, there'll be my word also. Rachel will put something on her shoulder, and I'll take her immediately to the Protector of Slaves to make a complaint."

"Don't be hasty now. Listen to me. Let's talk about this."

"There's nothing to talk about." He turned to walk away.

"I saved you from the hangman, Harman Kloot," Andries's voice cut him short. "You're angry now, but what will happen after you make a complaint? All that will happen will be a fine. I've done you a turn. You can do me one now."

"You want me to save myself at her expense? After what both of you did?"

"You have to believe me. I had no idea Marieta would throw the water at her. I tried to stop it."

"Maybe you did, but you put Somiela in that position, you forced her to do things she didn't want, you forced her to wash you. Why? You don't stand naked in front of someone for no reason. You had lecherous intentions."

"I'm not going to argue about her interpretation of things. Marieta shouldn't have done what she did, and for that I am sorry. I'll make sure that her shoulder gets looked at by a doctor. It won't happen again. I can also alter some things in the house. But to go to the Protector. What will that do? Think about it."

Harman heard what he said, and was shocked to learn that a fine would be all that would be exacted for such a crime. He'd thought that perhaps some time in a jail cell, or the slave being set free, or put with more lenient owners – he didn't know what he'd thought, but certainly not just a fine. What would that do for Somiela? How would that restore her? She would still be in the house, and probably worse off for having complained.

The next words issuing forth from his lips shocked even him. "On one condition. That you sell her to me."

Andries's mouth fell open with the ludicrousness of the idea. He laughed, a horrible, ugly laugh. "You're mad. I'll do no such thing."

"Then that's that. When I return, I'll get off your premises."

"I wouldn't be so hasty if I were you. I know where to get in touch with those men."

With that statement, Andries de Villiers cut the last lines of respect between them. "Do it, then," said Harman. "It's the girl's freedom, nothing less. And I mean what I say. I'll pay you your price. One year's work without pay. That will solve your problem of a foreman for twelve months. After that, Somiela's mine. I want it in writing, Martinus one of the witnesses."

Andries was astonished at the ease with which all this flowed from Harman's mouth. "My wife was right about you – you're dangerous. Do you think you can come here and negotiate a slave's freedom as if it were a sack of flour?"

"Isn't it?"

"It isn't, and I don't let my workers dictate to me."

"It's your decision. I'll take my story elsewhere."

"You're putting yourself to a lot of trouble for a slave."

Harman had said his piece, and wasn't going to say more. He waited.

Andries examined the dirt under his fingernails. "What about the maleier? What does he say?"

Harman noted his tone. It was the voice of one ready to negotiate. "The maleier has both you and your wife in his eye teeth right now. I'd stay far away from him, and far away from his stepdaughter."

Andries took his time. "One year's preposterous. One and a half. We'll round it off to the date officially set for emancipation, December 1st, 1834. That's a little more than a year and nine months. She won't have to serve the apprenticeship. That sets her free four years before the others. I won't let her go before. You work for free until then. That's my offer. And if you still want to go to the Protector now, go ahead. I'll have a fine, and she'll be here long after December 1st to serve the four years."

Harman hid his surprise. He hadn't expected that the farmer would agree. And twenty-one months wasn't so far away. "Agreed. I'll go to Martinus and ask him to come here tomorrow and draw up an agreement."

"I don't see why it's necessary to involve him in this. He's my son-in-law now."

"And my brother. Without him, the agreement's worth spit."

He left and walked down to the men. He couldn't believe how he'd spoken to the farmer, but felt no guilt for it. The man was a pig, and his wife no better. Harman wondered how he was going to stomach them.

"Listen, Sangora," he said when he reached him. "We can't undo what happened. It happened, and we can't call it back. The first thing is Somiela's safety, and how we can turn this to our advantage."

Sangora eyed him sceptically. "This doesn't sound good."

"I went up there threatening to report him to the Protector of Slaves. But even if they were to believe all of us, all he'd get would be a fine. I managed to do something even better. I negotiated Somiela's release. I will give De Villiers a year and nine months' free labour in return for her freedom. She'll be free December 1st next year, she won't have to serve the four years."

There was a murmur of disbelief.

"You mean she can leave here in twenty-one months' time?" Sangora asked, not quite believing him.

"Yes."

"And you've offered to work for him for free?"

"Yes."

"I don't believe it."

"Believe it."

"He won't keep his word," Salie said.

"He doesn't have to. I'm going to Martinus to draw up the papers. If he goes back on it, I'll take him to court."

"But what about what he did? Standing naked in front of a girl and asking her to wash him! And that dog burning her with hot water! Did you ask him about that?"

"Don't get angry with me, Sangora. Of course I asked him. That's why I went up there. He denied everything. Talked about misunderstandings and accidents." Harman put a hand on Sangora's shoulder. "He'll never admit to anything. We have to move past it. This way they know the law's over their heads. Somiela's safer now than she's ever been. He's also promised to have a doctor look at her shoulder, and to make some changes in the house. Really, Sangora, I thought you'd appreciate what I did. In twenty-one months she can walk away from this place a free woman. No one will own her after that."

"I'm sorry. I'm just angry."

"I'm angry too, but I have to put that behind me now. I'm leaving to go to Martinus. You people carry on with your work."

They watched him leave for the stable.

"So he negotiated her freedom," Salie said, "But there's no guarantee. A year and nine months is a long time. You can't let those bastards get away with what they did. And she would just go from one owner to another. *He* owns her after that."

"You always have to piss on everything," Arend said. "What about what he just did?"

"What did he do? We can all make promises. You trust these pigs. Your mother works in the kitchen, you get things."

"What things do I get? When she sends food, everyone gets."

"Your mother's just lucky she's inside."

"Don't talk about my mother, I don't like it."

"I'll talk about her if I want."

"Stop it!" Sangora interrupted. "I don't want to listen to the two of you."

"You going to let them get away with it, Sangora?" Salie persisted. "Your wife's child? You going to turn the other cheek? It's an eye for an eye."

"Jesus changed that."

"What're you talking about?"

"Never mind." Sangora walked away. He couldn't listen to more. A tightness was forming in his chest. He reached the jongenshuis and threw himself down on the mattress. Hanibal was lying groaning a few feet away, but Sangora paid no attention. He wanted to sort out his thoughts. It was time to pray, but he was too worked up, too angry for God.

Arend came in. "We're going to get our food. You want me to get yours?"

"Give it to someone else." After Arend left, Sangora went to the barn where he scratched about without being able to apply himself to anything. He walked to the door and looked out at the men sitting under the tree eating. A few minutes later, Marieta de Villiers emerged from the kitchen and walked to the washing hanging on the line.

"Somiela!"

Rachel appeared in the doorway.

"Tell that girl to come here," Marieta shouted. "She left these sheets out too long. They're bone dry."

"Her arm's hurting, she can't do anything. I'll get it."

"Tell her to come here!"

Sangora watched. He felt a horrible, horrible rage. He stepped out of the barn and started walking. Up to the house. Not fast. But purposeful. He wouldn't lose control. He had no business addressing her and asking questions, but he wanted to know why, what Somiela had done. He wanted to understand. He needed something to make the rage go away.

But Sangora wasn't able to ask anything. When Marieta saw him approach, she started to scream. "Get away, heathen! Andries! Come out here!"

Sangora stopped. Then everything inside him exploded. All he was aware of were people shouting, running in all directions, pulling at his clothes, Marieta de Villiers choking. Shots ringing out over his head.

Harman arrived at Martinus's house and found his brother working on some documents he'd brought home from work.

"Elspeth is at a neighbour's," he informed Harman who enquired after his wife. "There's a new baby. I'll warm up the coffee. Have you eaten?"

"No. I'm thinking of going to Bessie's house for an hour or so after I leave. She's always accusing me of not having anything with them after I come from here. But I'll take the coffee. I could use some."

He followed Martinus into the kitchen. "When last have you seen her?"

"The wedding was the last time."

"You don't visit?"

"Haven't had time. And you know Bessie. She always wants you to come to her. I don't think she likes Elspeth too much."

Harman said nothing. People like he and his sister recognized right away the vapidness of someone like Elspeth.

"So what brings you here on a Saturday afternoon? It's not your day off."

Riding to Martinus's house, Harman had thought exactly how

to present the problem to his brother. He'd had time to think since his confrontation with De Villiers.

"Something terrible happened at the farm," he started. "Andries forced Somiela to wash his naked body this afternoon in his room. Marieta arrived home unexpectedly, came into the room, and threw a kettle of boiling water at Somiela. Somiela's whole shoulder's burned. The – "

"What?"

"That's right. The place is in an uproar."

"I don't believe it." Martinus was horribly shocked. He knew his father-in-law to be capable of cruelty, but had never considered him likely to go after a female slave. And his mother-in-law burning the girl! It was a serious crime.

"I went up to him and challenged him. I wasn't going to stand by and do nothing. He told me that even if I reported him, and Somiela was believed, all he would get would be a fine. But I knew he valued his name, and didn't want this to come out. There was also that business about keeping Sangora in chains when he first arrived at Zoetewater. So I negotiated with him. I offered not to report him to the Protector if he sold Somiela to me. I said I would work without pay for a year. He agreed, but demanded I work for twenty-one months. December 1st, 1834, the official date, Somiela's free. I came here because I want you to draw up the agreement and witness it."

Martinus was dumbfounded by the request. "You're asking me to be a witness against my own father-in-law?"

"You're not a witness against him, just witnessing an agreement."

"I'm married to his daughter, Harman, we're family. Think of what you're asking me to do."

"For God's sake, Martinus, can't you see what he is? Just because you're married to his daughter, doesn't mean you have to be blind to everything."

"What does that mean, everything?"

"Listen, I've come a long way, I'm tired. I don't know what I mean. I'm sorry. I just want you to do me this favour."

"It's not just a favour, Harman. You're putting me in a spot. Have you thought this out? I mean, it's good to care, one feels

186

sorry for these people, but why are you putting yourself out to this extent? Why do you want to buy her?"

"I want her."

"You want her?" Martinus asked, not quite understanding.

"Yes."

"You mean, you *want* her?"

"Is there an echo in the room? For heaven's sake, Martinus, I want her, for myself, for a wife. And I told Pa already. He knows."

"You told Pa?"

"You keep repeating things, Martinus. Get to what you want to say."

It was all too much for Martinus to grasp. His father-in-law's behaviour, the slave girl burned, his brother's request and ridiculous notion to purchase a slave to have as a wife.

"But she's a slave. You can't marry a slave. You're a Kloot. You want to dilute the strain? What would happen if there were children?"

"You mean if one of them came out black?"

"Yes. That's exactly what I mean."

Harman laughed. "Have you never wondered why I look different from you and Beatrix and Karel?"

"What do you mean?"

"I mean, there's bosjesman blood in the family."

Martinus got up angrily. "That's enough!"

"Dance around all you want, it's true. Pa had another woman before Ma. I'm the result."

"*Our* Pa?"

"It's not rinderpest he has, Martinus. Pa told me himself. When I was sixteen. His moment of truth. Imagine that – my birthday present, finding out that my mother was Sonqua. Ma raised me from the time I was born, before she was even married to Pa, and to me she's the only mother I know, but I'm not pure. Whether you like it or not, your own brother's a baster."

Martinus was horrified. A part of him believed that Harman was speaking the truth, but another part wanted to deny it. He would never accept what his brother had told him.

"Listen to me, Harman," Martinus said, coming to sit next to him, "maybe all this is true, but I don't want to hear any more about it. Here's my advice. This isn't the Karoo, and you're not Pa. Pa's a whole law unto himself, he doesn't care what people think. It's different here in the Cape. The community's a closed one. They don't stomach outsiders. You're in or you're out. I'm talking to you as a friend now. We never talked much when we were younger, but you're my brother and I don't want to see you mess up your life. That girl's something to look at, don't think I haven't noticed. One would never say what she was. But what will it bring you? Grief. Rejection by your own people. No one will accept you. In the end, you're alone with a house full of unbaptised children. You've just been here a few months. This is the first girl you've seen. There're others. Of the same ilk, language, and God. Don't be unequally yoked."

"Are *you* equally yoked?"

"What do you mean? We're the same kind."

"*Are* you?" He got up and put on his hat. Martinus's words had cut deeply into him. He had always admired his younger brother, and could've told him about Boeta Mai and Soleiman and really soured the milk in his coffee, but had chosen not to. "Will you come tomorrow night? Yes or no?"

"Can't you see where this puts me?"

"If you say no, I'll have nothing to support my claim in a court of justice, if it should ever come to that."

"I'll have to speak to Elspeth about it."

"I have my answer then."

"What does that mean?"

"It means that she cannot possibly agree that you should draw up an agreement holding her father to his word to let Somiela go at the end of twenty-one months. And I don't think she'll have too much sympathy for Somiela, being just a younger version of the one who birthed her."

"That's enough!" Martinus said, getting up. "You'd better go. I never thought I would hear something like this from my own brother. And all because he can't get what he wants."

The afternoon had faded when Harman got back on his horse, but he would take a chance and see if Bessie was home. He could talk to Bessie. Even if she disagreed with what you had to say, you could reason with her. Bessie had a way of seeing things clearly, not mixing or confusing issues even if they were closely related.

Harman arrived at the small house with the two steps and apple tree near the sea and found his half-sister talking to a woman at the gate.

"You've come to visit!" she exclaimed, saying goodbye to her friend. Her hair was the same colour as his, and was combed out down her back. He noticed that she had put on a little weight, and wondered if that signalled a pregnancy. He knew Bessie had trouble carrying beyond the third month and had already had two miscarriages.

"Only for a few minutes, Bessie. I come from Martinus. I went to see him about something important. Where's Braam?"

"Gone fishing. He should be coming back any time now."

"Actually I'm glad you're alone. I wanted to talk to you. Family business." He knew Bessie would not take that to mean that Braam wasn't family, only that it was a matter for the two of them. They often discussed things other members of the family didn't know about.

"Have you eaten? I have some ox tongue."

"I'm starving. Martinus offered me something, but I said I would come here. I didn't want to hear you complaining again that I always eat with Martinus and not with you." He followed her into the kitchen where she went directly to the pot on the stove with a plate in her hand. Bessie helped him to three slices of tongue, some roast potatoes from a separate pan, and boiled carrots. She came to sit with him at the table.

Harman told her what had happened at the farm, and of his visit to Martinus. Bessie listened without interrupting, her eyes narrowing like their father's at certain passages, their colour changing from a water blue to stormy darkness.

"You can't blame Martinus," she said at last. "He's in the middle. He must please his wife, and support his brother. It's a difficult situation."

"I know, and I feel bad about what I said to him. I expected too much. But it plagues me. No one understands."

"What is it that you want them to understand?"

"How I feel about Somiela."

"How do you feel?"

"I don't know. I mean, I know, but I don't know where I can go with it. Everything seems so against it. Even Pa seemed put off by the whole thing, and Pa should be the last one to speak. You're the only one I can talk to. What do you think, Bessie? Am I being foolish?"

Bessie looked down at her hands and stroked her fingertips. "You know, Harman, I'm closer to you than to the others. We understand each other, even if it doesn't make sense to anyone else. We're the first two. Maybe that's it. Maybe because they all have the same mother, and we don't. I don't know." She paused to look at him. "Braam isn't what Pa would've chosen for me. There's no farm he will inherit, no money. Braam works for a boss. But we're happy together. I didn't think I would like it in the Cape, so far away from everyone, but when Ma died, it was easier. I've made friends here. And Braam's friends are my friends. What I want to say is, if you allow others to influence you, you mustn't even think of this girl. It'll hound you to your grave. But if you take her, you must know that it won't be easy. You'll be alone except for a few who will stand by you. I'll be one of those who'll support you, but you'll not have many supporters. People in our own family might reject you." Bessie watched him slice up a piece of tongue. She could tell he was listening intently. "What I'm saying is, if you feel strongly about this girl, you must do it. We only have one chance to be happy."

Harman felt buoyed by her response. "You agree?"

"If you feel strongly about her, yes. No matter who she is."

"She's also Mohametan."

"What does that mean?"

"It means she will not come to my faith. They're strong about this point."

"Does it mean she'll want you to come to hers?"

It was the thing heaviest in his heart. And if he couldn't say it to himself, he had to say it to Bessie, and have his conscience speak back to him. "Yes."

Bessie didn't show her surprise. She spread her hands on the table, and inspected her fingers as if she would find there the answer to his dilemma.

"You have nothing to say?" he asked.

Her eyes looked deep into his. "What do you want me to say?"

"You know we have Mohametans in the family, even though no one talks about it. I told you."

"Yes, but we were raised with the Word of the Lord, and when it comes to the Lord, there's no compromise. I don't know what to tell you. I don't want to be punished for telling you the wrong thing."

"Do you think Pa believes in the Lord?"

Bessie smiled for the first time. "You know Pa. He believes in Neeltje, and counting the sheep every night, and coming up with the same head count. Pa's lord of his world. I wasn't raised by him, and I wasn't raised by my ma. My ma never said six words to me the whole time she lived. I was raised by her sister, Tante Diena, and my grandmother, Elsie Joubert. Everyone knows Elsie Joubert. She had the biggest Bible in the Karoo. She and Tante Diena are the strongest supporters of the Lord. You can't ask me this question, Harman. Here you must examine your own conscience. I want you to be happy, but I don't want you to go to hell. And I don't want to go to hell with you."

Harman rode back to Zoetewater with a heavy heart. Martinus was right, Bessie was right, everyone was right. What exactly did he feel for Somiela? What did he want? Did he know? He wasn't going to remain in the Cape, and would return to the Hantam when the time was right. Life there was hard and enduring, with few luxuries. He needed a woman who would develop an understanding of the land, one who understood silence. A strong woman. One who could look after him, love him, one he could love in return. Bessie was right. He *had* been raised with the Word of the Lord, but if there was one Lord, then they were all His, and the Lord surely wouldn't be aggrieved by a man wanting kinship with a woman of a different belief if He had created them all. What did it matter how they worshipped Him as long as they followed His code and honoured His name?

And so Harman rode back to Zoetewater, the Lord dwelling uppermost in his thoughts. He had left there to ask Martinus to draw up an agreement, gone to Bessie and discussed his own fears, and come back more confused than before. One thing he didn't know was how much Bessie still hurt over her mother. He wondered if Bessie knew the truth of what had happened between her mother and their father – that Roeloff Kloot had never loved Soela, but had set himself upon her in the foaling barn while she was engaged to his brother, David. Bessie had never known the man her mother had married – he'd been shot by his father, Willem Kloot, before Bessie was one year old. And the one who'd fathered her had seen her when she spent weekends at Kloot's Nek, but had never really said who he was. It was Neeltje who had done it. Neeltje who was the explainer and comforter and mediator between her husband and his many children. The past was wild and turbulent and bloodied. Roeloff Kloot may be worshipped by the Sonqua and respected by neighbouring farmers, but he had taken greedily in his youth, and had hurt many people including Bessie's mother, and Harman's mother. Sanna, the old Koi-na servant, had told him that Soela's silent sickness was directly related to her broken heart, and that Zokho had been the only one to pay the young Roeloff back – cruel and heartless as it was – leaving her infant under a tree to be claimed either by jackals or to die of exposure.

Harman reached the entrance to the estate, and was so engrossed in his thoughts, that he almost trampled over Arend as the interpreter came running towards him.

"Seur! Stop!"

"What is it, Arend?" He brought the horse to a halt.

"Something terrible's happened! Sangora attacked the nooi in the yard!"

"What are you talking about?"

"Salie worked him up. He kept telling Sangora he was a fool, that he should do something. The whole thing happened while we were eating and the nooi came into the yard shouting for Somiela to come out and take the sheets off the line. My mother said Somiela's shoulder was sore, *she* would do it, but the nooi said she didn't care what was wrong with Somiela. That's when Sangora comes walking up to her from the barn. I don't know why. Then before he even gets within twenty feet of her, she starts screaming and calls him a heathen. The next thing we know, he has her by the neck and she's choking."

"No . . ."

"He was mad. I tell you, you had to see him. The seur came out with his rifle and fired. Sangora ran off like a dog with a jackal after him, and no one's seen him since! Seur's threatening to give all of us twenty-five strokes! He thinks we put Sangora up to it. Gumtsa's missing also. Seur's accusing him of helping Sangora. He's going to ask you to track him. You mustn't do it, you can't bring him back. You have to go after him and help him get away. That's why I waited here to catch you before you went up to the house. If you turn around now, no one will know you know anything. If Gumtsa's with Sangora, they're heading for Hanglip. You must help him get away from there. That's the first place the seur will go looking if he calls in the kommando."

"You're asking me to help a fugitive?"

"If they bring him back, they'll make an example of him. You can't let that happen. If you don't help him, he's dead."

There was the sound of a wagon coming down the drive.

"Who's at the house?"

"Van Heerden and his wife, visiting. Now I'd better go before they come looking for me."

Harman watched Arend as he dodged between the trees and disappeared. Then he stood for a moment, not knowing whether to go up to the house, or after Sangora. One thing Harman did know. His agreement with the farmer had now been greatly compromised.

Andries heard him arrive and came out into the yard. "The most dreadful thing's happened!"

Harman dismounted and listened to the farmer relate the events as if he were hearing them for the first time.

"He just attacked her for no reason?"

"Well, of course he had reason; his stepdaughter, what happened this afternoon. We all know that. But you can't go around attacking people. It's a serious offence attacking a white woman. I want you to go after him. Tell him I want to talk to him. Tell him I understand he wasn't in his right mind after what had happened to his stepdaughter. Bring him back and I'll deal with him. Better me than the authorities."

"What makes you think I'll find him?"

"Because you don't want to see him shot in the back."

"Maybe it's better then if the whole thing comes out and he goes straight to a landdrost to tell his side of the story."

"If that's what you want." Andries had had enough. He, too, had had time to think of Harman's arrogant confrontation with him that afternoon, and regretted that he'd agreed so hastily to let the half-breed go at the end of the following year. But he was firm on the matter of Sangora. No one was going to undermine his authority and disturb the order on Zoetewater. Marieta was still his wife, and he was still master of his home and his own senses. The maleier wasn't going to escape punishment.

Harman recognized the challenge in Andries's words. Andries would go after Sangora himself and take the law into his own hands. "You're asking me to deliver a man up for punishment," Harman said softly. "One who's been sorely provoked. What kind of justice can he expect?"

"I want to know why he did it."

"You just said you knew why he did it. But I don't agree that that's the only reason. I know Sangora. If it was his intention to attack anyone, he would've done it this afternoon after Somiela was burned. He wouldn't have waited. But if he was taunted, or provoked, that's something else. A court of justice will take that into account. Perhaps you should ask the slaves." He paused. "I'll bring him back if you give me your word you'll listen to his side of the story. If you find that he was justifiably provoked, you'll only give him a warning."

"They hang a man for what he did."

"What did he do? He's your best slave. He makes money for you, you couldn't replace him. Surely you understand a man stretched to the limit the way he was this afternoon."

"It was revenge. Nothing less. My biggest mistake was to take off those chains."

"Those chains were illegal. That's another thing he could complain of to the authorities."

"Just bring him back."

"What if I don't find him?"

"I'll call in the kommando, and our agreement's off. Bring him back and our agreement still stands."

Harman left for his room in the yard and went straight to bed. It had been a hard and horrible day, and already the events of the afternoon seemed like a distant memory. He couldn't get Somiela out of his thoughts, her red and swollen shoulder. He had made little fuss so as not to alarm her, but he'd seen burns like that. They cooked the skin and left ugly scars. What Andries and his wife had done was unforgivable, and something which Harman would never forget. He'd controlled his emotions when explaining to Sangora what he'd negotiated with the farmer. To let the carpenter see his real anger would've incited rage, and fired up the men into mutiny. If it wasn't for Somiela, he would've washed his hands of the whole affair and left Zoetewater once and for all. But he couldn't. In the time Harman had been there he'd seen the true nature of the man – the farmer could hide nothing from him – and thought him an unfeeling bastard, but never a molestor. This was a new threat. A snake whose venom he wasn't yet familiar with. How did he know it wouldn't strike again? How could he prevent it? He was a hired hand with no powers. He couldn't do anything. He was grateful for someone like Rachel in the house. Rachel had even less power than he, but Rachel had eyes in the back of her head. The aia had appointed herself guardian over Somiela and was fiercely protective. Still, Harman wasn't entirely at ease, and didn't know what he feared most; Andries's carnality, or Marieta's hatred. And now, Sangora attacking the woman and running away simply added more wood to a fire that was already blazing out of control. Why in God's name had he done it? Perhaps if Harman hadn't gone to his brother's house that afternoon, it might not have happened. The problem now was where to look for Sangora, and what to do when he found him. Would he deliver him up to Andries de Villiers like an ox led to the pit to await slaughter? Harman had no answers, only a dull pain which had started at Bessie's house and resided in the left side of his head. Eventually, his eyes closed and he slept.

Shortly after midnight, he came awake. He looked about him in the dark and took a few minutes to orient himself. Harman wondered whether the men were still up. He knew that they spent long hours talking at night, and after what had happened that day, were probably too worked up to sleep. He swung his legs over the side of the bed. His body was heavy with fatigue, but he forced himself to get up. He stood for a full minute in the doorway looking at the moon, then crossed the yard quickly to the jongenshuis. Everything was in darkness. He tapped on the door.

"It's me," he called softly.

The door opened and he saw the candle on the floor, the men sitting around it with long expressions.

"You're not sleeping . . ."

"We're very worried," Arend said. "Mijnheer didn't go after him?"

"No."

"What's going to happen now?" Tromp asked.

Harman kneeled down next to the old shepherd. "I'm leaving at dawn to see if I can find him. You think he's gone to Hanglip?"

"If Geduld's with him, yes."

"How do you know Geduld's gone with him?"

"We just know. Geduld was leaving anyway. He's a few days still from the end of the month, but that's all the same to the bosjesman."

Harman nodded. "How do you get to this place?"

"You can go along these mountains until you come to Muizenberg. From Muizenberg you travel east along the shore until you come to a big rock hanging over the sea. That's Hanglip. You can't miss it. Just don't forget to go east from Muizenberg. There're woodcutters hiding out in the area. If they let themselves be seen, ask them. They may even know something. The drosters in the Vishoek mountains often travel to Hanglip to visit friends or to trade."

"How's Somiela? Does anyone know? You've seen her, Arend?"

"They got the doctor. There's a plaster on her wounds. The doctor said she was not to do anything that would inflame the area, not to lift anything, and not to work. Salie spoke to her for a few minutes."

"She's all right," Salie said scornfully. "More frightened of the moerneukers than anything. But Rachel hasn't smiled since this thing happened. They know that look. We all know it. We get cold pap if she's cross with us. God knows what she'll put in their food after this."

Harman got up and walked to the door. "I'd get to sleep if I were you. He's going to be ringing that bell in a few hours – it's almost morning already. I'll see you all when I get back."

"What will Mijnheer do when Mijnheer finds him?" Arend asked. "Will Mijnheer help him escape, or bring him back here?"

"Sangora doesn't need me to help him escape. He needs to tell his story to a landdrost and clear himself, or he'll be on the run for the rest of his life."

"His story?" Tromp scoffed. "Who'll believe it? If you bring him back, he's a dead man. There's a landdrost married into this family. Did he do anything about Sangora's chains?"

Harman turned red.

Arend saw that Tromp had offended Harman. "Sometimes you don't think before you open your mouth, Tromp. Mijnheer isn't liable for his brother's actions."

"You don't have to defend me, Arend. Tromp's right."

When the door had closed behind him, the men went into fresh argument.

"You shouldn't have said that to him, Tromp," Arend charged the old shepherd. "You hurt his feelings."

"Yes, Tromp, that was cruel," Petroos agreed. "He treats us all right. We wanted him here. He's not responsible."

Tromp threw himself back on the mattress and stared up at the ceiling. "You're making too much fuss. It's good for him to know how we feel. And what feelings? He's a white bosjesman."

"Who told you that?" Arend asked, eyeing Salie. He had only told one person what Geduld had told him about Harman's mother, and that person was Salie.

"Why're you looking at me?" Salie asked. "Geduld told everyone. His mouth runs over when he drinks." He pulled the blanket up to his chin, and turned to face the other side. "You're all worked up over Sangora. Go and sleep. Sangora's survived much worse than this. He has God, and a set of big feet. The inlander will find him. I have no doubt of that."

I was ingeboeked for ten years, when I was so young (here showing his height then), to my baas Dawid van der Merwe in the Camdeboo – my baas promised then to bring me up and instruct me as his own children – but I had to lie among the dogs in the ashes – I was many a time lifted out of the ashes by the arm and flogged well so that when I ran from the hearth the ashes were strewed and the coals after me, and the dogs, alarmed, would pursue me – I got no instruction and no clothes – I know nothing – my mother was obliged from the bad treatment to run away and leave me – and my father soon after – and when he would attempt to get a sight of me, the dogs were sent after him – O! my poor father!

(The Hottentot, Magerman, recalling his experience between 1812-1815)

"These chickens are starting to stink, Gumtsa. How much farther?" Sangora asked.

Gumtsa had stolen the hens the previous night from a farmyard at the foot of the Vishoek mountains. The plan was to eat one when they had put enough distance between themselves and Zoetewater, and take the other with them as a gift to those who lived where they were going. They had walked for hours along the dune-trimmed shore, the rolling ocean on their right, the wind almost ripping them off their feet. They looked back frequently to see if anyone was coming, moving quickly into the dunes when they suspected anything. But behind them was only the wind tossing up silver sandstorms.

Sangora wasn't feeling too good about himself. Hiding out in the Vishoek mountains the previous night, he'd been too charged with the first flush of freedom to truly understand the trouble he was in. But this wasn't freedom. Waking up under a bush with mist in your hair and the wind in your ear was a different reality. His soul ached. His conscience pricked him. He'd allowed his emotions to get the better of him. A moment of blind rage, and the course of his life was irrevocably changed. He'd attacked a white woman. How had he allowed such a thing to happen? What had snapped inside him to make him lose his iman? He'd allowed

198

the hatred in, and made room for the jinn. Now he was on the run, with nowhere to go – the law on his tail, the unknown ahead.

"How far still, Gumtsa?" he asked again.

"We're only at Macassar now," Gumtsa said, walking ahead of him. "We'll stop when we reach those rocks. A holy man's buried up there, one of your people."

Sangora nodded. Everyone knew the story of Sheikh Yusuf who had come to the Cape at the end of the 17th century. Of noble birth, and a political exile, the Sheikh was brought from Ceylon where the Dutch had had enough of him, and thought him better out of the way at the Cape of Good Hope. He was settled with his forty-nine followers at Macassar, near the mouth of the Eerste Rivier where he was housed on a farm, the settlement becoming a sanctuary for fugitive slaves. But the life of the community was shortlived: just five years later, the Sheikh died, and the whole contingent, with the exception of two followers and a daughter, was shipped back.

Under different circumstances, Sangora would've liked to explore the area and see what he could find of this early Mohametan community, but they had to press on. Gumtsa wanted to reach Gordon's Bay by late afternoon, he said, and be at Hanglip before nightfall. Sangora would never have thought that Gumtsa had more energy than him, but he fought to keep up with the apricot-skinned hunter. Gumtsa didn't walk like most men. Dressed in his little leather flap, the quiver with the six arrows on his back, a digging stick in his right hand, his sturdy little buttocks lifted left, right, left, right, as he trotted at a half run, his small feet hardly touching the sand. That's how they did it through the desert, he said, covering long distances. A bosjesman learned to walk very fast when the sun burned down on his head and water was two days away. Silence preserved the last juices left in the body. And so the two of them walked in silence; the little nomad in front, eyes squinting to the distance ahead, the taller, darker man in pantaloons following with a dead chicken in each hand.

"We'll stop here, out of the wind," Gumtsa said. "Don't look so miserable, Sangora. You're free."

"This isn't freedom, Gumtsa."

Gumtsa squatted down on his heels behind a huge boulder. He

took one of the chickens, stuck his hand into the cavity and pulled out the guts. Then he made a small fire and threw the chicken, feathers and all, on top of it. "They would've found us already if they knew anything. They don't know where we're going. Do you see anyone coming? Of course not."

Sangora was up on the boulder, his eyes travelling slowly over the expanse of the sea, the silvery shore below it stretching east, the rocks, pools, the wild flowers in dazzling yellows and purples in between the dark green bushes hugging the cliffs. The waters were rich with fish along these shores, and they had walked all the way from Muizenberg to the squawking of hundreds of birds. He watched them for a moment, his thoughts far away. What would he ever tell his wife? He had promised her that Somiela would be safe as long as he had breath in his body. And his body had been too stupid to control itself. The aia was right. One couldn't make promises. Harman's negotiations with the farmer had troubled him, but he saw now that the inlander had had foresight where he'd only reacted in revenge. Somiela couldn't stay one day longer at Zoetewater than she had to. He watched the birds, gathered like soldiers on a dune to his right. Something disturbed them, and they lifted off into the sky in a blaze of wings over his head. A few hundred feet away they floated down to the ground again in a soft whisper and settled like a snowy blanket on a dune further away. *That* was freedom, he thought.

He climbed down and stood up to his waist in a little pool with the water rushing in gently between the rocks. He lowered himself, rinsed his mouth, washed his face, ears, arms, elbows, running a wet hand along the top of his head, doing everything three times, mumbling something under his breath.

Gumtsa watched him. He knew what the Mohametan was doing; he was taking abdas, the ritual ablution before performing his prayers. "That's salt water, Sangora. Your skin will be on fire once we get back in the wind."

Sangora looked at him turning the chicken over on the fire. "What if there're no people at this place where we're going? Will you leave me there and go on?"

Gumtsa laughed. "I don't believe you're afraid, Sangora. There'll be people there, don't worry. That's why we're taking this chicken. They're a suspicious lot, so you want to share something with them."

Sangora left him for a sheltered area between two rocks a few feet away. Facing east, he took a moment to compose himself. Presently he touched his thumbs to his ears, *Allah hu Akbar, Allah hu Akbar*, and started prayers. He performed all his rak'ahs, and two extra, for God to have mercy on his miserable soul. When he was done, he sat for a few moments in silence with his eyes closed. Then he recited the opening verse of the Koran again, even though he had recited it ten times already as part of his prayers. The verse was of special significance and always brought him peace. It was not a long verse, lasting less than a minute, but by the time he reached the end of it, a calmness had settled over his heart. He thanked God for his health and the health of his family, he thanked God for Arend and Salie and Rachel who were with Somiela, and especially, he thanked God for the arrival of the inlander at Zoetewater, who he now believed had not arrived there by accident. *On no soul do we place a burden greater than it can bear.* The Almighty had not abandoned them. It wasn't for nothing that Harman Kloot had come to Zoetewater. It was God himself who'd put him there.

"Is that chicken almost done, Gumtsa?" he asked when he had had his consultations with his Lord and felt at peace again.

Gumtsa took the chicken off the fire, broke it in half with his hands, the head dangling down one side of it, and returned it to the coals. "We will eat better than the richest farmer today. It is too bad that there are no uintjies to put next to it on the coals."

Eventually, the chicken was roasted, and he and Gumtsa shared it, devouring every last morsel, even chewing the bones. Gumtsa asked only for the feet which he said he would like to take with him after he'd left Sangora at Hanglip. Sangora was only too happy to let him have them. He had not even expected that he would have food that day. What would he eat tomorrow? The next day? Would they have caught him by then?

"Come, Sangora," Gumtsa got up, kicking wet sand over the coals, looking quickly around to see that they had left nothing behind.

They walked for hours in silence. Late in the afternoon they reached Gordon's Bay, where the sea was so calm that it didn't seem part of the same ocean. The landscape changed slowly, from a wide creamy shore, to a narrower stony one, to thick bush, until the mountains crowded close to the shore and they found themselves high up on a ridge.

They drank their fill from a trickling stream, and continued on, stopping occasionally when Gumtsa stuck his digging stick into the hard ground to unearth a tuber or plant.

"There it is, at last," Gumtsa pointed to a massive rock leaning over the sea a few miles away.

"Where are we now?"

"At Rooi Els. Wait here, I want to check one of the caves to see if anyone's there. Crouch down behind one of these rocks. Don't let yourself be seen."

Sangora looked about him. He was scratched and torn from wading through the bush, and didn't relish being attacked by drosters or wild animals.

"What about snakes?"

"You didn't get bitten so far, Sangora. What snake will want to bite you now? Be more scared of the leopards."

"Leopards? You didn't say there were leopards." Before Sangora could say anything more, Gumtsa had jumped over a rock and disappeared.

Sangora lowered himself out of sight and tried not to think of where he was. The mountain had an eerie silence. Nothing stirred. Except for the roar of the sea thundering against the rocks below, the stillness filled up his ears. It was a quiet, desolate place with no paths, no sign of movement, not even the squawk of a bird. The weather was overcast, and a grey mist hung over the peak.

Gumtsa popped up behind a bush as suddenly as he had disappeared. "I found an axe and a rope and some bones. It's occupied, but you don't want to go there. It's safer at Drostersgat."

"Why?"

"Here there's no place to run. Remember the story I told about the two white children? It happened here, in that cave. At Hanglip you have lots of places to hide."

"Is it far? We've walked the whole day."

"It's just around the bend, where that rock hangs over the sea."

They walked for a while along the mountain, until finally they passed the stream Gumtsa had mentioned earlier, and stood on top of a cliff, looking down at the sea.

"We're here," Gumtsa said, putting his few belongings down on the ground. "This is Hanglip. Drostersgat's somewhere near here."

Sangora looked around. It was a vast, isolated area populated with thick bush between the mountains and the sea.

"Where're the people? It's very quiet."

"They've seen us, don't worry. There's a path up there where they keep a lookout. That's how they're able to evade anyone who comes looking for them. There're many caves, but only two entrances to the ones that lead underground. Once they're in those caves, no one can reach them. Look down. See all those rocks? It's too dangerous for boats or ships to come in this way. At low tide, you can climb down and walk in, or go down Drostersgat. You can see why this is safer than Rooi Els. Look at all these hills. You have many places to hide."

"Don't turn around," a voice said suddenly behind them. "Who are you?"

Sangora felt the hairs rise on his arms. It was a harsh voice, coarse, unmannerly.

"Sangora Salamah. The one with me is Gumtsa."

"Why are you here?"

"I was told this was a safe place for someone who doesn't want to be found."

"Why don't you want to be found?"

Sangora hesitated. He didn't like answering questions without knowing who he was speaking to. From the age of the voice, he made the speaker out to be an older man. Sangora took too long to respond and felt a sharp object pushed into his back.

"I asked you a question."

"I attacked someone."

"Who?"

"A white woman. For burning my stepdaughter with boiling water."

"Turn around. You only."

Sangora turned slowly and looked straight into the face of a man about the same age as him. What startled him was the man's clothes: a torn and filthy blue and red jacket with three shiny buttons, obviously a stolen uniform. He figured him to be a runaway slave or a sailor.

"How do I know you're not here to spy on us, an informer?"

"If you place any value on the word of someone who believes in God, you'll know I'm speaking the truth."

The man laughed suddenly, showing a bank of broken teeth. "God? That's a good one. All right, you have a choice. You can stay, or go with this bosjesman. And don't turn around, you," he said in Gumtsa's ear.

"He's a friend," Sangora pleaded.

"Not to us. A bosjesman will sell his soul for a dop. We don't want his sort here."

Sangora turned to Gumtsa. He didn't know what to do.

"You must stay," Gumtsa said. "I brought you. You'll be safe here. I'll go north. You can't come with me there."

"But – "

Gumtsa picked up his possessions. "You have several lives, Sangora. You've only used up one of them, you'll survive." Without looking at the man behind him, he walked off.

Sangora felt a crushing panic. He was on his own. With the clothes on his back, and a dead chicken. For a moment he almost wanted to run after Gumtsa. Gumtsa was the last thread to his other existence, to the people on the farm. With Gumtsa gone, there was no connection. Sangora turned around to talk to the man in the stolen uniform, but he, too, had vanished. There was no sign of him. Sangora stood shivering in the wind, not knowing what to do next. He was close to the edge of the cliff and looked down at the white breakers slapping against the rocks hundreds of feet below. An uncontrollable urge overcame him. How easy it would be. How swift.

"Come!"

He turned in the direction of the voice. The man had re-appeared, and was now calling to him. Sangora walked away, stepped between a few bushes, over some rocks, and came upon the man rolling up a thick coil of rope. They were a good distance from the edge of the cliff, but the sea roared in his ears as if he were standing right over it. He saw why: a wide, open slash between the rocks, plunging down to the raging currents below.

"Drostersgat," the man said, seeing where he was looking.

"This is the Drostersgat people talk about?"

"Yes. Down there, there's a cave."

"The rocks are so flat, I didn't even see the opening."

"Unless you know where to look, you'll walk right past it. But you can hear the sea. It's louder than thunder."

Sangora felt dizzy looking down the deep hole. A huge, round boulder was stuck in the opening with the rope fastened around it, and ten or twenty feet down, great big waves of slapping foam. "It looks dangerous to go down here."

"It is. You wouldn't think that anyone would, but it's high tide now. We go down at low tide with this rope."

"The rock won't come down on your head as you lower yourselves?"

"It hasn't moved in a hundred years. It was used by others long before us. I'm removing the rope now, just in case. We haven't had strangers sniffing around these parts for a very long time. But you're here now. Others might follow."

Sangora watched as he kneeled down, untied the knot and tucked the end of the rope into the thick coil. "You've been here long?"

"Almost eight years. I don't stay here all the time. My name's Hendrie."

"Where do you go when you're not here?"

Hendrie looked up at him. "We go on raids. There're six of us. One of them's a woman. We eat what we fish from the sea, occasionally a tortoise or a rabbit from these bushes, but mostly we have to go out and steal."

"A woman lives here with you in these caves?" Sangora was surprised that the man was answering his questions and offering so much. But Hendrie, despite his wild appearance and filthy clothes, seemed friendly.

"Yes. Let's go. We'll go in the other way."

Sangora followed him up the mountain. He noticed that Hendrie chose to follow a more difficult path despite there being an easier way to get to the top. He saw the sense of it. It left no trails, no tell-tale signs, and it dissuaded the casual visitor too.

They came to a bush growing up against the face of a large rock. Hendrie pushed the branches aside and squeezed past it into a hollow grotto. Sangora followed. The cavern was small and had a tunnel leading into the darkness beyond.

"Hold onto me."

Sangora hid his disgust at the thought of touching the droster's clothes. His own clothes were soiled, but had at least been washed the previous week. Hendrie's clothes were sweat-stained and greasy, crusted with dirt, and stank of goat piss. Gingerly, Sangora took hold of the end of Hendrie's jacket. Minutes later he could see nothing in front of him and was glad to be holding onto anything that would bring him out the other end.

Hendrie walked steadily, feeling his way along the bumps and crevices he recognized. Sangora moved like one blindfolded. He felt things under his feet and didn't want to know what they were, and he had the sense of moving downwards. Several times he stumbled. They were burrowing deep into the bowels of the mountain.

"How long is this tunnel?"

"Long."

"There're no animals lurking in here?"

"Not now. In the hot months, scorpions and cobras. You just have to be careful."

"How can you be careful? It's dark as a grave."

"It's better dark. You don't want to see."

"Why not?"

"Bones. Human remains. There's a cave leading off here somewhere with skeletons. Old. No one goes near it."

Sangora didn't want to know more. Presently they started downwards, and he heard the roar of the ocean.

"We're here," Hendrie said. They turned a corner and came onto a platform of raised stone, the sea dribbling into the mouth of the cave a good distance away. It was a cavernous area containing all the worldly possessions of the group: blankets, untanned hides, pots, bowls, farming implements, firewood, rifles, and on a bundle of old clothes, a whimpering infant. Two men, dark brown in colour, sat around a small fire fashioning fishing hooks out of bits of iron and bone. A woman squatted nearby, rocking back and forth on her heels studying the infant but making no attempt to console it. The condition of their attire was no different from Hendrie's, and all appeared to be in desperate need of soap and water. The air reeked of sweat, smoke, and animal fat.

One of the men got up. He was short and squat, with a big head, and a pelt of matted hair.

"It's all right, Dikkop, he's safe," Hendrie said. Hendrie turned to Sangora. "Dikkop's quick on his horse. He guts you first, then asks questions."

Dikkop looked at Sangora curiously, with piglike eyes.

Sangora felt uncomfortable under his stare, and imagined he was called Dikkop for the size of his large head, with a wild set of ears. "I am Sangora," he said.

Dikkop ignored him. "Why'd you bring him here?" he asked Hendrie.

"He's in trouble, he needs to hide. He attacked a white woman. A bosjesman brought him."

"He tells you things and you believe him? It could be a trick. He could've been sent here by someone who wants him to spy on us." Dikkop turned to Sangora. "Does anyone know you've come here?"

"No," Sangora replied with all the earnestness he could muster in his voice.

"You'd better not be lying."

"I'm not."

Dikkop looked at the chicken in his hand. "What's this?"

Sangora realized he was still holding the dead bird. "For you. It was killed yesterday."

"He comes with a gift," the man at the fire laughed suddenly.

"That's Aron," Hendrie said. "Aron doesn't go out with us. He stays here with his sister and looks after things. There's also Boegie and Plaatjes. They're out looking for food."

"My sister's name is Venus," Aron said, still concentrating on the hook in his hand. "Venus lost two babies. She'll lose this one also."

Sangora looked at Hendrie.

Hendrie confirmed his suspicions. "Aron's not right in the head."

Venus got up and came to stand in front of him. Sangora handed her the chicken. "What's wrong with the child?"

She didn't answer.

"Babies don't live long here," Hendrie said.

"You know something about babies?" Dikkop asked.

Sangora knew then that Dikkop was the father. "I had an infant. It died."

"What of?"

"I don't know. God's will."

Dikkop looked at Hendrie, then back at him, "God's will?"

"Yes."

Dikkop laughed. "A believer, Hendrie. Perhaps his God knows of a way to get us food and clothes and gunpowder. Who's your God, then? Jesus?"

Sangora was exhausted from his travels. "Jesus isn't God."

Dikkop glanced at Hendrie. Even Aron looked up from his work.

"What're you?"

"Mohametan."

"A maleier!" Dikkop exclaimed. "Get him out of here, Hendrie, he's bad luck." Then he checked himself. "Wait! Maleiers have magic. I've heard of your magic. It's said a good doekoem can do anything. True?"

"I don't know."

"You can't make this infant better?"

"I can pray for him."

Dikkop walked over to the small bundle and picked it up. "Here, he's six days old. His mother has no milk. I'll give you a chance to prove your God to us. Make him better and we'll all believe in Him."

Sangora didn't bother to say anything. He took the bundle into his arms. The infant was swaddled in an old shirt, and the first thing he saw when he unwrapped it was the wound where the umbilical cord had been severed. It was raw and distended, and had a clump of leaves with some sort of paste plastered over it. The child was hot and feverish, and it didn't take an expert eye to see that he was seriously ill.

"What do you think?" Dikkop asked.

Sangora didn't have the heart to tell him what he believed. And anyway, he was not God. How could he say whether the child would live or die?

"We must pray for God to help him."

"That is your solution? To utter words? Or your God has told you already it's no use?" He walked away and disappeared behind one of the rocks.

No one spoke. Aron returned to the hook in his hand, Venus held the chicken over the flames to singe off the feathers. Hendrie took off his jacket, revealing an even dirtier shirt underneath, and went to squat near the others at the fire.

"You can take one of those hides over there," he said to Sangora who had said a long prayer in Arabic for the infant and laid him back down on his blanket. "And don't let Dikkop upset you. He's not bad once you know how he thinks. He's lost two babies before. The woman's not one to figure out things. She dunked this one in the sea thinking it would cut its fever. When it didn't, she put him down and lost interest."

Sangora took a sheep hide, threw it on the flat rock near the fire and stretched himself out on it. He wanted to put down his head and sleep, but he was in strange surroundings with very strange people. He watched Hendrie, who despite being younger than the shepherd, reminded him of Tromp, his weariness and disdain. Dikkop still had the anger. The anger kept him alive. But it was a dangerous anger. There wasn't room for error.

Sangora's eyes closed against his will. When he opened them again, he realized that he had slept. The rush of the sea had woken him. The level had risen and was several feet high; swirling, eddying, angry floods of twisting waves crashing about the walls of the cave. They were safe where they were although not out of reach of the spray. It wasn't dark yet and he saw the roasted chicken leg and boiled cabbage on a tin plate near his head. It was for him, he thought. The drosters had kept him his share. Again he would have chicken. Again God had seen to him.

A sobbing sound made him turn. It was the woman, with her head down, sniffling. Dikkop had his arm around her shoulder, Aron was staring sightlessly at the fire, Hendrie at the cave wall, leaning his weight against it, watching. Sangora didn't have to be told what had happened.

Hendrie saw that he had woken up. "The child's dead," he said.

Dikkop turned. "It's your doing, maleier. Bringing your bad luck to us. He must go, Hendrie."

"He's fed you this night."

"You're defending him?"

"I'm not defending him. We're only six. There's strength in numbers."

Dikkop opened his mouth to say something, then slumped back into place next to Venus.

Sangora was not disturbed by the exchange. Dikkop had said the words, but there was no power in them. It was something he had to say. His heart was heavy with the loss of his child. And Sangora felt an empathy for these people. They were no different from the displaced ones at Zoetewater. Their clothes stank and they lived in a cave, but there was the same tie that held them together in grief.

"We should bury the child," Sangora suggested. "We can't leave him lying here. It's still light."

They all looked at him.

"It's better for his soul," he added quickly.

"His soul?" Dikkop asked, not understanding.

"Yes. He has a soul. His soul is with God. He's free now. Even if you don't believe, let him have the dignity of his grave."

Dikkop's eyes shone like glass. He got up, and picked up the bundle to his chest. "Come, Venus."

Hendrie picked up a shovel and followed. Sangora brought up the rear. Aron remained at the fire.

They were halfway through the dank channel when they stopped abruptly at the sound of voices travelling towards them.

"It's Boegie and Plaatjes," Hendrie said. "Someone's with them. Listen."

The noise got louder. Minutes later they were face to face in the dark tunnel.

"What's all this? I could hear you from far," Dikkop said.

"We found this bastard sniffing around."

"Who?"

"We don't know. Keep still before I gut you!"

"You're making a mistake," a new voice said.

Sangora's heart leapt. "Harman!"

"Who's this?" someone else asked in the dark, hearing Sangora's voice for the first time.

"Go back outside. We can't see anything."

When they got out into the light, Boegie and Plaatjes saw the dead child for the first time, and Sangora saw the knife held at Harman's side. Dikkop also got his first look at the intruder.

"Who are you? What're you doing here?"

Harman jerked himself free from Boegie. "I came for him. Sangora and I know each other."

"Is that true?" Hendrie asked Sangora.

"He's the kneg on the farm where we work, a friend."

"Why are you here?" Dikkop asked. "To hand him to the hangman?"

"We have to talk," Harman said to Sangora, ignoring Dikkop. "You're in trouble."

"That's enough talking," Dikkop interrupted. "What're we going to do with him? It's getting dark. We have a child to bury."

Hendrie spat on the ground. "Let him go."

"They'll give us away," Plaatjes said.

"Why would we?" Harman asked. "This slave's a fugitive. I wasn't here. You never saw me. No white man or slave came this way."

"What do you mean?"

"I mean I don't want anyone to know even that we passed through. I came here to help Sangora."

"Why should we believe you?" Dikkop asked.

"You don't have to. *He* has to. Ask him."

Dikkop tried to read the white man's eyes. They were strange eyes. He'd not seen eyes like that on a white man before, and they didn't tell him anything. His manner said more. The way he stood unafraid before a pack of drosters who could kill him in an instant. Dikkop felt uncertain about this man, but he knew the maleier trusted him.

"The devil get your mother if you betray us," he said finally.

"Go now, before he changes his mind," Hendrie added.

"Wait!" Dikkop stopped them. "Come with me first. There's something I want the maleier to do." He started down the mountain towards the sea in the gathering mist with the child in his arms. They followed him to a clump of rocks a few hundred feet from the edge of the cliff. The ground was hard and stony, and he selected a place between a rock and a bush. Hendrie took the pick axe, and struck into the earth. Boegie and Plaatjes got down on their knees and scooped out the earth with their hands. Venus walked away and went to stand at the edge of the cliff, looking out to sea.

It was all too unreal for Sangora. The small vault, waiting for its earthly deposit. The mist creeping down the slope. The woman at the edge of the cliff, her dress billowing in the breeze. A string of faces, all tied together by grief. He looked at Harman at the back of the group, standing deep in thought.

Dikkop stepped into the grave and laid down the child. "Say a few words for his soul."

Sangora realized that Dikkop was talking to him. "He's facing the wrong way."

"Which way should he face?"

"East."

Dikkop picked up the bundle and turned it the other way. Sangora looked up briefly at the darkening sky. He cupped his hands and started to pray. The men stood solemnly around the grave listening to the strange words, trusting that they would convey the right message to the right powers.

"He's with God," Sangora said finally. "Nothing more you can do."

When the grave was filled and covered with rocks, they stood about for a few awkward minutes, not knowing what to say to each other.

"You can go now," Dikkop said to Sangora. Then without another word, he started to walk away, Hendrie and the others following silently behind. Venus remained where she was, at the edge of the cliff.

"I can't go back, Harman," Sangora said as soon as they were alone. "You know what they're going to do to me, no one's going to believe my side of the story, no one. I can't. You mustn't ask me to come back. It was a bad thing that happened – but it all happened so quickly. I was so angry, and when she started to scream, everything inside me broke loose. I'd never been so angry, I lost control."

"You're not going back," Harman reassured him. "I have a plan. I don't know how good it is or if it'll work or fool anyone, but I have no other ideas, so we'll have to try it. Who's that woman over there?" he nodded to the lone figure at the edge of the cliff.

"She's with Dikkop. She's not right in the head."

"It might help us. Now here's what I want you to do. Listen."

Sangora listened carefully as Harman outlined his plan. It was the most outrageous thing he had ever heard, fraught with danger. It depended on many factors coming together to make it work, and even then there was no guarantee that the law wouldn't eventually catch up with him. But there was no other plan, no time to work out another, and this one was so ridiculous that they had to plunge into it right away before they thought better about it. Sangora trusted Harman who was putting himself in jeopardy. If Harman Kloot didn't think the idea mad, Sangora thought there had to be a remote chance of success.

"Are you ready?"

"Yes."

Harman looked at the woman a few hundred feet to their left. "Hurry now, before she turns this way."

Sangora clambered quickly over the cliff. Several minutes later there was a loud scream.

Harman peered over the cliff. "Oh, my God! No!"

The woman heard the screams, and turned.

"The stupid fool jumped! Sangora jumped!"

Venus stared at him blankly. She walked slowly over to the spot where Harman indicated, and peered down. But there was nothing to see except the waves rolling and crashing against the rocks. Whatever had fallen down there had already been swallowed up by the sea.

Harman was frantic. "You have to get help. Oh my God! I don't know why he jumped. One minute he was talking to me, and the next, he flung himself over! Maybe he's still alive!"

The woman just stared at him.

"Please, I beg you, get the others. We have to go down there."

"He brought a chicken," she said.

"What?"

"He couldn't save the child."

"Please, go and call someone. There's a man down there! Perhaps we can still save him. Tell them to bring a rope!"

Venus turned back to the sea. Her face was childlike and calm. She stood for a few moments, then drifted silently into the fog in the same direction the men had gone.

Harman settled down on a boulder. He would wait. He hoped she would tell Dikkop and the others about Sangora's disappearance and that they would remember what she'd told them. But maybe she would say nothing at all. She was strange enough. He waited and waited. No one came. The sky closed and the silence settled around him. When he couldn't see his hand before him in the dark and was convinced no one would come, he leaned over the edge of the cliff.

"Sangora . . ."

For a moment there was no answer and his heart leapt with fear.

"I'm here," the voice came, not too far down.

"Thank God, you're all right. Get up here."

"They're not coming?"

"I don't think so."

Sangora clambered up over the edge. "I tore my pants on a branch. Half of the one leg's gone." He indicated the torn fabric ruefully. "You think they'll believe it?"

"We can't think of that now, we have to get away. I have the horse hidden, let's go. The woman will tell them what happened."

"She doesn't speak."

"She told me about a chicken."

"She did? I heard you tell her to get help."

"And just like I suspected, she didn't. But at some point she'll say something, I'm sure of it."

Sangora felt a flicker of hope. Perhaps Gumtsa had been right. Perhaps he would have a chance.

Boeta Mai was in a deep sleep when an urgent knock on the door woke him up. At first, he thought it was the wind, then he heard it again. Someone had died, he thought. That would be the only reason for a call in the middle of the night. He thought immediately of his sister and her family. But he'd seen them just two days ago, they were all well, no one was sick. Maybe it was the law. But what had he done? Had Soleiman done anything? All this raced through his mind as he got out of bed and walked with bare feet down the passage.

"Who is it?" he asked, leaning his head against the front door.

"Boeta Mai?"

He recognized the voice. "Harman? My goodness."

"Yes."

The door opened.

"I'm sorry to disturb you at this hour. So sorry, but it's urgent. Can we come in?"

"Of course," Boeta Mai urged them to enter. "What happened? Why are you here this time of the night?"

"A terrible thing's happened. Sangora's in big trouble, and I couldn't think of anyone else. I'm so sorry to bring this to you, but perhaps you can help us out."

Boeta Mai closed the door. "Let's go talk in the kitchen."

Sangora started his story, beginning with Somiela running out in the yard screaming after being burned with boiling water, ending with the staged suicide at Hanglip.

Boeta Mai shook his head in disbelief, both at what had transpired at Zoetewater, then at the sheer courageousness of the plan. He was so astounded by the two men before him, their unbelievable tale, he couldn't think of anything to say. Did the son of Roeloff Kloot know what he was doing? Helping a slave escape? Was he mad? Sometimes naivety worked in your favour, but not always. He and Maryam had talked many times of Harman's visit to their home. They did not know the other children, but agreed that he was definitely his father's child. There was the same compassion for people who couldn't defend themselves. Also the same foolhardiness and blind bravery.

"We got away without being seen," Harman added. "And no one saw us come here."

"I can't believe what I'm hearing. To even think of it. It's very daring, and might just work. Sometimes it's better not to examine a thing too closely or you won't do it. Still, the whole thing rests on what the farmer believes when you tell him. That will be the crucial moment. For all that you are the brother of his son-in-law, he might not believe it, and might still call in the authorities to investigate."

"I've thought of that," Harman said. "He probably will do it. But I had no choice. I can't take Sangora back to Zoetewater, and can't have him still on the run and hunted. Staging a fake death was the only thing I could think of. That's the first part. The second part is, where do we go now, where to hide Sangora. There, I have no ideas – other than coming here for advice. I can't go to my brother, he's bound by the law. He's also tied by marriage to the farmer. And I can't go to my sister and involve her and Braam in something like this. Also, I have an agreement with De Villiers. What Sangora did, compromised that agreement." Harman paused. "I'm counting on the woman at Hanglip to back up my story. She's not right in the head, but I think she believed what she saw, or what she thinks she saw, and it might still work in our favour if the authorities ever go out there and question her. It's a daring plan, I know, but we've done it, we can't go back on it now."

Boeta Mai had listened to every word. The more he listened to Harman, the more he felt in sympathy with the young man. Still, he had to point out to him that it was no frivolous matter. "It's dangerous to harbour a man on the run, you know that. A man like me could lose everything. My family would suffer. At the same time, I can't stand by and do nothing."

The two men waited.

Boeta Mai drummed the fingers of his right hand on the table. He was thinking. "I know a freeman in Tulbagh," he said at last. "He and his sons look after a small wheat farm for a widow. He hires people. You may be able to lose yourself there."

"It's safe?" Sangora asked.

"Safer than here. I could put you up in the shop in Long Street, but you don't want someone spotting you and reporting it. It would be safer for you in the country."

"What if this man doesn't agree?"

"He will. He's a friend. Sollie will take you tomorrow night. I'll take care of the arrangements. You need clothes, shoes. A new name. Sangora doesn't exist after tonight."

Harman and Sangora looked at each other.

"So my name gets changed once again."

"This time you have no choice, Sangora," Harman said. "This might be the thing that saves you in the end, erasing your identity."

"My real name will still be in the slave book."

"We don't know that. It might, it might not. I'll see what I can find out about that."

Sangora turned his attention to the older man. "I can't thank Boeta enough."

"Don't thank me yet. I'm just the man with the plan. We still have to do it. The rest is luck and chance."

Harman arrived back at Zoetewater a few hours before dawn, unsaddled his horse and walked wearily to his quarters. Halfway across the yard, he saw the kitchen door open, and Andries de Villiers step out with a lamp in his hand. He had hoped to have a night's sleep before having to deal with the farmer, but it was unavoidable now. He had taken his leave of Sangora after giving him ten rix dollars and promising that he would keep in touch through Boeta Mai. Harman had been on the road for three days now. His body felt heavy, his head ready to drop off his shoulders with fatigue.

"Harman, is that you?"

Harman prepared himself. Everything depended on how convincing he was, the farmer's receptivity, his mood. He would know immediately whether the plan had a remote chance of succeeding.

"It's me, yes."

Andries walked up. "I've been going mad here with worry. I thought I would wait up just in case you came back tonight. Did you find him?"

"The news isn't good."

"What do you mean?"

"I tracked him all the way to Hanglip. He killed himself."

"What?" Andries's voice went up a pitch.

"He didn't want to come back, and jumped off the cliff into the sea. I couldn't stop him. I didn't know he was going to jump."

Andries grew red in the face with disbelief and rage. "I don't believe it."

Harman sighed. "I'm sorry. I'm very tired. If you want to talk about it in the morning . . ."

"What do you mean he jumped off the cliff? Didn't you talk to him? Didn't you tell him what I said?"

"I didn't have a chance. I reasoned with him. He didn't believe me. The next thing I know, he's gone over."

"But what man would do such a thing?"

"I don't know," Harman replied, trying to keep the sarcasm out of his voice. "I rode back immediately to come and tell you. The best thing is to go to the authorities. His body might still be there, but I doubt it. The sea's very high where he went down. And very dangerous."

Andries found it hard to accept. "This is all very confusing. You find him, and he ends his life. How can that be? You know what this means."

"I don't."

"We don't have an agreement."

Harman looked at him. The lamp had a dull glow, but he could see the pig eyes clearly. "Our agreement was the last thing on my mind. I would've thought Sangora's safe return would've been your first priority also. But I hear you, and will rethink my situation at Zoetewater." Without waiting for a response, he picked up his things and walked off.

"Wait a minute!" Andries called after him.

Harman continued. He really didn't care. He had done what he could. As Boeta Mai said, everything now was luck and chance. And help from God. In his room, he pulled off his boots and fell wearily into bed. There was a knock on the door.

"Who is it?" He wasn't in the mood for questions now.

"It's me, Arend," the voice whispered.

"Come in."

Arend entered and stood awkwardly before him. "Sorry to

disturb you, Mijnheer, very sorry, but we heard you come back, and we're all anxious to know what happened. If you found Sangora."

"Sangora's dead," Harman said flatly. "He jumped off the cliff at Hanglip before I could stop him. I don't want to talk about it right now. I'm too tired."

Arend's body rested heavily against the back of the door. He couldn't process what he'd just heard. "He's dead?"

"Yes. Please, I'll talk to you all in the morning."

"But – "

"Arend, please. In the morning. He's dead, there's nothing anyone can do about it."

Arend left, and Harman fell instantly asleep. When he opened his eyes, the sun was out and there was a knock on the door. His head felt heavy, his throat dry. "Who is it?" he asked for the second time in less than six hours, not bothering to get out of bed.

"Somiela," the voice came from the other side of the door.

"Come in," he said.

Somiela opened the door gingerly and looked in. "You're still sleeping," she said, surprised to find him still in bed. He was usually in the kitchen when the first bread came out of the oven. "I heard what happened. Is it true?"

"Yes. Come in. I don't feel too good this morning. My head feels like there're stones in it. Sit down."

Somiela came in, highly agitated, but didn't sit down. She felt uncomfortable being in his room, and kept the door open. "What happened? It's hard to believe that he did this. Not Sangora. We don't believe in this kind of thing – there's punishment for taking your own life." She clasped and unclasped her hands. "And Sangora, who's so religious, how could he do it? He must've been very disturbed. Did he speak to you? Say anything?"

"I don't want to talk about it, Somiela, not now. It's all too fresh in my mind. I will ride out to your mother and inform her as soon as I can. But listen to me, this is going to change things around here."

"What do you mean?"

"I may not stay here for long."

"You mean, you may leave?"

"I may have to."

She was silent for a moment. "And me? You'll forget me."

"I'll never forget you, no matter what. But my hands are tied. I tried to work out something with Andries, and it didn't work. I can't think right now, my head's full. Has he said anything?"

"He's gone for the fiscal. Left as soon as he got up."

Harman closed his eyes. So the fiscal would come. Would this be to report a suicide, or to investigate? His head throbbed. He needed something to clear it. He hadn't eaten all of yesterday, and now he had the men waiting under the tree, waiting to start work, waiting for an explanation. He didn't know where to start.

"I need coffee. Is there any going in the kitchen? And some bread?"

"Yes. There's last night's meat and potatoes. I'll get it ready for you."

"Perhaps a good breakfast will open my head. But I don't want to see anyone in the house."

"I can bring it to you."

Harman threw back his blanket and sat with his legs over the side of the bed. He was still in the clothes he'd travelled in, crumpled and dirty. "I've never been this tired before. Not only my body. Everything feels heavy." He stood up and came to stand in front of her. "Now listen to me, Somiela," he said, looking deep into her eyes. "I want you to trust me. Don't ask too many questions just now. Just trust me. Whatever happens, whatever you hear, just know that it will all work out."

She raised her eyes to his. "I trust you."

"How's your shoulder? With all of this, I forgot to ask."

She touched her hand lightly to the spot. "Sore. But the doctor put stuff on it. It's helping."

"She's not bothering you in the house?"

Somiela knew he meant Marieta. He had long ago stopped using seur or nooi when referring to the farmer and his wife. "He's warned her to leave me alone. Rachel heard him talking to her in the voorkamer, she told me. And Rachel's in trouble also, for standing up for me. So there're two of us. I'd better go and bring you your breakfast. Do you want it here?"

"Yes," he nodded, sitting down on the bed again. "I need a few more minutes before I go out there and see all those angry faces."

Andries returned with three men late in the afternoon and came straight to where Harman was in the pressing house.

"They want to ask you some questions. Let's go outside."

Harman followed them out to the stream where he was introduced to them; two Afrikanders, and the fiscal, an Englishman. He hid his surprise, and wondered how it must've annoyed Andries de Villiers to find out that the very fiscal whose help he sought belonged to the race he hated so much.

"Tell us what happened," the fiscal said.

Harman told them how he had tracked Sangora to Hanglip, and begged him to return to Zoetewater. Sangora was afraid he wouldn't get a fair hearing. The next thing he knew, Sangora had hurled himself over the cliff.

"We've just come from there," the fiscal said. "We found a strange woman wandering about. We tried to get her to talk. She wouldn't. We don't know where she's from, but she responded to our questions. She pointed out a spot where someone had gone down."

Harman waited with his heart in his mouth. He knew there was more.

"Fanie and Koos climbed down to investigate, and found a torn piece of clothing on one of the bushes. But there was nothing to indicate a body had crashed onto the rocks."

"It could've fallen directly into the sea."

"It could've."

Harman looked the Englishman cold in the eye. It was obvious to him that the man wasn't convinced. "Are you doubting me?"

The fiscal didn't respond to his question. "Were you friends with this man?"

"We liked each other. I would've done many things for him, but I don't think I would've helped him over a cliff."

"You could've helped him escape."

"Is that what you've come here to tell me?"

"No. We haven't come here to tell you that. We're *not* convinced that he went over that cliff, but have nothing to indicate that he didn't. The matter's closed. Sangora van Java drowned."

Harman tried not to show his relief. He turned to the farmer who had watched him intently throughout. "Does this alter anything between us? Our agreement?"

"It alters nothing. There's no agreement."

"Well, then, it's the twentieth today. I'll work until the end of the month, and then I'll be gone." For just a moment he was tempted to lay bare the whole rotten mess; to tell the fiscal why Sangora had run away and tell him also that De Villiers had had him in chains when he first came. Harman tipped his hat to the men, shook hands with the Englishman just to aggravate the farmer, and returned to the pressing house.

That night, long after Harman had gone to his quarters and the men in the jongenshuis had fallen asleep, one of the slaves got up quietly from his mattress. He went outside and relieved himself near a tree. When he was done, he looked suspiciously about him, then walked quickly to the stable. Andries de Villiers was already there, waiting for him.

"So? What did you hear?"

"He's dead, Seur."

"It's true, then."

"Yes, Seur. The inlander's so upset, he can't even talk about it. He was friends with Sangora."

"What else is he saying?"

"Nothing, Seur. He walked around with a long face all day. Doesn't say anything."

"And the others?"

"What does Seur mean?"

"They're aggrieved?"

"They can't believe it. Everyone liked Sangora."

"Who has the Mohametan taught to write?"

"No one," Hanibal lied.

"Has he converted anyone, or tried to?"

"No, Seur. He talked about his faith, but never tried to convince us of anything."

There was a moment's silence. Hanibal waited. He hated the position he was in. There had been no one reporting on the men since Kananga's departure, and Andries de Villiers had cornered Hanibal one Sunday afternoon when the others were out. The farmer had told him in no few words what he wanted, forcing him into betrayal against his own friends. Hanibal was determined never to say anything that compromised a man's safety, but the deception weighed heavily on him, and was the cause of his headaches and fevers.

"And the girl?"

"Seur?" He was surprised by the question as he knew nothing of Somiela's doings. Somiela wasn't his concern. She was the inlander's and Salie's and Arend's. They were the ones always talking about her. And Andries de Villiers had never before asked about her.

"Are any of them – is there anything going on?"

"Oh no, Seur," he said quickly, honestly, almost adding that Somiela was the inlander's, but stopping himself just in time.

"What else can you tell me?"

"Nothing, Seur."

"Come, come, I know you all talk. What're they complaining about? Slaves are always complaining, there must be something."

Hanibal thought desperately of something to tell him, something small, to satisfy the farmer without getting anyone in trouble.

"Well, the mattresses, Seur," he said, daring to say it.

"The mattresses?" Andries asked incredulously. "What about them?"

Hanibal backed off slightly at the rise in the farmer's voice. "They're thin, Seur, we can feel the cold right through them. And Petroos didn't get a jacket this year."

"This is what you're all talking about, mattresses, and jackets, and what you didn't receive?"

"Yes, Seur."

"Who's talking about it?"

Hanibal thought quickly. "All of us, Seur."

"There's no trouble brewing over the maleier's death?"

"Trouble, Seur?" he pretended not to understand.

"No one's talking strange things, talking of making trouble?"

"Oh no, Seur, people are sorry that the Mohametan's gone and killed himself, but there's no trouble."

Andries was silent for a moment. "Well, keep your ears open. And don't let me find out you're keeping anything from me."

"Yes, Seur."

The news came first from the kitchen, and spread quickly. Harman and the farmer had had words, he was leaving Zoetewater at the end of the month. From where they sat under the mulberry tree eating their last meal of the day – they were eating there rather than under the apricot tree, so that they were out of view of the kitchen window – the slaves watched Harman at the water barrel washing himself. They sat quietly wiping their bread around their plates, their eyes missing nothing. They felt aggrieved. He'd told them that first day that he would treat them in the same fair way that he wanted to be treated. Was it fair to leave and not say one word to them? Were they to hear this from the kitchen, or from the farmer when he was already on his horse riding away? Why was he leaving?

Harman looked in their direction briefly, nodded, then crossed the yard and left.

"How could he just leave us like this?" Hanibal asked. "Zoetewater's cursed. People getting sick, running away, killing themselves. Everyone's leaving. What's going to happen to us now?"

"Someone has to talk to him," Tromp said.

Salie collected the empty plates. "Arend can do it. He's the best one. The inlander and I don't see eye to eye."

"Whose fault is that?" Arend asked.

"Alright, you two," Tromp interrupted. "Arend, you'll do it?"

"If I have to. When?"

"The sooner the better. We don't want him to get used to the idea that he's going. The longer we leave it, the stronger will be his intention to get away."

"But he hasn't even told us that he's going. Maybe he'll even change his mind. Maybe my mother's wrong."

"Your mother's never wrong. Tonight, Arend," Tromp insisted. "The end of the month is a week away."

Salie took the plates up to the house and the men moved from the mulberry to the apricot tree where they had a clear view of the

224

back door. When they saw the kitchen door open and Harman emerge, they waited a few minutes, then slipped quickly across the yard to his quarters. Outside the door, Arend turned to them and motioned with his hand that he wanted them to stand just behind him, not to crowd into the room. He knocked on the door.

Harman opened it almost immediately. "Arend. Is something wrong?"

"We don't know, and we hope that we're the ones who are mistaken, but in case we're not, we've come to beg you to change your mind."

Harman looked at the group of men, and stepped outside. "Change my mind?"

"Yes. We heard that you're leaving, and we're distressed by this news." The men had talked earlier of what Arend would say and while they knew the real reason Harman was leaving, had decided to take the blame – anything that would make Harman Kloot stay. "We know we haven't always listened," Arend continued, "but we'll be more obedient if you give us another chance. Even Tromp wants you to stay. And Salie. All of us. We're grieved by what happened to Sangora and still can't believe that he's dead. And if you leave also, we'll have no one."

Harman looked at the expectant faces. He wished he could tell them the truth. "It's not any of you, you haven't done anything. Things change. Circumstances force you into doing things. I have no choice."

"But the seur will win if you go. You need work, and we've got used to you. He'll get a mandoor again. What cruelty can we expect then? Our numbers are getting smaller. He's lost his investment with Sangora, he'll take it out on us, make us work twice as hard. And what about Somiela? Are you forgetting? Sangora's not here any more to protect her. Who'll protect her now?"

Harman smiled. "*You* will watch out for Somiela. Your mother will watch out for her. Salie. And what would Sangora say if he were here? He would say that God will watch out for Somiela. I can't do anything for Somiela if I can't do anything for myself. I'm sorry to let you all down. I got used to you also."

"You are saying you are going then?"

"I'm afraid so."

"So we'll go back to where we were, before Sangora came, before you came, and have no snot of an inkling as to what we can expect for a kneg."

Harman was surprised by the interpreter's tone. He could see from the other faces that they were relying on Arend to persuade him. "Don't make this worse, Arend. You know that's not true. You've gone on from that. Sangora's made you all stronger. He's given these people something to think about. You're not the same people you were a year ago. His courage speaks for a lot."

"It doesn't speak for anything if he threw himself off a cliff," Tromp interjected with a snort. "What did we learn from that? That a man has a breaking point, that despite his God, his God couldn't save him?"

Later that evening in the jongenshuis, the men were restless and querulous. Arend's pleading had done nothing, and one blamed the other for Harman's departure.

"It's not anyone's fault," Tromp said wearily. "Arend did the best he could. It's not his words, or lack of them. Can't you all see why he's leaving? You all think yourselves such experts on what goes on in his head. He's leaving as a matter of principle. We know that he had words with the farmer. The moerneuker went back on his word, blaming him for Sangora's death, as if he had told that hard-headed maleier to jump off a cliff. Why'd he do such a stupid thing, anyway?"

Salie didn't like the way the old shepherd referred to Sangora. "He's dead, Tromp. We don't speak ill of the dead."

"The dead have no ears."

"Doesn't matter. If a heathen has no respect, we have. And from the way you challenged the inlander, I didn't think you would defend him."

"I'm not defending him, but it's no use trying to blame him. The place is cursed, and that's it. There's no mystery. We should kill those moerneukers in their sleep."

"Right, Tromp, a good idea. Then we can all hang by our necks."

A young voice at the back of the room spoke for the first time.

"We're not going to do what we said the other night?"

They all looked at Hanibal.

"You mean you thought we were serious?" Salie laughed. "Get it out of your head. It's too dangerous. Don't even think it."

"We all had too much to drink when we discussed it," Petroos added. "We weren't thinking. Can you imagine what they would do to us if we were found to be responsible?"

Hanibal raised himself up on his elbow. "So all that talk was for nothing."

"Sometimes it's just good to talk and let it out, to dream," Arend said. "We can dream. Dreaming's not dangerous. But I don't know about the others, I don't want to speak for them. I'm out."

"Me too," Salie said quickly.

"And me," Petroos added.

"I'm too old for this shit," Tromp sighed. "But if I had twenty more years . . ."

Elspeth was knitting on the stoep when she saw Harman come galloping towards the house on his mare. What was he doing there, she wondered? It wasn't even Sunday. Sunday was when he liked to come, when he visited his brother, and afterwards dropped by his sister's house. She rested the knitting on her lap and watched him approach. He cut a striking figure with his long hair floating back off his shoulders, and she wondered what it would be like to be held in those strong arms. Would it be like being held by his brother? No, she thought, there was a fire that burned inside Harman. That fire would consume her. She didn't delude herself that Harman had any grand feelings for her. Despite his civility, there was dislike. She sensed it, in the coldness of his eyes when he smiled, in the way he kept silent when Martinus referred to anything that involved her. He came because of his brother, and tolerated her because she was the wife. She didn't know whether she liked any of the Kloot family, or whether they even liked her. The father, especially, had a way of looking at you that made you immediately want to own up to your sins if you had any, and it was remarkable how much Harman resembled him in manner. It was this manner that unnerved her.

227

But she'd tempered her feelings. Harman no longer held for her the same fascination he once had. Men, she had discovered, were really all the same – she had only to look at her mother's unhappiness, or listen to Van Heerden's wife's complaints. Her belly was growing heavier with Martinus's child. Martinus was busy day and night with his papers, and she spent most of her time alone. This gave her time to think. She was happy to be married, but it wasn't what she'd thought. Living in town was different to living on a farm. She lived on a street with other people, but had only made one friend, and longed for her mother, the mischievousness of the twins, the bustle and activity of Zoetewater, even the firm remonstrations of Rachel who sometimes forgot she was a slave. There had always been a neighbour visiting them with news, a story someone had to tell, a quarrel with the slaves, a new lamb in the kraal. Her days with Martinus were marked with the same boredom and loneliness. Martinus got up, he went to work, he came home with papers and worked some more. She was hoping the baby would make him a little more attentive. And when the time neared, she would speak to her mother about Somiela. Somiela could come and help with the child. Yes, she thought, brightening. Her house would take on the semblance of a real home with laughter and voices and servants and the smell of good food. She had always liked Somiela's cooking, and no longer felt threatened by the girl. A few months of marriage had clarified things. Men had a few moments of delirium when they called you every pleasurable thing under the sun, then they pulled up their pants, and dismissed you until the next time. She felt more threatened by Martinus's work than by any interest he might have in a slave.

"Afternoon," Harman greeted, tying the reins to a hook in the stoep wall. "How are you?"

Elspeth got up from her chair to show him her condition. It was obvious now in the new dress.

"I am well. What brings you here on a Wednesday afternoon?"

"I was in town on some business for your father. It's my last week at the farm."

"Your last week?" This was news to her. "I didn't know. Something's happened?"

"Yes. Your father will tell you."

"I'm sorry to hear that you're leaving," she said, meaning it. "What will you do now?"

"I don't know. Martinus is home?"

"Yes. He's got some papers spread out on the big table in the kitchen. He has a document he has to prepare for tomorrow."

"I'll find him," Harman said. "Please don't let me disturb you."

Harman stepped into the house and found his brother with his head bent over a pile of documents and open books. He knew from Elspeth's demeanour that Martinus hadn't told her of his last visit, and was grateful for that. He'd spoken rashly, expecting the impossible. But would he be even more impossible now? Dare he?

Martinus looked up, surprised. "Harman."

"You're surprised to see me."

"Yes. I thought after the last time . . ."

Harman pulled up a chair and sat down next to him. "It wasn't fair, what I asked."

Martinus was relieved to hear that he'd been forgiven. He'd suffered his own guilt over it, and hadn't forgotten either what else Harman had told him about their father, the Sonqua woman, and himself. "I'm glad you understand. I really wrestled with it. I was in such an awkward position."

"Well, don't speak so quickly. I'm here to give you a real sleepless night now."

"What do you mean?"

Harman looked towards the passage. "You have to give me your word, Martinus, that what I'm about to say, whether you agree or disagree, will stay between us."

The smile went slowly from Martinus's eyes. "Am I going to regret what I'm about to hear?"

"Very much."

"Then why tell me?"

"Because you're a landdrost, you know the law, you can help me. You're also blood."

Martinus sat motionless for a minute, looking at his brother. "What is it?"

"I have your word?"

"You have it."

Harman nodded. "All right. "When I left here the last time and arrived back at the farm, the whole place was in an uproar. Apparently, Sangora tried to talk to Marieta to find out why she'd burned Somiela, but as he was approaching her, Marieta screamed, and he lost all control. He attacked her, your father-in-law came out with the rifle and fired shots, and Sangora ran away. I was sent after him, to bring him back. I tracked him all the way to Hanglip. I found him there with a band of drosters." Martinus was listening with the concentration of a judge, and Harman paused to give him time to digest what he'd said and to prepare him for the next jolt. "I was in a terrible bind. I knew what had happened and knew what would happen to him if Andries got his hands on him. Sangora's a good man. His stepdaughter was compromised. He was provoked. I couldn't bring him back. He wouldn't have a chance." He paused again, willing Martinus to understand what he was about to say next. "I staged a suicide."

Martinus sat back in shock. "You staged what?"

"I staged a suicide, yes, at Hanglip, then took him in the middle of the night to some people I knew. And I'll tell you more about them another time. These people helped him. They took him the next night to a farm in the country. He's there under another name. I returned to Zoetewater and told Andries that Sangora threw himself over a cliff. He called in the authorities. They went out there, then came to see me. I kept to my story. They're not convinced, but they can't prove anything. They've closed the file, and have recorded him as drowned. Now my questions are how Sangora can go about setting up a new identity for himself without being caught, and if his name will now be removed from the slave book."

Martinus was stunned by the disclosure. "You are mad, Harman. I'm convinced of it. You've aided a fugitive! Helped him escape!"

"Martinus, don't preach at me now. Please. I'm serious."

"I'm serious also. I'm a landdrost, for heaven's sake! Look what you've done. Don't you have any regard for the law? What do you think will happen if they find out? You're in serious trouble. And now you want to involve me. I could lose everything I've worked for."

Harman closed his eyes and leaned back in his chair. When he spoke again, his voice was tired, resigned. "I don't want to involve you, Martinus. I only need your advice. You need never admit to anything, and I'll never say I came to you. I helped a man. I have no regrets. I want to know how he can go about establishing a new identity for himself. You're a landdrost, you have knowledge I don't have. I'm asking you for advice, not to get involved. Just advice." He stopped and weighed his next words carefully. "I realize that I expected too much last time. I expected you to choose between a wife and a brother. It was wrong to expect such a thing. Still, Martinus, I want to know in my heart that my own brother has feelings for other people. I couldn't bear it if he turned out to be just an upholder of the law, whether or not that law was fair. I want to know that you're fair in your heart. I have to know that you're just. I have to know that you're my brother first, and that no matter what, blood is blood, and no law will dilute it. Maybe I'm selfish, maybe I expect more now than the last time, but I need to know we're on the same side."

"You *are* selfish."

"And you *are* my brother."

Martinus leaned back in his chair. He didn't speak immediately. "Do you know what you've done?"

"Yes."

"I'm privy to this knowledge now."

"I know."

"If the truth ever comes out, my life's ruined."

Harman said nothing. He waited to hear what was next.

Martinus got up from his chair, and walked to the stove. "You want coffee?"

Harman relaxed. "Please."

Martinus poured a thick black liquid into two cups, stirring three teaspoons of sugar into them. "I wonder what Pa would say to something like this."

"You want me to tell you?"

"Tell me."

"He would not say anything. He'd think about it. And act with his heart."

In the kitchen a few days later, Somiela sat with the twins at the table, reading to them from a book they'd brought home from school.

She liked reading to them. It was a chance to discover new material, and it was also one of the times when there was no division between them. The girls liked it when she injected her own imagination into the tale, and made things up. And she could make up quite a lot. She'd hatched a whole story around Harman. How he would love her, how he would convert to her religion, how they would live happily ever after with a house full of children, twelve chickens, and a cow. The imagination was a safe place. She alone made the rules and supplied the action. But Harman was leaving, and had his own story. Of what use were her dreams now? Her dreams couldn't control what he wanted to do. He said he wouldn't forget, but that did little to still her fears. There were lots of women casting about for husbands – women more suited, of the same ilk; women like Van Heerden's two daughters, who although plain as potato dumplings, had property and status. What chance did she have? Harman liked her, and did have feelings, but were they enough to commit him to a life as an outsider with a half-breed? Men said a lot of things, her mother said. What they said in the heat of passion held little value in the cold light of day. Three times he had taken her to see her mother. Who would take her now?

"Somiela . . . I asked you a question," Annie prodded her arm.

Somiela turned. "I'm sorry. What did you ask?"

"I asked whether you could change the ending. You told us that one already."

"I did, didn't I? Maybe tomorrow. I can't think right now."

"But you promised."

"I know I did, but it's getting late. I have to set the table."

Rachel was at the stove, stirring beans into one of the pots. She heard the exchange.

"You two, go and wash your hands. And go tell your mother and father the food's ready."

The girls got up reluctantly and left the room. Somiela took out the plates and set them out on the table.

"Don't brood," Rachel said. "Things will work out."

"You don't understand."

"I don't? You think Rachel wasn't young once? You think I don't know what it's like to want something and not be able to have it? I was once where you're now. It's not a good place to be."

"If things didn't work out for you, how will they for me?"

"The inlander's turned the world upside down for you already. He's not one to give up."

"By leaving, he's giving up."

"He's not leaving. He's doing what he has to do."

"Sangora said that pride's not good."

"Maybe it isn't, but it's what makes the inlander what he is. And maybe it's not pride. Maybe it's principle."

"His principles aren't good for me."

Rachel became impatient. "Stop thinking of yourself only. Now, help me here with these potatoes. Dish them up, around the meat. And stop thinking so much. Let the thing flow where it must."

On his last afternoon at Zoetewater, Harman stood in a blustering wind saddling his horse and saying goodbye to the men. The village was in the grip of a terrible southeaster, and the men stood clutching their jackets about them, some still hoping that there would be a change of heart at the last moment and that he would stay. Spirits were low. Few words were said. Their eyes seemed to accuse him. He wished he could tell them that Sangora was safe.

"Here he comes," Salie said.

Harman watched as Andries de Villiers, head bowed into the wind, crossed the yard to come towards them. Just as well, Harman thought. It would save him a trip to the kitchen to get his wages.

"So this is it," Andries said, coming up. "I regret that things ended this way. In any event, there'll always be work here for you if you decide to come back. There's no need for bad blood. Like it

233

or not, we're related. I'm sorry you let personal feelings get in the way."

"You reneged on your word."

"You didn't bring him back."

Harman's eyes froze into his. "I did what you asked. I had no control over his actions."

"You knew I wanted him back."

"It didn't matter what I knew. It's what I was able to do, what I had control over. I had no control over a man who had it in his head to kill himself. He didn't say to me, 'Harman, I'm going to jump,' and give me a chance to stop him. He just did it."

Andries slid his hand into his pocket and took out the money he'd counted out earlier. He handed it to Harman. "I'm sorry things didn't work out."

Harman took the money and put it in his pocket. He got on his horse.

"Seur, look!" Arend shouted suddenly, pointing to a column of smoke.

"Good God!" Harman jumped off his horse. The fire was coming from the woodworking barn, huge flames, leaping into the sky.

"Get the buckets!" he shouted. "Ring the bell!"

Men ran in all directions.

Harman raced ahead of Andries. Why hadn't they seen the fire, smelled it on the wind? He raced across the yard, but it was already too late. The barn was a blistering inferno with giant flames licking at the walls through the roof. Nothing was going to save it.

"There's a bigger danger!" Harman shouted to Andries over the roaring crackle. "The outbuildings all have thatched roofs. With the wind and the trees and flying sparks, the fire can spread to the house!"

Andries had never seen anything this serious before. "What do you suggest?"

"We have to stop it here." Before Andries could ask how, Harman ran off to the shed. He searched around and found what he was looking for: a folded wagon-sail on one of the shelves; old, full of holes, but big enough for what he had in mind. He

234

returned to the fire and found the men with buckets and barrels, dangerously close to the heat, the women farther back, watching.

"Somiela, you and Rachel, get in there behind Tromp. You too, Annie and Leentje, pass the water up to the front. Hanibal, Petroos, Salie, wet this sail, and come with me!"

They ran to the wagon house. "Get up there and spread the sail over the roof. I'll pass up the water. Keep the sail wet and don't let go of it in the wind. We want to prevent flying sparks from igniting the thatch."

The men did as they were told. Harman heard the sound of wagons approaching, and turned; it was neighbours who'd heard the bell and seen the flames on the horizon. Several men jumped off with leather buckets and ran to the stream.

For an hour or more, men and women worked side by side, bringing buckets of water, passing them up to the front, and at last the blaze was brought under control. When the last bucket of water found its mark, all that remained of the barn and everything in it were three posts sticking out of a pile of blackened debris, and a smouldering dampness rising out of the ground.

Harman walked over to the men standing on one side, their sooty faces streaked with sweat. "Does anyone know what happened here?"

"I know nothing," Arend said.

Harman looked at Salie. "Me neither."

"Tromp? Do you know what happened?"

"Nothing happened," the old shepherd said. "It's a fire."

Harman turned to Hanibal. "Hanibal?"

Hanibal's eyes were shot with fear. His left hand trembled. Someone coughed. They all turned as Andries walked up with two neighbours.

"I don't know how this thing happened. We've never had a fire here before. The whole barn gone. Arend, did you see anything? Anything at all that looked suspicious to you? No one left a lamp going, or flint, or – or did someone start a fire in there?"

"No, Seur."

"All of you were together?"

"Yes, Seur. We were saying goodbye to the mijnheer."

Harman thought he should say something. "We've had very

dry weather and treacherous wind. Lots of tinder and coal lying about in the sun."

Andries wasn't convinced. "A fire doesn't just start on its own."

"I know, but I can't see how else it could've happened. With this wind, anything's possible."

"I've seen it happen," one of the neighbours said. "Remember the fire that almost destroyed the whole of the Cape a hundred years ago? It wasn't in our time, I know, but the story's still told. Spreading down the mountain, five houses gone in the blaze. Chickens roasted in their pens, it travelled so fast. All from the wind." He turned to Harman. "That sail was a damn good idea. There could've been real tragedy here."

"Yes," Andries agreed. "You saved this place from burning down."

"Well, it's over. And a good thing the sail worked. The men took a chance on that roof. I think some of them burned their feet. Perhaps there's some salve in the house." He put on his jacket.

"Get mijnheer's horse," Andries said to Arend.

"It's all right," Harman said. "I want to say goodbye to some people."

The three men watched him walk away.

"He's leaving?" the man to his left asked.

"Yes."

The man waited for more, but Andries didn't say anything. Andries was feeling something pass out of him, he didn't quite know what. Two men had come to Zoetewater. One had caused him grief from the start, and had then killed himself. The other was worth his weight in rix dollars, and was leaving him now. Where had he made his mistake?

It was very rainy that morning. My master had not asked me to remain in his service and therefore I did not know what he intended with us and I did not like to question him about it. In the early morning of that Monday I looked after the cattle as usual and after I had sent the cattle out of the kraal my master called me and told me to bring my tools – a spade, pick axe, and sickle to him which I did; he then told me that I was winding up the people to leave his place and ordered me to mention to all the others that those who intended to leave the place must do so immediately; we thereupon left the place tho' it rained very much; I did not ask my master to remain on the place until the weather cleared as I perceived he was angry.

(The apprentice, Jan, C.A., CO 476, no. 127, January 1839)

On a rainy morning in the winter of 1833, Andries stood knee-deep in mud with Salie and Tromp, trying to decide what to do with the cow lying groaning at their feet. Tromp had led the cattle down the slope, when the cow had lost its balance, slipped, and broken a front leg.

"I'm sorry, Seur," Tromp said. He knew he had caused serious damage. The cow was one of only three milk cows, significantly contributing to the milk and butter in the De Villiers household.

Andries was red-faced, livid with rage. "Sorry? What can sorry do? You don't care." It was three months since Harman's departure. The new foreman had worked half a season, then, fed up with a clutch of unruly men, had left for a job with a neighbouring farmer. Word had spread. Andries had heard the rumours himself: a slave with broken ribs, a half-breed getting burned, a suicide, a mysterious fire, a disgruntled kneg, rebellious slaves. No one wanted to work at the estate. He didn't hire anyone after the foreman had left and tackled the job himself, but it proved too much. His mounting weight had slowed him down and it was an effort sometimes just to get on his horse.

"You should've brought them down the other way, but that was too long a way for you. Now all you can do is stand there and say sorry."

Tromp's hooded lids flickered briefly. The insults didn't hurt any more. He hardly listened to them. What could the farmer do? He would dig his own grave if there were any more incidents at Zoetewater.

Andries took out a knife and handed it to Tromp. "We'll have to put it out of its misery."

Tromp nodded his head vigorously. "Can't we shoot it?"

Andries pushed the knife into his hand. "We're not wasting a bullet. Get a spade, Salie, and bring the others."

Tromp wanted to stand out of the rain while waiting for Salie, but remained where he was so as not to antagonize the farmer any further. He knew he would cough his lungs out that night.

Salie arrived, dug a pit near the cow's head, and took the knife from Tromp. "I'll do it," he said. With his left hand he gathered the jugular vein between thumb and index finger, and with the right hand, quickly drew the sharp knife across it. Blood spurted out thick and fast, and hit him in the chest. He held the head down until the jerking stopped and the cow's head came to rest over the pit.

It was midday by the time the carcass was disembowelled, quartered, and carried up to the house. The slaves got the head and the tail. After burying the guts, they made a fire behind the jongenshuis where they grilled the brain on the coals with small onions they'd dug up from the garden, and ate it while waiting for the head to roast on the spit. The tail they skinned and chopped up with an axe, and gave it to Somiela to stew for them with onions, tomatoes, green chillies, and cloves.

Later that same afternoon, still fired up over the loss of the cow, Andries was drinking coffee with Joost van Heerden on the stoep. They were discussing the problems at their respective farms. Joost had come to hire two of the Zoetewater slaves, and was bitter about the changes, which almost certainly would take place the following year. Andries had already had the news from Martinus. During parliamentary debates, several schemes had been presented which proposed a transitional period during which slaves had to be prepared for responsibilities after freedom. This would be done through manumission of deserving slaves, freedom for children born of slave women, and special self-purchase schemes. These measures were intended to promote self-help and incentive without throwing colonial society and production into turmoil. The slaveholders had long ago rebelled against this; Andries and Joost themselves had been part of the protest meetings against Ordinance 50. This ordinance had fixed limits to the amount of punishment owners could give their slaves, established the office of a Protector of Slaves, and given slaves the right to complain. The farmers were outraged that the law could give to a third person the odious power of interfering in the arrangement of private affairs. These officials were independent of and superior to slaveholders and struck at the heart of the master-servant relationship, undercutting their power that they were the sole source of protection and discipline. Slaveholders in turn proposed limited measures of gradualist abolition, such as the freeing of new-born children which would not threaten their control. An event which persuaded them that gradualist abolition might be necessary, and even desirable, was the slave revolt evoked by the uprising of slaves and hottentots against their owners on a remote Bokkeveld farm in 1825. This, together with the increasing assertiveness of slaves who were bringing complaints against owners and demanding rights of liberty beyond those prescribed by the amelioration laws, showed the slaveholders that something had to be done or they would have real rebellion. They understood that emancipation was inevitable, but wanted it carried out fairly, and wanted the assurance of adequate financial compensation. The problem was that slaves saw the four-year apprenticeship as a tactic on the part of owners and the authorities to perpetuate slavery beyond its final end. Many of them were starting to run away, staying away for longer periods of time, some of them never returning.

Joost was at Zoetewater that afternoon to hire July and November because two of his own slaves had deserted, and a crippled hottentot, called Dikbeen, indentured to Joost for twenty-five years, had also taken it into his head to abscond. Joost had lied to the authorities when Dikbeen had first come to the farm, saying he was eight when Dikbeen was already fifteen, thereby binding him to a longer period of service. Dikbeen, encouraged by the cheeky behaviour of the slaves on the farm, was now, ten years later, showing his own strength.

"Nothing good's come of their interference," Joost complained. "Nothing."

Andries hated the English as much as Joost did, if not more. "And it'll be worse when December first comes. Are you letting any of yours go?"

Joost gave a short, barking laugh. "I can hardly manage now, I need every hand. What about you?"

"Maybe the old one. I can't afford to keep him under the new laws. He's becoming expensive to keep. This morning I had to slaughter a cow because of him. He let the cow fall down the slope. It broke its leg. And there's an insolence amongst them. They were always insolent, but they cared to hide it before. You knew what went on in their heads, but they didn't dare show it."

"I know what you mean. If I wasn't so short of labour, I'd let that maleier of mine, Moensat, go. The other day, when I told him that he'd better take the medicine I suggested for the cold in his chest and get back to work, he had the nerve to tell me that he wasn't a jong, his name was Moensat, and sticking his finger almost in my face, said, 'We've been created by one God, and I'm as good as you.' I nearly fell off my horse."

"What did you do?"

"I wanted to take the skin off his back, but I didn't. I put him in the kraal for three days shovelling shit. I have three runaways. I didn't want to make matters worse." He got up wearily. "I have to get back. Thanks for helping me out."

"I can spare them for a few weeks."

Andries saw him off, then went into the kitchen where Marieta was sitting at the table close to the stove, knitting a yellow bonnet for the coming grandchild.

"I'm riding out to Martinus," he said.

Marieta looked up from her knitting. She knew why he was going. It wasn't to see his son-in-law or stepdaughter, but to see what he could work out with the brother who was visiting for two days. He was ready to humiliate himself.

"Elspeth can't come out any more in her condition. Maybe I should come along. It's been weeks since we've seen them."

"Yes, Pa, can we come too?" Leentje asked. "We'll be good."

"I'll be home late, and you have to be up early for school."

"But we won't see Elspeth now, until after the baby."

"I know, but Pa has things to discuss." He turned to Marieta. "You will go there next week, anyway, or the week after. It's due then, not so?"

"Yes. Did you think more about what I said? She'll need help for a few months with the baby."

"Why doesn't she have the child here?"

"It's not a good idea. And how long could she stay? She has her own home to see to. It doesn't pay for a woman to be away from it for too long. Not at a time when she's disinclined to perform all her wifely duties anyway."

Andries blinked. Wifely duties. When was the last time she'd performed hers? Where was the enthusiasm of the early days? Getting anything now was like walking uphill against the wind – only to get to the top to find it so disappointing that you wondered what had motivated you in the first place.

"All right. I'll tell them they can have Somiela. I'm going to discuss that other matter also. I can't put it off any longer."

"You're inviting the devil back in, you know that. It'll give him too much power."

"It can't be helped. The work's fallen behind. Vines have to be pruned and cut, the soil fertilized. Also new vinestocks have to be planted. The slaves aren't working, I can't find a replacement. He *did* save this place from disaster, don't forget." Andries glared at her. "If you have a better idea, let me know what it is, and I'll do it."

Marieta recognized the sting in his voice. She said nothing. She knew when to let go, and this was a bad time to press her point. Things had calmed down in the house, but there was unrest amongst the slaves. They were cheekier since the maleier's death and Harman's departure six months ago, and Andries came in exhausted at night. She had noticed the strain, and preferred a live husband to a dead one.

On Sunday after the midday meal, Somiela stood with Rachel on the stoep and watched the family wagon depart. The De Villiers family would be out the whole afternoon visiting friends. She and Rachel had the house to themselves. And she had plans.

"I'm going to take my bath now, Rachel."

Rachel nodded. They were not allowed to make use of the room where the family washed themselves, and this was the signal to Rachel who would occupy herself with knitting or sewing in the front room while Somiela had her bath in the kitchen.

Somiela took the tin tub from the wall and set it in front of the stove. She didn't want to think too much about the afternoon ahead – her fantasies never worked out. Harman was working in Paarl. On the last Sunday of each month he rode into town where he met Arend in Dorp Street at the masjied, and sent her a message. He said little. His mother and father had come to see him. His sister, Beatrix, had married a Steenkamp. Karel had broken his leg in a riding accident. But nothing about him, when he would see her, how he felt. As the months passed, hope fluctuated like a faulty barometer; high after hearing from him, low towards the end of the month. Then a few weeks ago she had received a handwritten note. He would be in the Cape for two days, and would come to Zoetewater on Sunday afternoon and meet her outside the gate.

She poured steaming water into the tub, and added a sprinkling of the green crystals she'd pinched from the bottle in the medicine chest. An apple fragrance filled the room. She laid out a clean dress over the back of a chair, closed the back door, took off her clothes, and kneeled down in front of the tub to wash her hair which had at last grown to her shoulders. Then she stepped into the scented water, sat down, and allowed the hot water to soothe her skin. She had a bar of carbolic in her hand, but didn't want to spoil the apple fragrance, and put it down on the floor. She took a handful of water, and stroked herself from the neck, slowly across the breasts, down to her navel, between her legs. She felt a swift and pleasurable pain. Her hand stopped. What was she doing, touching herself like that? She picked up the carbolic and scrubbed vigorously between her legs.

She got out of the water, dried herself, and combed out her hair in front of the fire. When she was dressed, she draped the yellow shawl her mother had sent with Harman so many months ago about her shoulders, and went into the front room.

"I'm going now, Rachel."

Rachel looked up briefly from her knitting. "The kitchen's clean, you put away everything?"

"Yes."

It was a cold day, with a thin mist hugging the slope. Somiela reached the end of the drive and settled down on a rock between two oak trees at the gate. She watched the road from both sides. A few wagons with families rumbled by, going out or returning home. But no horseman.

"Somiela," a voice said behind her.

She turned.

Salie came through the trees. She had noticed something different in him the last months. He'd cut his hair, and it made him look younger than his twenty-two years, less wild. But it wasn't his appearance. It was a withdrawal she'd sensed. He no longer pursued her. Why could she not feel for him what she felt for Harman? He was handsome, and they were bound by the same code. There were no Mohametan slaves where she had been at the previous place, and it wasn't every day you had such a chance. With him she need never apologize for her faith.

"What're you doing out here on the road?"

"Waiting."

He came closer, and looked at her. The new dress, her hair shining in the dull afternoon light, and something else. An intimate scent. Not one he recognized or had smelled before, but one he knew by instinct. "For him?"

"Yes."

They stood for a moment watching the oncoming wagon. It passed them with a grinding of wheels.

"He's a Christian, Somiela. You think he'll marry you? You can't change who you are."

"Who said I wanted to?"

"And can't expect him to. Or perhaps, you will change to his faith."

"I won't change for anyone. And you don't have to be the same faith to be someone's friend."

243

"Oh, you're waiting out here, to be his friend? That's all you want?"

"There's something wrong with that?"

"You're starting to lie to yourself, Somiela." He burrowed his hands deep into his pockets. "Wait for him, then. And be his friend. Maybe just being his friend will make you happy." He gave a thin smile, and wandered off.

Somiela watched him turn into the entrance. There was something very final in the way he walked away, something sad, and she felt suddenly depressed. His words hurt, but he was right. She couldn't change who she was, and couldn't expect Harman to do so. She was harbouring false hope, clinging to something which in the end would only bring her pain. Could she not learn from Rachel's mistake? And why was she still standing out here on the side of the road? It was obvious he wasn't coming. He would know that close to nightfall she would have to be back in the kitchen to serve the Sunday supper. She saw the family wagon come up the road and cut quickly through the trees and returned to the house.

Rachel was busy at the table cracking eggs over mashed potatoes. "I'm making potato pudding. Set the table. They'll be home any minute now."

"They're here already," Somiela said.

They heard the crunch of the wagon rolling up on the hard ground outside. A few minutes later, the back door opened and Andries de Villiers and his family stepped into the kitchen.

Leentje moved to close the door behind her father.

"Don't close it," Andries said. "Someone's coming."

Somiela moved quietly about the kitchen, taking out dishes, setting out the food on the table while the family gathered around. She was carrying a platter of fried meat when she heard a sound at the door. The platter slipped from her grasp when she saw who it was and she just managed to catch it before it went clattering to the floor.

"Come in, come in," Andries said. "We're just sitting down to eat. Did you get wet? It was starting to drizzle when we pulled up."

Harman dropped his bedroll at the door. He looked awkward

standing there wearing clothes they'd never seen him in before, his hair even longer, a new pair of boots on his feet. He took off his hat.

"I didn't catch any rain, no. Evening all. Somiela."

Somiela felt everyone in the kitchen looking at her. She nodded, not trusting herself to speak. She couldn't believe it. He'd come back. And spoken to Andries de Villiers as if nothing bad had transpired between them. Why was he there? He had come with his bedroll, he was planning to stay. What had the farmer promised him? She was so preoccupied with her thoughts, she missed most of the conversation going on at the table.

". . . we haven't said anything . . ."

". . . perhaps it's better if I . . ."

". . . no . . ."

"Somiela . . ." Andries de Villiers turned in his chair

"Yes, Seur?"

"We've arranged for you to help the kleinnooi with the baby which is due any day now. When you're done here in the kitchen this evening, pack your things, and make everything ready that you will need to take with you. Arend will take you first thing in the morning."

"The kleinnooi, Seur? Me? I'm going there?"

"Yes. You'll live with the kleinnooi and Mijnheer Martinus from tomorrow onwards."

"Tomorrow, Seur? *Live* there? For how long?"

"Don't be asking questions!" Marieta scolded.

"It's all right," Andries said. "Not long. Six months or so."

Somiela was horrified. "Six months!" How could they do this to her? Move her to a strange house and separate her from the people she'd come to know and considered almost as family? At Zoetewater she at least had the aia, and the men to talk to in the yard. She looked at Rachel. Rachel couldn't meet her eyes.

"Six months isn't long," Andries continued. "You'll only be at Zoetewater until December first of next year anyway. You'll be glad to hear that you'll be free after that. You won't have to serve the apprenticeship."

Free? It was a strange word on her ear. Was the farmer talking

245

to her? Somiela looked at Harman. A single glance told her. He'd negotiated her freedom. It was why he was there, to fulfil his side of the agreement. When December 1st arrived, the other slaves would have to serve the four-year apprenticeship, but she wouldn't have to. She wouldn't belong to anyone after that. She didn't know whether to laugh or to cry. Her slave days were numbered, but she and Harman would be apart yet again.

The meal passed in a muddle of glances and stilted conversation. When it was over, Harman took clean bedding from Rachel and went to the room in the yard. Somiela cleaned up the kitchen, stunned by the turn of events. No one had told her that she would be traded from one house to another. And what would she do all day alone with Elspeth? She put away the last of the dishes, and started to pack the dresses and underclothing she would take with her to the landdrost's house. She set the small bundle on the bench ready for the next morning, then brought out the mattress on which she and Rachel slept in front of the stove.

"They're sending me away, Rachel. Just like that. Without warning."

"A master gives no warnings. He does what he wants. But you'll be all right. The landdrost has a good heart."

"His heart doesn't protect me from his wife."

"Elspeth? I know that girl. She'll have a new thing to play with. The baby will change her, you'll see. Maybe she's changed already, being away from here."

Somiela was quiet for a moment. "But why now, Rachel? Just when he's back?"

"The baby's due now. I heard them talking about your going there some time ago already, that Elspeth wanted you to come."

"You knew and never told me?"

"It might not have happened. Why upset you?" Rachel pulled her nightdress over her head. "And perhaps it's better for you to be gone while he's here."

"No, Rachel, it's not. Who is it better for? He's been gone a long time, I never forgot him. And he never forgot me. Look what he did. I'm only here until December next year. *He* did it. No one else." She picked up her shawl and drew it around her shoulders. "I'm going to him."

Rachel lowered her huge body onto the mattress. "You're going to his room?"

"Yes."

"You be thinking about what you're doing now."

"I'm not going to be doing anything." She opened the back door and stepped out. The overhead lamp had been extinguished, there was no moon, but she knew the grounds. She walked quickly, without hesitation, almost stumbling over a barrel someone had left in the yard. Tomorrow she would go away. Tomorrow she had time to think. Now she wouldn't think of anything.

She passed the wagon house and saw the glow of the lamp in the window of the buitekamer. He wasn't asleep. She knocked on the door and went in. He was on the other side, naked, silhouetted against the lamplight.

"Somiela . . ."

Somiela stared at him. She had seen Andries de Villiers without clothes; an old wildebeest, wide around the girth, flabby, glutinous, a fat pig of a man whose unsightly physique turned her stomach. This was a magnificent body – hard flanks, strong legs, and . . . her eyes feasted on him until she forced them away – his manhood speaking to her in a language her own body understood. She could feel his heat reach into her and spread like hot liquid across her belly. Her head swam. Her hand ached to reach out and touch him.

He came forward. "I came back for you, Somiela. I told you I wouldn't forget. I told you I would come back for you. I've come."

"I know, I know. And now they're sending me away."

"They can send you where they want. I'll have you when the time's right."

Somiela thought she would faint. His hands were in her hair, his breath hot on her face.

"You have feeling for me, Harman?"

He turned her face up towards him. "Still, you don't know? Look at me, Somiela. My body wants you. My heart. My soul. You will ask me such a thing?"

"I'm afraid."

"Don't be." He drew her close, feeling the length of her body against his. "I want you, Somiela. I can't wait any more."

Somiela knew she could no more still the ache inside her than she could wish the sun to rise in the west. The dress slid easily off her shoulders to the floor. There it lay bunched around her ankles. Their bodies touched. His hand found her. She moaned. Cried out once. Then the night calmed and passed into stillness.

The weeks dragged by slowly for Somiela. The routine at the landdrost's house was the same every day. Martinus rose at cock crow and had breakfast. He left for work. There was another breakfast when Elspeth got up, the baby's bath, the soiled clothing and nappies, the midday meal, housework, ironing, supper, the dishes, a quiet time by the fire, and finally bed. Occasionally there were visitors and she had an hour's respite reading a book in the yard. Martinus had given her permission to borrow books from his collection as long as she put them back in the same place when she was done. And twice Harman had come on a Sunday to visit and take a walk with her in the Company Gardens. She had been strangely apprehensive to be seen with a white man in public, but no one had stared at them. Life wasn't hard, and crept along at a predictable pace. There was enough to eat, a warm place to sleep, and the landdrost was pleasant although he never, even in Harman's presence, communicated with her in a manner other than that of master and servant. Rachel had rightly predicted that Elspeth's separation from her family would bring change, but it wasn't overwhelming, and Elspeth still became impatient and raised her voice at her. She had learned to recognize the signs – how Elspeth behaved when she got up in the mornings – whether the baby was colicky or not – whether the landdrost was sympathetic when she complained of her fatigue.

Still, Somiela noticed a tiredness in her own body of late. A soreness in her breasts. And the smell of food sometimes disturbed her. The afternoons were easier, and by the evening meal, she was herself again. One morning, seven weeks into her stay, she got up as usual to put the bread in the oven and get Martinus on his way. She was fine until Elspeth came into the kitchen with the baby and said she wanted eggs. Somiela cut three slices of bread, poured Elspeth's coffee, and cracked three eggs into the pan on the stove. The smell hit her nose, and she felt a wave of nausea rise up. She rushed from the kitchen to the sloot at the side of the house, and threw up.

Elspeth eyed her warily when she came back in. "You've been sick every morning for days now."

"It's the smell of the eggs. I can't stand it."

"Do you know why?"

"No." Somiela took the pan off the stove, dished the eggs onto a plate and set it on the table for Elspeth. "I'll take Pietie now," she said, carrying the infant to the small bath set up on a side table. "His water's all ready."

Elspeth continued to eye her. "Have you been with him?"

The question caught Somiela off guard. "What does Kleinnooi mean?"

"You know what I mean."

Somiela lowered the infant into the water. Her silence filled the room.

Elspeth looked enquiringly at her body. Somiela was wearing the dress her mother had given her which had caused all the trouble that first day at Zoetewater. It still fit loosely around the narrow hips, but had grown snug across the bodice.

"I think you're growing a child."

"A child?" Somiela gasped. "It can't be."

"You are. I'm sure of it. When was your last flow?"

Somiela was too disturbed by this horrible prediction to think clearly. Her mind reeled. How could she be growing a child? She'd only been with him once. But she'd felt recently that something was wrong. She was never sick, and her body had a different feeling now, a fullness. She even smelled different between her legs. What would she do if Elspeth was right and she really was pregnant? What would she tell her mother? Her mother who'd talked to her so many times? She knew right away that she couldn't tell Harman. Then there was Rachel, who'd warned her repeatedly. She could hear the aia's voice now. She dried the infant, vaguely aware of Elspeth's displeasure.

"I have to get rid of it."

"It's not yours to get rid of," snapped Elspeth. "It has to be born. My stepfather owns you. The child's his."

Somiela looked at her. If the child was going to be born at all, it wasn't going to belong to anyone else, least of all Andries de Villiers. But she had other, more pressing fears.

A few days later, Somiela asked if she might visit her mother on Sunday afternoon. Elspeth granted the request. But Somiela didn't go to her mother. Instead, she visited a crippled slave, an old woman, Saartje, at a house situated between the establishments of an ironmonger and a carpenter on Graave, close to Spin Street where she and Sangora and her mother had been put on the block behind the Slave Lodge. Saartje, who'd befriended her at the market two weeks before, was surprised to see her, and spent the afternoon listening to her tale. When Somiela had poured out her heart, the old woman nodded understandingly.

"Is there something I can do to make it go away?" Somiela asked.

"There may be, if it's not too late. It depends on how far the seed's travelled, how deeply embedded it is. How late are you?"

Somiela had worked it out beforehand. "Two months."

"Two months is long. But we'll try. It won't hurt to try. I'm giving you seven onions. Now, this is what you must do."

Somiela listened carefully.

"Every day, for seven days. It's better last thing at night."

Somiela thanked her and promised to follow the instructions. But she could not go back to the landdrost's home yet. She hadn't been gone long enough, and didn't want Elspeth to get used to her returning so soon from a visit; it wouldn't be good for next time. She usually stayed at her mother's until an hour or so before dusk.

She left the house and stood in front of it for a moment, wondering which way she would go. She decided to go up to the masjied on Dorp Street, just to see if she recognized anyone outside, and then look for Pepper Street and see where Boeta Mai's house was. Saartje's words and manner had calmed her, given her hope. The remedy of the seven onions must've proven itself already on others. The woman wouldn't pull this remedy out of the back of her head, surely.

Feeling much better now than when she'd left the landdrost's house, Somiela walked leisurely up Bureau Street to Wale Street where she admired all the people strolling into the Company Gardens; the fine Sunday afternoon dresses of the women with their colourful shawls, the tailored jackets of the men. She could tell the English from the Afrikanders. How, she did not know, she just knew. Their clothes were different, their hats, their manner. She looked at her own dress. It was one of the newer ones her mother had made for her; nicely fitted, but unpossessed of lace or satin cuffs to avoid trouble in the house. Would they think she was a slave, she wondered? The shoes Andries de Villiers had given her all those months ago were long gone, and hadn't been replaced, but the family had said nothing when she appeared with a new pair on her feet provided by her mother. She suspected that they'd got used to seeing her in shoes and simply hadn't noticed when the old pair had been replaced by the new. She realized, walking in the street with these shoes, that they affected the way in which passers-by regarded her. Some people even greeted her. Then she realized something else. Some of those people thought she was white. White! Why else would they greet her? Almost unconsciously, she straightened her shoulders, and kept her head more erect as she continued on her way up Wale to Long Street, where she turned left, walking slowly to browse, scan, and look into all the windows.

Long Street was a street filled with merchants, and she read some of the signs on the shops that she passed; a soap boiler, a tanner and hatter, a cooper, a butcher, an undertaker, a boatman, a public notary, a wine merchant, a silversmith, a tailor, an English teacher. This last one caught her attention. Arend could speak this language and she had learned a few words from him, but she would like to learn more so she would be able to read things in English. She wondered how much lessons would cost, then realized that she had been so engrossed that she had passed Dorp Street and arrived at the lower end of Pepper Street. She stopped for a moment on the corner, then started to walk up the hill. Harman had said number sixteen, if she remembered correctly, and that there was a fanlight in the door. She found it easily, and passed it without stopping. But she had seen enough.

The front door was almost on the street, with just a few steps in front of it. The windows had curtains. A palm tree in a pot stood outside. There were no wagons or people in front of it.

Somiela continued up the road to Bree Street, turned right, came down Dorp Street, passed the masjied. She did not recognize anyone, and walked at a leisurely pace until she reached Long Street once again. Then she turned left and went on as far as Greenmarket Square where she continued all the way down until she was once again on Keizersgragt and saw the landdrost's house. The visit to Saartje and the walk through town had refreshed her, and she did not even pay attention to Elspeth when the woman complained that she had been away a long time.

That same night, after the last meal had been served and the dishes washed and put away, the infant changed and put in his crib, and the landdrost and his wife installed in their bedroom, Somiela boiled water on the stove. She waited until everything was quiet before she got out the spare chamber pot that the family provided for overnight guests. She peeled and chopped up one of the onions, put it in the pee pot, and set the pot on the floor. Then she poured two cups of boiling water over the onion as Saartje had said, and lowered herself over the enamel chamber, the fullness of her skirt acting as a seal. The steam scalded her skin, but she remained on her perch. She felt her pores and passages expand, the fiery vapours reaching deep inside. She got up and inspected the contents. Nothing. It was only the first time, she told herself, she had to be patient.

She performed this ritual seven nights in a row. Nothing dropped into the pot. Not a drop of blood, not a clot. The thing gripped tight as a tick to her guts. To add to her misery, the morning vomiting became worse. She felt achy and bloated, and kept on spitting out her saliva, chewing on mint leaves to change the taste in her mouth. When she could no longer get her mother's dress over her breasts, she accepted for the first time that she would have a child. She was in a terrible state, and her fears multiplied when she learned that Harman was coming for Sunday lunch. Her hair had grown limp, she felt nauseous, and imagined herself fat as a cow.

On the afternoon before his visit, she waited for Elspeth and

Martinus to finish their coffee where they sat talking together on the stoep, then asked Elspeth if she could visit her mother the following day.

"But you were there just a few weeks ago. You can't go gallivanting on your day off every time you ask."

Martinus poured more coffee into his mug. "You look sick, Somiela. Is anything wrong?"

Somiela didn't know whether Elspeth had told him about her condition, but along with Harman's seed growing inside her, she had developed a strange kind of boldness. "I'm going to have a child."

Martinus's face changed colour. He had expected to hear that she had a headache, or an upset stomach. "A child? Whose child is it?"

"Harman's."

He choked on his coffee and it sprayed from his mouth. "My brother's?"

Elspeth rolled her eyes. "Don't look so surprised, Martinus. Don't pretend you don't know what's been going on."

"But – "

"There're no buts. She's three months already."

"You never said anything."

"I thought you knew, that he told you."

Martinus looked at her in surprise. "He said nothing."

"Maybe he doesn't know. You know how he doesn't hide things that can shock you."

Martinus turned to Somiela. "Does your mother know?"

"Not yet, Seur."

"But you were there two weeks ago," Elspeth said. "Didn't you tell her?"

Somiela had told one truth. She would tell another. "I didn't go to my mother. I went to see a woman to try and get rid of it."

"What?" Elspeth got up from her chair. "I told you it wasn't yours to get rid of. That child belongs to my stepfather."

"Sit down, Elspeth," Martinus intervened. "You went to see someone to get rid of the baby?"

"Yes, Seur."

"What did you do?"

Somiela was embarrassed to tell him. She glanced at Elspeth. "I sat on a pot of onions, Seur."

"You did what?"

"I used the pot you keep for the visitors. I put onions in it and boiling water. And then I sat on it."

Martinus shook his head in disbelief. "And what happened?"

"Nothing."

Martinus sat for a few minutes in silence, drinking his coffee.

"You know he's coming for lunch, tomorrow," Elspeth said.

"Yes, Kleinnooi. I can prepare everything, but I have to see my mother. I can't be here."

"You can't be here, or you don't want to be here? You can't hide this from him forever."

"Wait now, Elspeth," Martinus said. "If she doesn't want to tell him, she doesn't have to. And maybe there's still a way."

"What do you mean?"

"If she doesn't want it."

Elspeth looked at him in horror. "You can't. It's Pa's."

"Nonsense. Your father doesn't own everything. And Harman wouldn't allow it. The best thing is to help her out of this if she doesn't want it."

Elspeth looked at him. "You're only thinking of – "

"That's right. If my brother doesn't know now, perhaps it's better for him not to know at all. No need to embarrass the family. He's confused right now. Tomorrow he may wake up and realize he's made a mistake, and then what? Then it's too late."

Somiela felt sick. She turned slowly from them and went to sit in the yard. She'd made up her mind. She hadn't thought clearly before. She'd placed too much emphasis on what everyone else would think. The child was swelling her breasts, making her tired, and she was bringing up her food, but it was *her* child and no one else's. And if Harman was repulsed by the idea when she told him, he could go too. The Kloots could plan from now until Judgment Day. She wasn't going to let anyone take the child from her.

On Sunday morning, she woke to dull skies and gloomy thoughts. Elspeth and Martinus had both agreed that she could visit her mother, and it was she who decided not to in the end. She would get the thing with Harman over right away. But she wasn't feeling well. There was a bitter taste in her mouth and she wanted to go right back to sleep, but there was no time for sickness, no place to lie down during the day. She had Elspeth's baby to feed and bathe, the midday meal to prepare. And what was she to wear in her new condition for Harman's visit? She selected the ugliest dress she possessed. She didn't know what this recklessness meant, and didn't care. A wrong word or look could turn her, and it wouldn't take much to sour her mood. When she heard Harman at noon at the front door talking to Martinus, she told herself that he would take one look at her and immediately be aware of her condition. She wanted him to, so he could have his shock and leave, and she could get on with what she had created for herself.

But Harman didn't notice anything. "How are you, Somiela?" he asked, coming into the kitchen.

"Good," she said, not looking at him.

He came to where she was stirring the food on the stove. "Is something wrong?"

"Should there be?"

He took off his hat. "I was busy. I couldn't come last week. Are you well?"

"Do you mean, am I fat?"

"Of course not. Why would you say that?" He was confused by her manner.

The smell of the cabbage rose up from the pot and Somiela felt suddenly nauseous. She dropped the spoon on the table and ran outside. Harman followed her out and found her leaning against the wall, heaving into the sloot.

"You're sick," he said. "What's the matter?"

She looked up at him, her green eyes wet with her exertions.

"Tell him," Elspeth said from the doorway.

Harman looked at Elspeth, then back at Somiela. "Is something wrong?"

"Nothing," Somiela said. "And I can't walk with you this afternoon."

"Tell him," Elspeth insisted. "He has to know." She went back into the house.

Harman came forward and touched her arm. "What is it that I have to know? I know there's something. Tell me."

"I'm sick."

"I can see that you're sick. What's wrong?"

"I'm growing a child."

"What?"

"You heard me."

"You're going to have a child?"

"Yes."

Harman released her arm. He couldn't speak.

"There, I knew it. I knew this was how you would react when I told you. Now do you see why I haven't? I knew you would be angry."

"I can't believe what you're telling me. And I'm not angry. I'm shocked. How long have you known?"

"A few weeks."

"A few weeks and you only tell me now?"

"I thought I could get rid of it."

"What do you mean?" He was becoming more and more alarmed. "You mean you tried to kill it?"

"I didn't think of it as killing."

"What did you do?"

"I sat on a pot of raw onions and boiling water. It was supposed to open me up and bring it down. It didn't."

"Who told you to do it?"

"An old slave woman down the road."

It was so ridiculous, he wanted to laugh. But it wasn't a laughing matter. Somiela was standing with moist eyes before him, desperate, filled with fear. There was nothing funny about what she'd told him. "This is serious. I must think."

"Think? What's there for you to think about? I'm the one who's going to have a baby. There's nothing to think about. Nothing will stop it from coming. I'll have it, and that's that."

"I know you will have it."

"Then what's there for you to think about?"

"Ssshh . . ." He put his finger to her mouth. "You're sick, but your mouth doesn't stop working. I still have to think. We'll work this out."

The ride back to Zoetewater went quickly. The afternoon had sobered Harman, opened his head. One night had led to this situation. It was no longer a dream, no longer something he had time to examine with the heedfulness of a scientist. He would have a child. A flesh and blood child who would laugh and cry and grow up and carry his name. He had to know what to do. Not tomorrow, not next week. Now. Was this how it had been for Roeloff Kloot? The circumstances under which he, Harman, had come into the world? Had it been one night, or several? Had it been love? What had really happened between his father and the Sonqua girl? Had his father followed his conscience or his heart? What would *he* follow? Then there was his faith. He had thought long about Bessie's words, and much as he wanted to argue with what his father believed and what his own beliefs were, he was still Christian. He never read the Bible, but you never escaped the Words of the Lord. Always there was someone around, ready to remind you. But he liked the Mohametan philosophies also. Boeta Mai and his family seemed happy people, satisfied. People were all equal in God's eyes, Boeta Mai had said. God had created the universe and everything in it. Why would a slave be worth any less than a man who owned ten cows? It was man who had created slavery, not God. Harman was terribly confused. He loved Somiela more than anything else – nothing compared with his feelings for her – but was he doing the right thing? Would he be able to close his eyes at night and sleep happily? Would he betray God if he married a woman he loved?

He reached the gate. Arend was in the yard to greet him.

"Mijnheer. How is Somiela? You've seen her?"

Harman was shocked by the words which sprang uncensored out of his mouth. "Somiela's well. She's going to have a baby."

"A baby!" Arend took off his hat. "Somiela?" It was obvious from his expression that he wanted to ask more, but didn't know how far he could go. He had no business asking personal things.

"Yes," Harman said, not sure why he had told the interpreter. "Everything's all right here?"

"Yes, Mijnheer, and everyone's back." He took Harman's horse and led it to the stable. He saw Salie and Hanibal under the tree eating sweet potatoes they'd roasted on the coals of a fire.

"You won't believe it," Arend said, hardly able to contain himself. "Somiela's going to have a baby!"

Salie came forward. "What?"

"He just told me. Can you believe it?"

"It's *his*, you mean?"

"Who else's would it be? It must be. I can't believe it. The inlander a father!"

Salie threw the half-eaten sweet potato to the ground and walked off.

"What's wrong with him?" Arend asked.

"You know how he feels about Somiela," Hannibal scowled. "Couldn't you let the news come to him another way?"

Back in his quarters, Harman sat on his bed and wondered if he should go to the house and consult the farmer. It was Sunday evening, and Andries de Villiers would have out his Bible and be filled with the Word of the Lord. Whether he believed in those words or not, didn't matter. It was something he did on Sunday nights, and Harman was reluctant to disturb him on a personal matter. Still, he didn't want to wait until morning. He and Martinus had spoken on the stoep before he left, had come to an agreement. Harman wanted to discuss the situation with the farmer and go to bed knowing things would be all right.

He looked about the small room. Would it be big enough? Would Andries agree? He got up and crossed the yard to the kitchen. Rachel told him Andries was in the front room and went to inform him that he was there and wanted a word. Shortly after, Harman went in and found Andries and Marieta at the table, the Bible open in front of them.

"You're back already," Andries said. "Come in."

"I know it's Sunday, and I'm sorry to disturb you."

"It's all right. Sit down, please. There's a problem?"

"Not a problem. Some new developments. Not your concern, but something I wanted to discuss with you." He paused for a moment to formulate his next words. "Somiela's going to have a child. In five or six months."

"She's pregnant?" Marieta asked, the news coming as a total shock.

"Yes. Martinus tells me that they can get a woman close by to come and work for them, and that Somiela can return to Zoetewater. Somiela wants to come back, and so do I. I'm asking if it's possible for her to return. She doesn't have to be a nuisance in the house and can stay with me in the buitekamer. I'll take full responsibility. Her work will continue as before."

Andries and Marieta were badly shocked. Marieta was the first to find her voice. "How do you know – are you saying it's yours?"

"Of course it's his," Andries said. "Why else would he be here?" The half-breed had an opinion of herself, and Harman fancied himself her rescuer. There was no doubt in Andries's mind that the child was Harman's. The farmer closed the Bible as if the words uttered in the room would contaminate its contents.

"Somiela was not a nuisance in the house," he continued. "But do you realize what you're asking? You're asking for her to come back and to live with you as man and wife. I cannot allow it. You're family now, I can't have people talking."

Harman's eyes turned into slits. He waited.

"What you do is your own business, but not here." Andries softened his tone. "As someone who doesn't want to see you ruin your life, my advice would be to think very carefully before you go jumping into anything. Somiela can have the child, take it with her when she leaves. Why involve yourself in something you might regret? The child will not come tomorrow or the day after. Think about it. Think of what it will do to your family. Your brother's a landdrost. This will not be good for him."

Harman waited until he was finished talking. "Can she come back?"

Andries saw that he was firm on this point. "She can come back, but can't stay with you. She'll stay in the house. Or, if you prefer, there're huurhuisies just minutes from here. Rent one of those cottages and stay there. It will actually be better for the two of you not to be together on the same farm. But I won't insist on it. It's up to you."

"There's no money I can afford to waste on a cottage."

"As you wish. You're hard-headed, Harman. You won't take advice. But you don't know everything. Older people know some things better than you. You can't see around the corner. We've been there." Andries looked at Harman. "You can remain on Zoetewater, but Somiela stays in the house."

"You're saying she can return?"

"Yes. If Martinus can find someone to replace her. But her work remains as before. Not until December first next year is she free."

When Harman was gone, Marieta pulled the Bible towards her. Her mouth was pursed with disapproval as she spat out the words. "He wasn't raised with this book, that I can tell you. Whoever put the pap in his mouth, didn't put in the fear of God. He's come here and turned everything upside down. Look what's happened. The maleier goes and kills himself, and the half-breed gets herself pregnant by the white foreman – who's family now! What will people say when they hear about it? Why you bought these slaves and let that traitor come and work here, I don't know. I just don't."

Andries pushed back his chair and got up. "You don't know many things, Marieta. And you don't know when to shut your mouth. Shut it, now."

On a hot afternoon in November, a wagon with two horses and four occupants drew up in front of the house on Pepper Street. Harman was dressed in dark pants and a long-tailed jacket he'd had made by a tailor on Loop Street whom Martinus had referred him to, and had taken special care with his appearance that day. He had stood in front of the small mirror on the door of his room and taken a blade and shaved his face smooth, his freshly-washed hair first dried with a towel to remove all the dampness, then neatly combed and tied back with a new leather strip. Arend had insisted on polishing his boots.

"This is the house," he said, looking about him at the other wagons lining the street. "Looks like a lot of people. Everyone must be here." He helped his sister, Bessie, several months pregnant, and Somiela and Noria off the wagon.

Somiela felt nervous. She was wearing the new dress her mother had made – loose around her waist to accommodate her growing figure – her long hair held back modestly with a silk ribbon. A pair of hard-soled slippers with brocade adorned her small feet.

"I feel so big in this dress."

"You only feel that way," Noria said. "Nothing's showing yet. You look beautiful."

Somiela squeezed her mother's hand. How afraid she'd been to tell her mother, and how different her mother's reaction had been.

"Mama's happy? Not disappointed?"

"I'm happy."

Harman's heart warmed. He knew from the mother's spirit and nature what he could expect in the daughter. But there was sadness also in his heart. It wasn't how he'd envisioned it, that it would be his half-sister, Bessie, who would be there with him, the only witness from his family to such a major event in his life. Bessie had always understood the secret places of his heart, having herself spent a lonely childhood with a mother who until the day she closed her eyes at forty-three, had never uttered a word to her child. Bessie and he had shared the same isolation, a sense of aloneness their other siblings knew little about. It pained Harman that he hadn't yet told his parents and his brother, Karel, and that Martinus, who had fought him on the issue but had come through for him in the end, wouldn't attend. It was the one thing, he said, Harman had to allow him.

Boeta Mai and his family waited for them at the front door.

"Come in, come in," he welcomed them. "Everyone's here, we have a full house. Is this Somiela? Come in, Somiela. This is my wife, Maryam, and my son, Sollie."

Somiela allowed herself to be swept up and embraced.

Harman came forward. "And this is my sister, Bessie, my father's first-born."

Boeta Mai and Maryam greeted Bessie warmly. They noted her condition, but did not enquire after a husband. "Come in, please. And please, make yourselves at home." He turned to Harman. "He's here. Sollie fetched him last night. Let's go to the back first before we meet with the imam."

"Prepare yourself, Somiela," Harman said.

They followed Boeta Mai down the passage, past a room full of guests, and entered the bedroom.

"Sangora!" Somiela stood transfixed at the door. Her face was ashen and she gripped the door frame in shock. Her eyes were deceiving her, she thought. Sangora had killed himself. They had mourned him, prayed for him. How could he be standing here? "I thought you were dead!" she exclaimed.

Sangora smiled. He was dressed in real clothes, shoes, his long hair cut short. "I'm not, as you can see." He came forward and hugged her.

"But – we all thought – "

"I know. Harman couldn't tell you. It was the only way. Only your mother knew what really happened. She's kept in touch with Boeta Mai and the family. We couldn't tell you anything. It was a hard decision, but we had to do it."

"You didn't trust me?" Somiela asked Harman, still unable to believe that this was really Sangora standing in front of her.

"It wasn't that. I just couldn't take the chance. You might've said something to Rachel. It was safer for Sangora if no one knew."

"But where've you been all this time? I can't believe it. You're alive."

"In Tulbagh. Under another name. No one here knows me as Sangora."

"You've changed your name?"

"Yes. It's Sedick Samaai now."

"What about papers?"

"All taken care of. My name's crossed off in the slave book. His brother took care of everything."

"Martinus?" Somiela was even more surprised. "Martinus helped you? I can't believe any of this. Do you know how they talked about you? Arend, I think, took it the hardest."

"I think of them all the time. How's Tromp? Hanibal?"

"Tromp's not well. I think it's his lungs. Hanibal's still drawing. You heard about the fire?"

"Harman told me. How's Rachel?"

"Still the same. I wanted her to be here, but you know how it is. We can't both be away at the same time."

Sangora smiled. "And Salie?"

Somiela looked at Harman, then back at him. "He's fine. He wants me to be happy."

"That's good."

There was a knock at the door, and Imam Achmat, dressed in a black turban and a flowing white robe, entered. "Sorry to disturb you all, but is everyone ready? I have a doopmaal at five o'clock."

"We are," Boeta Mai said, leading the party outside. They went into the front room where the round table, dressed with a lace tablecloth, groaned under bowls filled with dates, peanuts, and sweets, platters of jam and coconut tarts, fancy butter biscuits in a half moon design, and in the centre of all of this, a high, round cake with hard white icing and a scalloped edge. The newcomers greeted the guests who consisted of Boeta Mai's sister, Latiefah, her husband and two adult children, a stout woman with a head covering who had helped Maryam with the baking, and two of Boeta Mai's friends. Harman and Somiela sat next to each other in front of the imam. Bessie sat on Harman's right, Sangora and Noria on Somiela's left.

Imam Achmat looked around at the people in the room and indicated that he was ready to begin. He recited a short prayer, then turned to Harman.

"We've met a few times, Harman, and talked a long time. Have you thought about what we discussed?"

"I have."

"And what's your decision?"

"I'll take the oath."

"You accept the one God, and the last prophet?"

"I do."

"You'll keep Somiela's honour and live by God's will?"

"I will."

Imam Achmat asked him to repeat a few words in Arabic after him. Harman was prepared. Boeta Mai had written these words out for him, explained them, and Harman knew what every word meant. He had practised saying them, and repeated them slowly.

The imam smiled. "You are now joined together in God's eyes. You are husband and wife. You've decided on a name for yourself?"

"Yes, Imam. I've thought about it. I will keep what I have. No matter what name I use, God will know who I am."

... *a number of processions of Coloured people parading Cape Town, singing a Dutch song in which every verse ended "Victoria! Victoria! daar waai de Engelschen vlag! (There the British flag is waving!)". My mother asked a Coloured girl to go on an errand for her. She said, "No, I won't. We are free today!"*

(A wealthy Cape Town citizen, later remembering December 1, 1834)

Somiela was sitting with Salie on the bench under the jacaranda tree near the stream, when she felt a sharp cramp in her belly. It was Sunday afternoon. No one had gone into town on their day off.

"Is something wrong, Somiela?" he asked.

"No. It must be something I ate. I've been having these cramps all morning."

Salie looked at her. He wasn't convinced. "Where's Harman?"

"At his sister's. She wanted him to come and fetch some things she's made for the baby. Her son, Roeloff, is three months old now, so she has spare things." Her face softened and she smiled. "He's so excited about it."

"And you?"

"Me too." She turned to look at him. "I've never wanted anything so much. I can't wait. I can't wait to see who it will look like."

"What're you hoping for? A boy or a girl?"

"Either one. As long as it comes out with two hands and two feet and is healthy. But I think Harman is hoping secretly that it's a boy."

"All men want a boy first." He looked at her for a moment, and smiled. "You are looking very beautiful, Somiela. Having a baby suits you."

"Thank you, Salie. You are happy for me?"

"Yes. The better man won."

"It's not true. There's no better man. I just – "

He put his finger to her mouth. "You don't have to explain. I've accepted. Even when I fought with him, a part of me liked him. And he's become Mohametan. Even if he did it for you, he'll be blessed for it, and you too. Have you thought of some names for the baby?"

"Yes. If it's a boy, we will call him Sangora. If a girl, Soemaya."

Salie smiled. "You have it all worked out."

"You have a name you like?"

Salie thought for a moment. "Sangora's a good choice for a boy, but I've always thought of you as a S'iam. Don't really know why. Your eyes, perhaps. The naughtiness in them. I wish I knew what the name meant. Sangora's good with meanings of names. You should ask him."

The mention of Sangora's name prompted Somiela to ask him a question. "You've kept the secret I told you?"

Salie looked at her. "Yes. No one here knows anything, but if they did, they would be very happy to hear that Sangora's alive, especially Arend."

"You can't tell any of them. Here comes the twins. They will want me to read to them. I promised."

"I'll go." He noticed her clutching her stomach. "You have another pain?"

"Not really," she said, leaning forward slightly.

"I don't think it's something you ate, Somiela."

"What do you think it is?"

"I think it's the baby." He turned to the twins, "Go tell Rachel Somiela's having pain."

"No," Somiela stopped them. "Don't go bothering Rachel for nothing. It'll be weeks yet."

Salie laughed. "Wishing it won't make it so, Somiela. The child will come whether you're ready or not."

"Must we fetch Harman?" Leentje asked. "He's just arrived. With so many parcels. He's putting them in his room now."

"No. Come, I'm going to read to you."

Salie walked off, smiling to himself.

Somiela was halfway down the third page, when another knifelike pain shot down the side of her belly.

"Oh, oh, oh . . . this one hurt."

"Salie's right, Somiela. It must be the baby."

"No," Somiela groaned. She held her abdomen with both hands, waiting for the pain to subside. "Let's sit on the grass over there. It's probably just the way I'm sitting." She got up from the bench, and felt a gush of heat at the top of her thighs. She lifted her skirt and looked in alarm at the colourless fluid dribbling down her legs.

"Call Rachel!"

Both girls ran to the house.

Somiela stared down at her feet. Her mother had sent a parcel containing towels and kapok and baby clothes, but had not told her what to expect. What was this water running out of her? She bent down and wiped the inside of her legs with a handful of grass, and remembered Elspeth's baby's birth, a long, painful process with Martinus pacing restlessly outside the door, and Elspeth screaming in agony. Who was going to be there for her? Slaves were left by themselves. There was no midwife. There was often no one to help. A girl on the previous farm had died when the baby came out feet first with the cord around his neck, and the mother had bled to death. Would this happen to her? Who would turn that baby around? She had never wanted anything as badly as this baby who had grown from a seed and would come from her body. She had counted the months, urged them to go by faster. And here the baby was, killing her insides, with only one way to come out. She squeezed her knees together, terrified at the thought.

"Somiela . . ." Rachel came puffing down the hill towards her. "Your water has broken?"

A sharp stab across the belly made her double over with pain. "Oooooo . . ."

"How far apart are the pains?"

"I don't know. Not far."

"We have to go inside. You have to lie down. The child's coming."

"What do you mean, the child's coming?"

"I mean the child's coming. You're going to have a baby, Somiela."

266

Somiela started to cry.

Rachel looked at her in exasperation. "This is a fine time. You want to stand here and cry, or you want to get on with it?"

"You don't have to be so mean, Rachel."

"I'm going to get meaner if you make this difficult. Come now, you have to lie down. When it's over, you won't remember any of it. We'll go to Harman's room. The nooi said when the time came, you could have it there. You can't have it in the house."

"Where will Harman sleep?"

"He'll find a place, don't worry about him. There's the wagon house, and the barn. Come, let's get these clothes off. You want him to be with you? He's inside the house, talking to the seur. Van Heerden and two other men are there also."

"I want my mother."

"Your mother's not here. I am. You want Harman to come?"

"No."

Rachel turned to the twins trailing behind. "You two better get to the house."

"We want to see, Rachel," Annie said.

"There's nothing to see. Somiela needs rest. And don't go telling anyone what's happening. She doesn't want the news broadcast yet."

The girls looked at each other. That was too big a promise to keep.

Somiela and Rachel reached the buitekamer and opened the door. Rachel hadn't been in it for a long time, and was surprised to see how Somiela had transformed the dull little room. Even though Somiela lived in the house, she spent Sundays with Harman, and over time had rearranged everything. There was a bowl of oranges on the small table, a lamp, a few books, a handful of dried purple flowers in an old mug, an embroidered coverlet on the bed, and the wooden crib Rachel's son had made, filled with things for the baby given by the slaves. There were no cupboards or drawers, except for the handsome storage chest with the floral design which Sangora, Arend, and Hanibal had worked on together, and the smaller geweerkis where Harman kept his rifles. Somiela's three dresses hung neatly next to Harman's good jacket and pants against the wall. One of Hanibal's farm drawings which evoked the mist over the stream was nailed to the back of the door above a small mirror.

Rachel pulled back the coverlet. Somiela sat down on the edge of the bed and removed her wet underclothing. "There's blood."

"Throw everything in here," Rachel said, bringing the bucket outside the door into the room. "I'll wash them. Do you have any clothes here?"

"I have some things in there," Somiela pointed to the chest.

Rachel opened the kist and was surprised to find it filled to the top with lace doilies, sheets, pillow cases, petticoats, women's underclothing, vests, shirts, and several pink, white, and lemon-coloured knitted bonnets, jackets and bootees for the coming baby. She wondered how they had accumulated so many things with so little money between them. Except for an embroidered table cloth, she'd never seen Somiela work on any of the things in the chest, and imagined that it was probably Somiela's mother who'd given them to her over the months. Somiela had been to see her several times, and once Noria had even visited Zoetewater so that she could see where her daughter lived. Rachel took out a nightdress and handed it to her.

Somiela slipped the nightdress over her head. A darting pain in the lower abdomen made her sit down again.

"Don't fight it. Breathe in deeply when you feel it coming. I'll bring your other clothes from inside, and something to drink."

"You'll be with me, Rachel? Throughout?"

"Who'll be with you if not me? I'll not leave you, child. Just do your part. Now try and rest. I'll be back in a few minutes." She looked at the twins standing at the door. They hadn't listened to Rachel's instruction that they go back to the house, and had followed the two women to the buitekamer. "Annie and Leentje, stay here with Somiela, and don't pester her."

Rachel returned to the kitchen where she informed Marieta that Somiela had gone into labour and wouldn't be coming in to help serve supper. "It *is* her day off, anyway," Rachel added.

"How far along is she?"

"The pains are coming quickly."

Marieta went to the stove and lifted the lid on one of the pots. "Food looks like it's done. You can serve supper early, then take

268

care of things at the back." She disappeared into the house and returned a few minutes later with a bundle of clothes. "They were Elspeth's, give them to her."

Rachel hid her surprise. It wasn't in the farm woman's nature to be generous, but Rachel had noticed Marieta's subdued manner since Somiela's return. Somiela's marriage to Harman had shocked all of them, the slaves also, and even though it wasn't recognized by the state, put her in a different stable. She had gone from work horse to one of value. She belonged to the kneg. The kneg was related by marriage. She looked at the little flannel nightdresses and knitted jackets. They were used clothes, washed and pressed, but still in excellent condition. Babies didn't stay small long enough for their clothes to get worn out. Rachel wondered why Marieta hadn't given them to her own daughter when the grandchild was born. Had she just forgotten, or kept them because she knew Somiela would have none? Rachel didn't think it was the latter. Marieta would bottle her sweat if she thought there was money in it, and a hardness of heart didn't just disappear overnight. But Rachel knew, too, that the heart had its own mysteries. She didn't believe for one moment that Marieta would ever accept Somiela as anything but a slave, but it was possible that the girl entering motherhood had softened, if only temporarily, Marieta's hatred towards her. Or perhaps it was because the child was the inlander's. Or because she had had a sudden revelation from the God she prayed to. Rachel did not speculate further. She had discovered long ago that it was impossible to take any single behaviour of the white man for granted. Just when you thought they acted one way, they went in another direction.

She took the clothes to the buitekamer, along with a mug containing a brew of boiled water and leaves. The twins were playing outside the door.

"You're not disturbing Somiela, are you?"

"No, Rachel," Leentje said.

"And we didn't tell anyone," Annie added. "Not even Arend."

"What do you mean, not even Arend. Was Arend here?"

"Yes. He came to put the pram in the room. They've got a pram also. He saw Somiela with his own eyes."

Rachel turned her gaze towards the house. Just as she expected.

269

Harman turned from conversation with her son in the yard, and came with great strides towards them. She hastened into the room.

"The nooi gave these clothes for the baby."

Somiela was in too much agony to appreciate anything. "The pains are killing me, Rachel. I didn't know there could be so much pain."

"What did you think? With all pleasure comes pain. But it'll soon be over. Don't strain yourself talking. Try to rest in between."

Harman appeared in the doorway, wild-eyed and anxious. "What's happening? Arend said that – "

"She's gone into labour."

"The baby will come today, you mean?"

"Yes. The pains aren't far apart."

He stood dumbfounded, not knowing what to do. It was going to happen. The baby was ready. It was no longer something that would happen in the future. He would be a father! He looked at Somiela in his bed. She looked huge and uncomfortable and not too pleased to see him. He came to sit on the edge of the bed. "Somiela? How're you feeling?"

Somiela glared at him through the pain.

He looked at Rachel, a hurt look in his eye. "She doesn't want me here, Rachel."

Rachel ushered him to the door. "Go back to what you were doing. Women get like this when they give birth. They don't want you around. Don't worry. She's strong. She'll come through this."

"I'll be just outside this door."

"Go back to your work. I'll call you."

The afternoon shadows grew longer, and soon it was dusk. The pains seemed heartbeats apart. Rachel worked by herself, wiping Somiela's forehead, holding her hand, helping her breathe through contractions, and all the time murmuring into her ear. "Keep strong, child . . . this is what separates us from them . . . men can't do this . . . here, we are alone . . . this is what makes us mothers, not what makes them fathers . . . we don't need them . . ." She put her hand between Somiela's thighs to feel

270

the opening. "You're getting bigger. Keep breathing. This child's in a hurry to get out."

Outside, Rachel could hear voices drifting towards her from where the men were gathered under the tree. They were all out there keeping Harman occupied, all anxious for news. He couldn't come in and had to be outside with them.

Just after sunset, Rachel stuck her head out the door. "Hot water, Harman. You and Arend get some from the house. The big kettle on the stove."

She returned to Somiela who was working through a contraction, her face purple with strain. She went to sit at the foot of the bed, and checked to see how far Somiela had dilated. "I can see the head. Put your feet on my shoulders, and when I tell you, you push. Hard!"

Somiela was blind with pain, and her body seemed to act on its own, bearing down naturally.

"Not yet," Rachel ordered.

"I can't, Rachel, I can't!" She planted her feet firmly on the aia's strong shoulders, and pushed.

"Again!" Rachel urged her. "The head's almost out. Breathe in now – push!"

Somiela took in a deep breath, pushed down with all her strength. Her screams were heard at the top of the hill.

"Rachel!"

Rachel ignored the banging on the door. She had the baby's head in her hands, and was easing out the shoulders. Moments later there was the lustful cry of a child.

"Rachel, I want to come in!"

"You can't come now!" Rachel shouted.

"Rachel, I will break down this door!"

Eventually, she opened it. Harman crashed past her into the room. "How is she, Rachel, how is she?"

"She's fine. She's got a girl."

On December 1st, 1834, Somiela rose early from bed, and dressed quietly in the semi-darkness so as not to disturb anyone. She hadn't slept. She and Harman had talked long into the night, packing their things, discussing their future. She'd waited long for this day, and yet had never thought it would happen. But here it was. The official day. Emancipation. How did she feel? Did she feel free? Any different from yesterday? December 1st didn't spell freedom for all slaves. For the majority it was only a freedom on paper. There were four more years. They would be bound by the same stringent laws. Despite the title of apprentice, they would still belong to owners who would work them all day and herd them into their kraals at night. No, she didn't feel particularly free. She was free to leave Zoetewater, but not free to enjoy it while others were still in bondage. There would be other masters who would set their slaves free, but not here. No slave at Zoetewater had been told anything. Arend said they hadn't even been told of their change in status, or what money they would receive as apprentices.

She walked quietly to the door, opened it, and looked out. It was a broody day for December, not what she'd expected. She had expected golden fires rising in the east, a special celebration from God. Perhaps God wasn't pleased. There wasn't much to celebrate. Rachel had told her she had no plans to leave Zoetewater when the apprenticeship period was up. Where would she go? She was an old woman now, with no desire for a new master and a new set of rules, for that was still what she'd be, a slave in someone else's kitchen even if she got money for it. But it was different for her son who still had his life ahead of him, and could start again. Arend talked of moving to town, looking for work as an interpreter. Hanibal talked of getting work on a ship and leaving the country. Petroos talked of learning a trade, and Salie of starting a tailoring business. But it was all talk. Four years was a long time. Anything could happen. For Somiela, things would change that day. She was no longer anyone's property. In less than three hours she and Harman would leave Zoetewater for good.

Where would life take her, Somiela wondered, and when would she return to the Cape? Harman talked only of going, not of coming back. The small room contained their worldly possessions, all that they shared. Now she would leave it, and leave Rachel, and leave the men who had been her friends, and perhaps never see them again.

She looked back at the sleeping figure of her husband, their six-month-old daughter, S'iam, asleep in his arms. She would never have thought that a man could be so attached to a child, that a baby could bring so much joy. God had blessed them with a red-haired fireball; one who laughed, who was seldom sick, who went from arm to arm to be cuddled and indulged. Who did S'iam look like? Like Harman or like her? A mixture of both of them, she thought, with her complexion the colour of new honey, and naughty grey eyes. A delightful child, greedy for attention and anyone who would have her. And there was no shortage of takers. The twins rushed home from school to push her around in the pram, stuffing blankets and pillows around her to keep her sitting upright, and spent more time than their mother wanted them to in the buitekamer, helping Somiela wash and dress S'iam. Somiela spent little time with her own child. When the work day was over, it was Harman's turn. He brought the baby out and sat with her under the tree where the men congregated to have their supper and talk. *Rooibossie*, they called her, for her reddish-gold hair. *The inlander's child.*

"Come to uncle," Arend would say, taking her from Harman.

S'iam's grey eyes would brighten. She knew who she liked. She liked Arend, but liked it better when Salie hopped her around on his knee, bringing tears to her eyes as she laughed. In the end, however, her little arms always reached out for her father.

She would miss the men in the jongenshuis, Somiela thought, miss their bickering and laughter, their gatherings under the tree, she would even miss hearing the slave bell. It was funny how she'd got used to it. It told her of another day. It told her that the men were getting up, that she was late or on time putting the bread into the oven, and all of these things had signalled life. Somiela closed the door and walked slowly up to the kitchen. She found Rachel already busy at the stove.

"I came to help you for the last time, Rachel."

Rachel said nothing. But Somiela could tell from the way she stood, her head bent, her lids heavy, that Rachel had cried, that she couldn't look at her just yet, as if one word would set off a flood of tears.

"What do you want me to make, Rachel? Eggs? Porridge?"

"I've made the men's porridge already. The family's having fried kidneys."

"Do you want me to make something special for the two of us? A last breakfast?"

Rachel looked up. "Make your tomatoes and eggs."

Somiela smiled. The aia was a good cook, but had found something she liked in Somiela's cooking. It was what Somiela quickly threw together in the pan for the two of them when last-minute guests finished all of the supper, or when they were alone in the house and felt like something to eat. It had become Harman's favourite breakfast also.

"I'll miss you, Rachel."

Rachel rattled the pan. "A person gets used to someone."

"My mother says that if someone's in your heart, you take them with you."

"Your mother's wise."

"But I'll still miss you, Rachel. You looked after me."

Rachel could bear it no longer. She turned from the stove and took Somiela in her arms. They held each other a long time. Both of them cried. "Look after that baby," Rachel said, wiping her eyes with the back of her hand. "First children suffer much."

"Why?"

"They see more. People don't know how to behave the first years they're married. It takes time. First children are there from the start. They see it all."

"You think there'll be more children, Rachel?"

Rachel released her. "If I know him, there'll be a brood. He looks like a man who'll want a house full of children. One for every day of the week, or for every task on the farm. Up there they have nothing to do. They put out the light as soon as it's dark."

Somiela laughed through her tears. "You make me laugh, Rachel, even when I'm feeling sad."

Rachel returned to the pan, once again composed, and turned over the kidneys. "There're no Mohametans where you're going, you know that."

"I know."

"You mustn't let it weaken your faith."

"You care about my faith, Rachel?"

"I care about your soul. You've gone through a lot to protect it."

At noon, Somiela stood with her baby and Harman in front of the wagon which Martinus had given them for a wedding present, saying goodbye. Rachel had provided food for the journey, and six jars of fig konfyt, Arend a small table with a drawer he said Harman could use to spread out his papers and work on, Hanibal a drawing of Somiela on the bench under the tree with S'iam on her lap.

Salie was the last one to say goodbye. He came forward and handed Somiela something wrapped in a cloth. "A piece of embroidered material. You can cut it into a dress for S'iam when she's bigger."

"Thank you, Salie."

"And two azeemaats," he handed her the tiny, cloth-covered amulets. "Sangora taught me how to make them. One for you, and one for S'iam. To protect you. You're going far."

Somiela's tears flowed freely from her eyes. She had affection for all the men, but especially for Salie. "Thank you for being my friend, Salie. Don't forget me."

"I won't."

She turned for the last time to the woman who had been her friend and protector. "All the best here for you and Arend, Rachel. The four years will pass quickly."

"The four years don't matter to me. Look after yourself. And look after her, Harman, she'll be far from her mother now."

"I will. You take care too, Rachel, and don't be so hard on Arend." He helped Somiela and the baby up onto the wagon, and got on.

Somiela settled down on the small bench in front. She saw Annie and Leentje come running towards them.

"My mother says to give this to you," Annie handed up a small pouch.

Somiela looked at it in surprise. She opened it. In the pouch were the wooden bangles which had been taken from her that first day on Zoetewater. It felt strange to see them again, to feel them in her hands. Sangora's hands had carved them, and scratched out her name in Arabic in the soft wood. Sangora wasn't there, but his spirit and wisdom would travel with them.

"We'll miss you," Leentje said.

"And S'iam," Annie added. "We'll have no one to play with."

"And I'll miss you," Somiela said kindly. She looked down at the men standing about the wagon, trying to look happy for her sake. She knew how they felt. She'd stood about enough wagons with her mother and Sangora at the previous farm, saying goodbye to slaves who were being sold. There would be few words, an emptiness for a while, then their lives would go on. Finally, she looked up at the house. Marieta de Villiers had come out on the stoep and stood next to her husband. Somiela took the bangles and slid them over her wrists.

"I'm ready."

The ride to the Hantam was uneventful, and took almost a week. Harman took things easy out of consideration for Somiela and the baby, and stopped frequently along the way. They had spent two days with Bessie and Braam, and their eleven-month-old son, Roeloff, before leaving the Cape, and the wagon was stacked to the roof with gifts and supplies. Braam had packed in a new rifle he wanted his father-in-law to have, and for Neeltje, a length of cloth, spices, and foodstuffs that were hard to get in the Karoo. Then there were Harman and Somiela's own supplies, and what Noria and Martinus and Bessie had given them. The wagon was loaded, they couldn't go fast. But the pace suited Harman fine. It was Somiela's first trip into the interior, and he wanted her to see and absorb the land through which his great-grandfather had travelled all those years ago to come and settle in the Hantam.

They passed through the greenery of Paarl, and Harman pointed out the granite domes, which he explained glistened so much in the sunlight when it rained that they were named the pearl and diamond mountains. They stopped in front of the Dutch Reformed church on the main street. Somiela looked around in wonder. She was fascinated by the quaintness of the street, all laid out with oak trees and houses, people walking about, children. It was a welcome change from the open land across which they had travelled so far. And she had never been inside a Christian place of worship.

"My father and mother stopped here for a service once when they passed through. My father didn't really want to, he said, but you can't argue with my mother when she has God on the brain. This here's the pulpit," Harman pointed to a wooden structure, "from where the dominee delivers his sermons."

Somiela touched the carved surface with her fingertips. "What will I call your mother?"

"Ma. I think she would like that."

From Paarl they travelled north to the farming community of the Wagenmakers Vallei. It was hotter here than in Paarl, and they outspanned early, moving on again the following morning. Approaching the outskirts of Tulbagh, Harman pointed to the little village coming up on his right.

"This is Tulbagh, where Sangora is."

"We're passing by?"

"Yes. We don't want to draw any attention to him. But we'll see him, when we come down and visit my brother in the Cederberg. I don't want to be too long on the road with you and the baby. I know you don't like sleeping alone with S'iam in the wagon."

"It's all right," Somiela lied, not wishing to tell him how she lay awake, listening to the cries of jackals and other night creatures, wondering if he would be eaten by lions in front of the fire where he guarded the wagon.

The fourth day saw them entering the wilderness of the Cederberg mountains, a rock-ribbed terrain sprinkled with wildflowers, waterfalls, caves, rock pillars, and fiery colours of unusual sandstone formations.

"Everything's so red!" Somiela exclaimed. "Even the sand."

"It'll get drier from here on. Karel's just on the other side, in the dip of the valley."

"Why don't we stop there, to rest? You haven't seen him in almost six months."

Harman looked at her, the baby asleep at her breast. He knew she was tired. "If we stop at Karel's, he'll keep us there for a week."

"I like Karel."

"Karel's easy to like. Not like Martinus, who has his head in a book all day long, and is always explaining everything to death, and not like me. Karel has patience. But he'll not let us go in less than a week. He'll want company, and when he sees S'iam, he'll find all kinds of reasons to delay us. We have a full wagon, Somiela. I'd feel a lot better once we got to Kloot's Nek and settled in. We have the rest of our lives. We'll come down here when S'iam's a little older, and visit Karel and Sangora."

They camped near a stream for the night, and the next day, picking up pace, they watched the vegetation change and the wildflowers and proteas and renosterbos dwindle and disappear as they entered the desolate terrain of the Karoo. The air got drier, the sun more fierce, the dust sitting thick and irritating in their throats. Somiela was weary. Two days she had sat up front on the small bench in the sweltering sun, waiting for the landscape to change. Harman had said it wouldn't, it would be like this till they got to the Hantam. A few miles on, he said, they would find the shade of a kareeboom, and stop to rest. She didn't know how anyone could be out here for long in the sun, or where they would find water, or what they would live on. Rocking back and forth with the child in her arms, her eyes drifting lazily over the rocky flatland stubbled with skaapbos and vygies and dried-out salt pans, she felt drowsy. Nothing stirred. Everything was silence. A yellow cobra with black flecks shimmered like polished brass where it lay coiled in the crook of a rock in the sun.

"That's the Hantamberge up ahead," Harman said at last. "We're less than a half day's ride from Kloot's Nek."

"We're almost there?"

"Yes," he smiled. "We'll rest at the foot of that rant. There's a tree. You can feed S'iam and wash your face. We have some water left."

The wagon rocked on. "Are you nervous?" she asked after a while.

Harman considered her words. Was he? He was coming home with a wife and a baby, and had given his family no time to get used to the news. His father had voiced his opinion at the time of Martinus's wedding, and not since; but he wouldn't be shocked, and his mother, also, might understand. Would they be as understanding of the other commitment he'd made? The thing that sat closer to the heart of the Boer than even the pull of the land, was the unquestioning belief in the Christian God. Would they understand that he had chosen another faith? There was no easy way to tell them.

"A little, yes." He looked down at the infant asleep at her breast. "They'll go mad for S'iam. There're no grandchildren at Kloot's Nek."

Somiela had a question, but didn't ask it aloud. How could he know the answer to what she wanted to know most, whether they might accept *her*?

He saw a spiral of smoke in the distance. "Look over there. Can you see it?"

Somiela squinted her eyes against the sun. "No."

"Someone's making a fire."

"Who do you think it is?"

"I don't know. It's on the other side of the rant. Maybe Sonqua."

"I thought you said they don't allow themselves to be seen."

"They don't, but maybe they've seen us, and want us to know. Or maybe it's just a trekboer heating his coffee." He flicked his reins, and the horses moved faster.

Somiela smiled. She'd sensed the change in him already. He was on old ground. His smile came quicker. Even his sweat smelt different.

He brought the wagon to a halt near a kareeboom at the foot of the mountain. "This is it. Last stop. We won't stay long. The horses need water, so we will have to get there soon." He got off and stretched his legs.

Somiela put S'iam down in the crib in the back of the covered wagon. "We have just enough bread left," she said. "Do you want that with tomato jam, or some dried meat?"

"The bread and jam. A last taste of Zoetewater." Already Zoetewater seemed very far away. "Do you miss the farm?"

Somiela thought about his question. She was with the man she loved, in a strange world, but there was also that other world, the one she had known all her life, the one she would never forget. The Zoetewater slaves had been her family for three years, and she missed them.

"Yes."

Harman looked at her. He was more relaxed now that the dangers of the journey were behind them. He had brought his wife and daughter to their new home. Tonight he would be reunited with his family. He touched a strand of hair which had fallen across her face, and moved it back gently behind her ear. The ride had roughened her a little, he thought, but she hadn't complained.

"You are glad you came with me, Somiela?"

Somiela looked up from the jam she was smearing on his bread. Her hands were dirty, her dress stained with her own smells and those of the baby. The Cape was very far away. She didn't have to see Kloot's Nek or its people to know that she was at the beginning of a new life.

"I will go with you anywhere."

Harman took the bread out of her hand and pulled her into his arms. "We've both given up something of ourselves, Somiela. I have no regrets."

Somiela wanted to cry. It didn't seem possible that she could be so happy under a miserable tree in the middle of nowhere.

A short, shrill sound reached their ears.

"What's that?" she asked. "It sounds like an animal."

"It's a bird call." He looked up towards the summit. This was a deserted and uninhabited land. There were no birds in these hills.

"Chirrrk . . . chirrrk . . ."

"It can't be," he smiled. "It can't." He put his hand to his mouth. "Chirrrk . . . chirrrk . . ."

He waited. A small, dusty figure with a bow and arrow appeared at the top of the rant. A handful of men, women, and children in loincloths and leather flaps rose up behind him.

"Tuka!"

The little hunter separated himself from the group and ran down the mountain towards him. "The son of Eyes of the Sky! You're back!"

Returning to the Hantam was the mistake he made. It wasn't long after that that they came. Ambushed him near the Oorlogsrivier where he had grazed the sheep. Shot him in the back. They'd carried that grudge all those years, never forgot. His father sat in the room for three days with the body before he put him in the ground. His mother took to her bed for a month. And there was Somiela, in strange surroundings, with no husband, and a baby. They asked her to stay. She stayed almost two years. Then the youngest brother, the one who'd inherited the Cederberg farm, brought her back. He liked Somiela, and they're still in touch. Strange how the one here never took to her. But I'm drifting. My head isn't what it used to be. Not long after she came back, she married. It was better for her and the child, and it wasn't a loveless marriage. The poor man had waited such a long time, and was very fond of the child. They have their own children, of course, all settled hereabouts, except for Somiela's first-born. Si'am never fully belonged to her mother. In the end, her white blood claimed her and she went off with a German to the new world. We receive a letter occasionally.

And look here. This one's of Zoetewater. Hanibal left out the barn, but captured the beauty of the land. See how these vineyards sweep up the Wynberg mountains? He was quite a good sketcher, Hanibal. Did I tell you that already? I only found out years later that it was he who'd set fire to the barn. He never said why.

That's Tromp sitting there under the tree. You know what happened to him. The morning after Somiela and Harman left for the Hantam, they found him hanging from the bell tower. The old shepherd always said he would never see freedom. He was right.

Arend and his mother stayed on, as I said. I believe Rachel was given a Christian funeral when she died. Can't say where Arend's now, if he even married. And no one ever heard from Geduld again.

This last one here's of my wife. You can see how young she still was. She died shortly after this was taken. A photograph, yes. The only one. We were together only four years when she came down with a fever and died with water in her lungs. Strange how it all turned out. Me outlasting most of them, even the twins. Sad about those girls, staying all those years by themselves. They died young, one two months after the other.

Hanglip? No, they never found out, and I never went back there. I think about it though. My night in the cave. How he came there and told me we were going to fake my death, and how young and reckless we were to think we could pull it off. It's better sometimes not to know how foolish you are, that's when it works. No, no one ever discovered the truth. I have that landdrost to thank. His duty to his brother won and he helped me with papers. Aah . . . here's Somiela and Salie coming now with the tea.

abdas: ablution in preparation for prayer
aia: wet nurse for farmer's children
ambulante hospitaal: hospital
as'r: third prayer of the day for Muslims in afternoon
atjar: mango or lemon condiment pickled in spices and oil
azeemaat: small square of paper with Arabic inscription, folded into a tablet, and worn by Muslims to protect them

basta: command to stop
barakat: plate of cakes to take home after a christening or merang
baster: half-breed
bilal: person who does the call to prayer from the minaret of a mosque
Bismillah: Arabic for 'in the name of God'; usually uttered at the beginning of meals
bobotie: curried mince, baked in oven
Boer: Afrikaner – farmer – peasant
booia: early slave word for father
borrie: turmeric
bosjesman: Bushman; today called San
beskuit: dried-out, bread-like type of cake that could be kept for a long time; used for long journeys
buitekamer: outside room

cabbage bredie: meat braised with onions and cabbage and potatoes

dagga: hemp, marijuana
dassie: small, harelike mammal

denningvleis: cubes of mutton braised with onions and cloves
dhania: coriander
doek: head scarf
doekoem: Muslim clairvoyant
dominee: preacher, minister
doopmaal: Muslim christening; refreshments served
dop: *tot*: usually wine
droster: runaway slave

gereedskapkis: storage chest for tools, hanging under wagon
geweerkis: chest for guns
grootbaas: term used by servants to address the master

half-naartje: derogatory term for half-breed
hottentot: name given to the Koi-na by the Dutch; today called Khoi or Khoikhoi
huurhuis: rental cottage

imam: Muslim cleric, minister
iman: faith
inlander: one who lives in the interior of a country, or away from the sea
inspan: to harness horses or oxen to a wagon

jeera: cumin seeds or spices
jong: derogatory term for male person of mixed race
jongenshuis: slave quarters
kalipha: Muslim cleric/teacher

kaparang: wooden thongs for feet worn by Muslims

kapok: cotton wool

kareeboom: indigenous tree species

kleinnooi: form of address used by servants for the master's daughter

kneg: foreman on farm; usually white and usually residing on premises

Koi-na: brown-skinned people of the early Cape; today called Khoi or Khoikhoi

kommando: group of farmers or burghers on horseback; usually used in a military context

konfyt: jam, preserve

koskas: kitchen cupboard

kraal: pen, fold for animals

krans: steep cliff, rocky ridge

kreef: crayfish (lobster)

landdrost: magistrate

Ma: mother

maleier: derogatory term for Muslim

mandoor: black overseer on farm

masjied: mosque

meid: derogatory term for girl

merang: prayer gathering/social function at which food is served, usually on a Thursday night

mijnheer: sir, mister - of Dutch origin

minnemoer: wet nurse/aia

moerneuker: mother-fucker

Mohametan: Muslim

nagmaal: holy communion

naai: derogatory term for sexual intercourse

naai-mandje: slut

neerslaantafel: folding table

nooi: young lady, or form of address for mistress of the house

oom: uncle

outspan: to unharness horses or oxen from the wagon

Pa: father

pap: mealie meal/porridge

rabanas: tambourine-like instrument

rak'ah: prayers consist of several rak'ahs; some two, some three, some four. A rak'ah would constitute two or three surahs from the Koran

rant: ridge of mountains or hills

ratiep: spiritual performance involving knives and swords – to the accompaniment of rabanases and drums

renosterbos: greyish blue-green shrub found in Karoo areas

riem/riempie: thong/s of softened rawhide used instead of rope for numerous purposes

rinderpest: infectious disease of cattle, and often sheep and goats characterized by fever and inflammation of the mucous membrane of the intestines

salat: prayer

salaam aleikoem: Muslim salutation/greeting

Seur: sir – form of address used only by the slaves

sjambok: whip made of thick rhinoceros hide

skaapbos: bush usually eaten by sheep

sloot: channel made by a temporary stream

snoek: marine fish common in Cape waters

soemba: early slave word for "swear on it" – to take an oath

Sonqua: Bushman; today called San

spoor: track, footprint, trail

stoep: patio, porch

tahajud: prayers performed after one has fallen asleep, and before sunrise

284

tante: aunt

tariq: to be gripped in a trance, or trance-like state

teetafel: tea table

toding: conical hat worn by slaves

toor: to bewitch

trekboer: farmer who moves from one place to another to find grazing for his cattle

uintjie; small onion

voorhuis: entrance hall of the house, usually large enough to be general sitting room

voorkamer: front room of the house designated for visitors

voorkis: storage chest for front of wagon

vygie/s: succulent plant found in arid land